Who's at the Helm?

Who's at the Helm?

Lessons of Lebanon

Raymond Tanter

Westview Press
BOULDER • SAN FRANCISCO • OXFORD

Copyright © 1990 by Westview Press, Inc.

Published in 1990 in the United States of America by Westview Press, Inc., 5500 Central Avenue, Boulder, Colorado 80301, and in the United Kingdom by Westview Press, Inc., 36 Lonsdale Road, Summertown, Oxford OX2 7EW

Library of Congress Cataloging-in-Publication Data
Tanter, Raymond.
  Who's at the helm?: lessons of Lebanon/Raymond Tanter.
    p. cm.
  Includes bibliographical references (p.   ) and index.
  ISBN 0-8133-0993-X
  1. United States—Foreign relations—Lebanon. 2. Lebanon—Foreign relations—United States. I. Title.
E183.8.L4T36 1990
327.7305792—dc20   90-12469
                                                                          CIP

Printed and bound in the United States of America

The paper used in this publication meets the requirements
of the American National Standard for Permanence of Paper
for Printed Library Materials Z39.48-1984.

10   9   8   7   6   5   4   3   2   1

To my parents,
Alice and John Tanter

Contents

Preface

In 1981-1982, President Ronald Reagan gave me the opportunity to work on the National Security Council staff; thus, I participated in foreign policy decisionmaking from a White House perspective. With my firsthand observations as a point of departure, I later conducted private interviews with American officials and foreign diplomats and consulted rich public sources, such as the *Foreign Broadcast Information Service* and the *Middle East Policy Survey*, to reconstruct the decisionmaking process.

Unfortunately, most of the former officials declined to speak for attribution. As a result, their views have been incorporated into the text under such euphemisms as "according to former officials." To avoid repeating such cumbersome phrases incessantly, they are employed sparingly and are often implicit, for example, whenever there are references to meetings or the views of specific individuals. I used multiple individual sources to enhance the validity of inferences and to validate assertions derived from "recall interviews" with public accounts in the press and memoirs of key officials. I also employed my personal experiences and recollections to choose among competing sources when they differed. I conducted telephone interviews and held face-to-face discussions from October 1982 to January 1983 and during June and July 1987.

My study is similar to works by other National Security Council officials, whose scholarship benefits from observing the management of foreign policy firsthand. In addition to the memoirs of national security advisers, such as Henry Kissinger and Zbigniew Brzezinski, there are the invaluable contributions of former NSC staffers Robert Pastor and Constantine Menges on Central America, Gary Sick on Iran, and William Quandt on the Middle East.[1]

The present inquiry stands with two authoritative works that also use primary sources: *Israel's Lebanon War* and *Under Siege: P.L.O. Decisionmaking During the 1982 War.* Each employs primary source evidence available from the government of Israel and the Palestine Liberation Organization (PLO) to reconstruct the Lebanon saga. Together with the present work, these companion volumes provide a relatively complete picture of the people, processes, and policies in the United States, Israel, and the Palestine Liberation Organization that combined to produce "Lebanon."[2]

The idea of studying the management of national security policy began with my fellowship during 1979-1980 at the Woodrow Wilson International Center of the Smithsonian Institution. I gratefully acknowledge that organization, as well as the University of Michigan Office of the Vice President for Research and its Institute for Science and Technology, for funds provided during 1985-1986. I am in debt to Professor Michael Brecher for a thoughtful critique of a draft version of this manuscript and extend special acknowledgements to research assistants Laura Eisenberg and Katherine Kress. Eric Baum, Kelly Doss, Leonard Greenberger, Michelle Miller, Casey Rosen, Ricardo Rodriguiz, and Betsy Rubinstein also deserve thanks.

I take this opportunity to express sincere gratitude to all those individuals who provided an occasion for me to observe governmental decisionmaking firsthand and who have been supportive of my professional development, including: Ronald Reagan, George Bush, Donald Rumsfeld; as well as former officials in the Reagan administration, such as Secretary of State Alexander Haig, National Security Adviser Richard Allen, Under Secretary of Defense Fred Ikle, and Ambassador to the Nuclear and Space Arms Talks Max Kampelman.

On a personal level, those who inspired me to complete this book include John, Judith, Kirk, and Shawn Tanter, as well as Wiebke Bielenberg, Dorothy Byrd, Dorothea Girke, Sarah Power, Maya Savarino, Jack Walker, and Charles Vest.

Raymond Tanter

Introduction

President Ronald Reagan's first secretary of state, Alexander Haig, posed a question concerning who leads national security policymaking:

> The White House was as mysterious as a ghostship; you heard the creak of the rigging and the groan of the timbers and sometimes even glimpsed the crew on deck. But which of the crew had the helm?[1]

Haig's query resembles one from a mythical survivor found drifting off the Azores without crew or captain, "Where the hell's the Captain?"[2] A similar question underlies this book on American decisionmaking regarding Lebanon, "Who's at the helm?" At issue is the topic of leadership. The heads of democratic states are accountable for both the process of decisionmaking and the policies of the government.

During 1986-1987, Reagan stood precariously at the helm of his ship of state. Although he valiantly struggled to retain control, a rising tide of public discontent about Iran almost overwhelmed him. This period stands out as a time in which his National Security Council staff was held responsible for a foreign policy decisionmaking process in disarray.

A half decade before the Iran fiasco, American policymakers encountered another crisis: the Lebanon conflicts of 1981-1983. These featured Israel's threat to use force against Syria and coerce Damascus to remove its surface-to-air missiles from Lebanon, an invasion by Israel to oust combatants of the Palestine Liberation Organization from Lebanon, an attempt by American diplomats to mediate among these protagonists, and the military intervention of the U.S. in Lebanon's factional strife. The Lebanon case provides insight into how people, processes, and policies interrelate in the wake of action-forcing events (e.g., warfare initiated by an American ally); thus, it is the focus of attention here. Although in many respects condemnable and difficult to justify after the fact, Israel's invasion of Lebanon did give the United States an occasion

1

to stimulate the peace process and enhance the security of its friends in the region.

Lebanon also provides an opportunity to study political and military aspects of national security. In this respect, this volume addresses three specific questions: (1) Which officials should regulate political and military affairs? (2) Why do leaders make decisions to combine or leave separate political and military actions? (3) What is the impact of crisis on process and choice?

White House officials are well positioned to coordinate an interagency process that combines the diplomatic activities of the State Department with the military operations of the Defense Department and the intelligence assessments of the Central Intelligence Agency (CIA). The president has occasion to referee the contest for dominance among the White House staff, State, Defense, and the CIA. When the president does so, the national security process may yield an appropriate synthesis of diplomacy and force.

It is incumbent upon a White House crew to think strategically and work in concert toward a presidential agenda in national security decisionmaking. Such a strategic approach would take advantage of a given situation to facilitate both the quest for security and the search for peace. Lebanon was a situation which provided an opportunity for the United States to achieve strategic goals vis-a-vis both the Soviet Union and the Arab-Israeli peace process. The White House was unwilling to sort out its priorities in the area and inspire the interagency process. Accordingly, the United States failed to take full advantage of Israel's invasion of Lebanon to enhance either security in the region or the peace process.

If Lebanon represents a misuse of the interagency process, then the Iran episode indicates a disuse of that process. White House staffers took advantage of the president's desire to get American hostages out of the grasp of Lebanese factions friendly to Iran. These officials saw a chance to create a strategic opening to Teheran and designed an arms-for-hostages deal; apparently on their own, the staffers diverted profits from the arms sales to support resistance forces in Nicaragua. Mismanagement regarding the interagency process in American decisionmaking on Lebanon prefigured the Iran situation that would occur five years later. From the perspective of an ineffective use of the interagency decisionmaking process, the legacy of Lebanon is Iran.

There is a delicate balance of power among the White House, the Department of State, and the Department of Defense in the interagency process. Consider standard operating procedures that may determine which unit "has the action" on a particular issue in a given situation. The State Department and the Defense Department share the responsibility for formulating policy toward and negotiating with foreign governments; they may lose the action to the White House if the situation is politically sensitive, involves high international stakes, or requires a significant degree of coordination.

As the Lebanon conflict intensified, Deputy National Security Adviser Robert McFarlane used the perception of high stakes to enable the White House to wrest control of policy from the State and Defense Departments. In contrast to his comparatively active participation during the initial stages of the Iran affair, President Reagan declined to challenge the initial consensus among his principal national security decisionmakers for a Lebanon policy of diplomacy that had little regard for the threat or use of force. Thus, before the crisis peaked, Lebanon policy was more the result of an unchallenged bureaucratic consensus for a diplomatic approach than the product of the president's long-held beliefs concerning the legitimacy of force in national security policymaking.

America's failure in Lebanon stemmed from an unwillingness to coordinate diplomacy with Israel's use of force, the inadequate orchestration of American diplomacy with the employment of U.S. military might, and the president's hasty withdrawal of American military power in the face of Syrian- and Iranian-supported terrorist attacks. The defeat in Lebanon set the stage for the Iran-Nicaragua affair fewer than five years later. Following the retreat of U.S. forces from Lebanon, administration officials sought to ransom Americans held hostage there by pro-Iranian groups with arms for the Ayatollah of Iran.

People and process are at the core of U.S. failures in Lebanon. President Reagan was only a part-time captain at the tiller of the American ship of state; consequently, others seized the helm. Special Middle East Envoys Philip Habib and Robert McFarlane were key actors for the United States at that time. Policy careened from Habib, as diplomatic troubleshooter for the U.S. Government to McFarlane, as artillery spotter for Lebanese factions. Forging an effective bureaucratic consensus around a diplomatic approach, Habib delayed Israel's use of force against Syria's missiles in

Lebanon, yet he was unable to capitalize on the situation to prevent war or to stimulate the peace process.

In contrast to Habib's successes, McFarlane mismanaged the intelligence and policy process for his own bureaucratic ends and to the detriment of national security. He also abused his position at the White House and as the president's envoy to the Middle East in short-circuiting the interagency process regarding the use of force. McFarlane acted unwisely in recommending to the president the widespread use of force in Lebanon without gaining the consensus of his Pentagon colleagues, coordinating such force with U.S. diplomacy, obtaining independent confirmation of the intelligence that prompted the decision to use force, and properly assessing the risks of force utilization.

The bottom line is that people such as McFarlane are at fault through their misuse of the interagency process. Chapter 1 thus begins with an overview of the bureaucratic politics of crisis involving American officials during May 1981.

1

The Missiles of May

Antecedents to Crisis

The Bureaucratic Politics of Crisis

The events of May 1981 gave American officials an occasion to use crisis as an opportunity for diplomacy. The threat implicit in the unfolding conflict between Jerusalem and Damascus about Syria's missiles in Lebanon could be used to enhance the prospects of peace and security there. Just as the Chinese character for crisis includes both danger and opportunity, some officials saw the threat of war as an opening for peace.

These Americans recognized that the history of the modern Middle East has been a cycle of violence and uneasy calm while diplomacy has been relatively unsuccessful, perhaps because it was not coordinated with the use of force. One focus of this book is the effort of these officials in Ronald Reagan's first three years in office (1981-1983) to alter the vicious cycle of war in the Middle East. They endeavored to seize the opportunities provided by the threat of warfare and actual hostilities to create new political realities conducive to the search for peace and security. These officials attempted to use the risk of war and fighting within Lebanon among Israel, Syria, and the Palestine Liberation Organization as a point of departure for creative diplomacy. So, a main purpose of this volume is to explain how and why diplomacy and force were used in the Lebanon conflicts that, in turn, became crises for the United States. In the bureaucratic politics of international crises, how force is combined with diplomacy is a core concern of the policy process.

Led initially by Secretary of State Alexander Haig and later by his successor George Shultz, those in the Department of State who wished to combine force and diplomacy in American policy toward Lebanon included U.S. Ambassador to the United Nations Jeane Kirkpatrick, Special Middle East Envoy Donald Rumsfeld, Director

5

of Politico-Military Affairs Richard Burt, and Director of the Staff for Policy Planning Paul Wolfowitz. In contrast to the first coalition, a second alignment in the State Department included Special Envoy for the Middle East Philip Habib and his deputy Morris Draper, as well as Assistant Secretary of State for Near Eastern and South Asian Affairs Nicholas Veliotes. This group was hesitant to reap whatever benefits there may have been for the United States in Israel's threats and use of force. Habib was sometimes a player in both camps; however, because he was more active on the diplomatic front than in the military arena, he generally acted in accord with the second group.

At the White House, allies of Haig and Shultz included Geoffrey Kemp, chief of the National Security Council's Near East Office and his deputy, the author, as well as my subsequent replacements for Lebanon, Lieutenant Colonel Oliver North and Howard Teicher. (President Reagan was a silent partner.) Unlike the NSC aides, a succession of National Security Advisers--Richard Allen, William Clark, Robert McFarlane, and John Poindexter--tended to straddle the two groups.

Although McFarlane often joined with Haig and Shultz against Secretary of Defense Caspar Weinberger, Clark frequently sided with Weinberger on issues regarding Lebanon. Allen was relatively neutral in the bureaucratic interplay, but because he reported to the president via White House Counselor Edwin Meese, Allen rarely received the credit for his unbiased approach to the interagency process. In contrast to Allen, Poindexter went outside of that process and ignored State and Defense when he felt the need to do so.

Generally lining up against Haig and Shultz on the issue of using force for diplomatic purposes were Weinberger and his Assistant Secretary of Defense for International Security Affairs Francis (Bing) West and, later, Richard Armitage, as well as their military allies on the Joint Chiefs of Staff. Like Allen, Under Secretary of Defense Fred Ikle operated across the two alignments. On the one hand, Director of Central Intelligence William Casey and the head of the National Intelligence Council, Henry Rowen, may be classified in the Haig and Shultz camps; on the other hand, regional officials at the CIA, such as National Intelligence Officer for the Middle East Robert Ames, tended to side with those who were reluctant to employ force in the service of diplomacy or who favored diplomacy over the use of force.

As Reagan entered office in 1981, officials in the Haig group and those at Defense concerned with Southwest Asian security sought to focus attention on the Soviet threat to the Gulf area. Events in Lebanon, however, conspired to induce the United States to redirect its attention away from the Gulf to the Arab-Israeli zone and to become enmeshed in the sectarian politics of Lebanon. The shift from the Gulf to Lebanon strengthened the hands of Habib and his allies who were less concerned with using crisis as an opportunity for diplomacy than was the Haig group.

The PLO in Lebanon

The 1981 Missiles of May crisis and the 1982 Lebanon War were policyforcing events that enhanced the bureaucratic fortunes of the Habib coalition. Israel entitled this conflict Operation Peace for Galilee, suggesting that one of Jerusalem's aims was to make peace. The invasion, however, allowed it to impose an accord, rather than to negotiate a peace between equals. Indeed, Lebanon and Israel signed a one-sided agreement of short duration in May 1983. To understand that accord, as well as the 1982 invasion, consider the role of the PLO in Lebanon.

King Hussein's victory in the Jordanian Civil War of 1970 resulted in the forced migration of thousands of Palestinians into Lebanon. A growing Palestinian armed presence there tipped the balance of power among the Lebanese factions and provided an incentive for Jerusalem's military interventions. Southern Lebanon served as a platform for launching attacks into northern Israel; consequently, some Israeli officials wanted to eliminate Palestinian troop concentrations in that area and even the PLO headquarters in Beirut. (Figure 1 is a map of Lebanon; southern Lebanon is the area north of the Israel-Lebanon border up to the Litani River.) The bottom line is that the Palestinian armed presence in Lebanon heightened Jerusalem's perception of threat from the northwest and contributed to its tendency to downplay the broader peace process in favor of narrower goals, such as enhancing the security of its border with Lebanon.

The PLO and the Lebanese Civil War

As a result of their growing numbers and increased arsenal, the Palestinians became a major variable in the Lebanese political equation. Indeed, the 1975-1976 civil war originated in a dispute

8

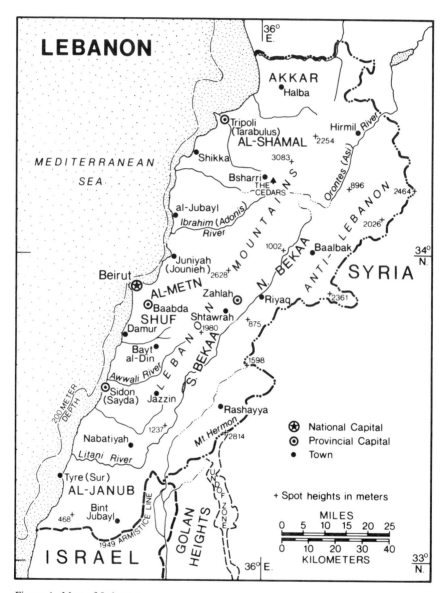

Figure 1. Map of Lebanon

Source: Colbert C. Held, *Middle East Patterns: Places, Peoples, and Politics* (Boulder, Colo.: Westview Press, 1989), p. 207. Reprinted with permission.

between Palestinians and rightist Lebanese militias over PLO freedom of action in Lebanon.[1] Rightist groups laid siege to refugee camps in East Beirut, most notably Tel al-Zaatar. The PLO mainstream transferred the majority of its fighters from southern Lebanon to West Beirut. One scholar of the Palestinian movement, Helena Cobban, notes that, with this shift, the destiny of the Fatah forces in Lebanon was coupled with the fate of the Lebanese oppositionists.[2]

As the civil war intensified, other groups chose sides. Leftist groups of the Lebanese opposition generally supported the Palestinian resistance and opposed hegemony of the Maronites (an eastern Catholic community of Lebanon associated with the Catholic church in Rome). Consequently, leftists joined armed Palestinians against a Maronite group known as the Phalange. The leftist coalition's impending success against the Phalange and its rightist allies paved the way for Syrian military intervention. Damascus preferred a balance among the contending groups to avoid a victory by any one faction. Triumph by a leftist coalition that included the PLO could have led to the establishment of a PLO-dominated state on Syria's border. Such an outcome would have decreased Syrian influence as Lebanon would be yet another state capable of provoking a conflict with Israel. Further, the timing of such a confrontation might not have coincided with Syrian interests but would have involved Damascus nonetheless because of its large numbers of troops in Lebanon.

The civil war ended in 1976 with the October 18 Riyadh Agreement, which was validated in Cairo by an Arab League summit meeting (minus Iraq and Libya) one week later. The accord ostensibly demarcated the parameters of the Palestinian armed presence in Lebanon. Despite this claim, the agreement merely institutionalized that presence and legitimized a virtual Palestinian state-within-a-state. Furthermore, by compromising Lebanon's sovereignty in the general Arab framework, the Riyadh Agreement strengthened the Palestinians vis-a-vis Lebanon's central government. Armed Palestinians then used Lebanon as a launching pad for raids into Israel, giving Jerusalem a pretext for its military incursion of 1978 and invasion of 1982.

The changing demography and power structure of Lebanon favored a leftist coalition in which the PLO became a key player. The inter-Arab agreement ratified demographic and political changes within Lebanon and formalized a Syrian armed presence under the guise of the Arab Deterrent Force, even further undercutting Lebanon's sovereignty. More exhausted than content with the outcome of the civil war, the antagonists reluctantly abided by an inter-Arab consensus to cease fighting, but they failed to resolve their political differences. Itamar Rabinovich, a leading student of Lebanese politics, observes that "both the underlying and the immediate problems that had unsettled the Lebanese political system and had led to the outburst in April 1975 remained unsolved and were in fact exacerbated and compounded by the [1975-1976] war and its repercussions."[3]

The civil war also ended with a reordering of the Palestinian movement's power structure. The conflict had not been as damaging to the mainstream leadership as it had to opposition groups, such as the Democratic Front for the Liberation of Palestine. The oppositionists took serious losses, especially in the early months of the fighting when the centrists opted to focus on recruit training and deployments along the border with Israel.[4] Just as radical Palestinians (e.g., the Popular Front for the Liberation of Palestine) took the brunt of King Hussein's crackdown in Jordan during 1970, they suffered more than the centrist Palestinians in the Lebanon Civil War of 1975-1976. The civil war severely weakened the coalition of oppositionists that in 1974 had criticized the Palestine National Council's endorsement of a diplomatic approach at the Rabat (Morocco) Arab Summit.

There are two primary causes of that internal war: a trend in population composition that favored a leftist coalition of which the Palestinians were central and the growing Palestinian armed presence itself. These same factors remained in the aftermath of the civil war. Additionally, external powers made little effort to devise a peace process for Lebanon that addressed the destabilizing effect of the Palestinian armed presence there. Rather, the powers acted on an unfounded hope that a Syrian military role would offer stability in the long run. Although Syria did help to end the eighteen months of fighting, its presence ultimately became a destabilizing factor in the Lebanese balance of power, further challenging the rightists' aspirations for continued domination.

Innovative diplomacy must take advantage of the political upheaval of war to facilitate the quest for peace. However, no peace process followed the 1975-1976 civil war in Lebanon, and the underlying causes of the conflict (such as the Palestinian and Syrian armed presence) were not confronted. The absence of a successful peace process left the door open for repeated Israeli invasions. And rather than mitigating the threat posed by external forces in

Lebanon, the powers acquiesced in leaving the Syrians in a favorable position in Lebanon's Bekka Valley. The war also ended with the PLO remaining in its strategically advantageous position along Israel's northern border.

The PLO and Israel's 1978 Incursion into Lebanon

On March 11, 1978, armed Palestinians, operating out of their southern Lebanese stronghold, attacked civilians within Israel along the coastal road between Tel Aviv and Haifa. As a result, Jerusalem launched the Litani Operation incursion into Lebanon three days later, occupying a six-mile-deep security belt on Lebanese territory along the Israeli border.

Jerusalem's goals in the Litani Operation were (1) to destroy PLO bases that were the source of rocket attacks on Jewish settlements in the Galilee area of northern Israel and of Palestinian raids into Israel, and (2) to extend the area controlled by Israel's Lebanese surrogate, Major Sa'ad Haddad, who led a local rightist militia recruited from the Christian and Shi'a Moslem population of southern Lebanon. (A dissident, underdog movement, the Shi'a sect is the second largest in Islam and includes some 10 percent of all Moslems but perhaps a majority of those in Lebanon.)

More than a retaliatory raid, this military operation up to the Litani River gave Israel's ally, Major Haddad, a chance to consolidate a buffer zone between the Palestinian fighters in southern Lebanon and Israel's northern borders. Although Israel technically withdrew by June 13, 1978, it continued to support Haddad's militia, which minimized PLO infiltration through the often porous United Nations peacekeeping military lines.

For Lebanon, the consequences of the 1978 Litani Operation were far reaching. After Israel defeated the PLO in the spring of 1978, Maronite rightist forces drove the Syrians out of East Beirut that fall, paving the way for large-scale collaboration between Jerusalem and the Maronites. Israel also began unrestricted arms transfers to the rightists via Lebanese port facilities that they now fully controlled. The Maronite militia's arms acquisitions placed the PLO in an increasingly vulnerable position. On the one hand, Jerusalem's invasion enhanced the benefits that the PLO mainstream would receive by aligning itself with Damascus. On the other hand, such an alignment exposed the PLO to Syria's manipulation and control.

Israel's 1978 incursion also had major consequences for Lebanese domestic politics, to the detriment of the Palestine Liberation Organization. Lebanon's President Sarkis had been elected with Syrian support in the fall of 1975, but after Israel's incursion, he began to reflect antipathy to the Palestinian armed presence characteristic of the militant wing of Lebanese rightists. Furthermore, the incursion gave the rightists a pretext for publicly advocating the repeal of the 1976 Riyadh Agreement, whereby Lebanon consented to the existence of an armed Palestinian presence. Finally, the 1978 incursion transformed the strategic balance in the area. In the absence of a forceful Syrian response to the invasion, Jerusalem successfully challenged Syria's efforts to control Lebanon, exposing the PLO to the combined military power of the Lebanese Maronites and the Israelis.

The PLO Versus Israel and the Lebanese Maronites

As the 1980s began, the PLO faced the prospect of being caught between an Israeli hammer and a Maronite anvil.[5] Although the Maronites failed to enter the war against the PLO as Israel expected, the PLO still believed it could be surrounded by two enemies. PLO Chairman Arafat compared his situation with that of an accordion: He feared that the PLO would be squeezed into a pincer movement between Israeli armed forces coming up from the south and rightists who would then control areas in the north.[6] In light of the Israeli-Maronite arms transfer relationship, a Soviet reluctance to help the PLO unless requested to do so by Lebanon, and Moscow's unwillingness to assist Syrian forces within Lebanon, the PLO accelerated its arms buildup.

U.S. Leverage on Israel in Lebanon

The Carter administration failed to address the massive PLO arms acquisitions and the organization's transformation into a virtual parastate within Lebanon. After going through the legal formalities of assessing Israel's compliance with American arms export legislation in the 1978 incursion, the administration then shifted its attention back to the Arab-Israeli Camp David peace process. As required by law, Secretary of State Cyrus Vance sent a letter to Congress stating that Israel might have violated the Arms Export Control Act of 1976 by using American-origin military equipment in the 1978 incursion.

Secretary Vance later wrote that the United States had little doubt that Israel's use of U.S.-origin military equipment had gone beyond the requirements of self defense. Because the Carter administration's main goal was for Israel to comply with the UN withdrawal order--and Israel was doing so--it did not want to trigger a counterproductive crisis.[7] Vance was correct to avoid a confrontation with Israel over the issue of U.S.-origin equipment. That administration, however, should have emphasized the requirements for a stable Lebanon--focusing first on the reduction of the armed Palestinian presence there. Indeed, Israel's withdrawal could have been made conditional on such a reduction.

Underlying the question of Israel's use of U.S.-origin equipment in Lebanon is the broader issue of Washington's leverage over Jerusalem. The reluctance or inability to impose effective sanctions against Israel is a recurring problem in America's Middle East policymaking. In the Litani case of 1978, as in similar situations, U.S. sanctions in response to initial Israeli misconduct could have impeded corrective actions. American sanctions also might inadvertently hamper Israel's withdrawal from territory it occupied in an invasion. The lesson for Jerusalem is that it can risk misdeeds if it takes ameliorative action before Washington policy circles can agree on punitive measures.

Thus, the focus of American attention regarding Lebanon in the spring of 1978 was on the narrow issue of Israel's potential violation of U.S. arms export legislation. An alternative policy, seizing the diplomatic opportunities created by Israeli action, could have concentrated on the broader question of how a peace process might address the spiraling Palestinian armed presence in Lebanon. But Washington chose to highlight the relatively minor issue of Israel's inappropriate military response to Palestinian provocations originating in Lebanon.[8] Moreover, as Vance acknowledged, even the administration's intense preference for a comprehensive solution to the West Bank Palestinian problem by way of a peace process was superseded by the policy problems associated with its concern for the security of Israel's borders with Lebanon.[9]

Lebanon could not compete effectively with the Arab-Israeli core zone for the attention of U.S. officials. With Washington actively involved in the Egypt-Israel Camp David peace process during 1978-1979 and Jerusalem's withdrawal of its military forces from Lebanon, the Syrian military presence left over from the 1975-1976 civil war developed into a dominant influence in Lebanese politics. Meanwhile, the ties between Syrian and Palestinian armed forces in the early 1980s began to have increasingly negative consequences for Lebanese rightists. Partly in response to this, the Maronite militias began a series of actions against the Syrians in Lebanon that produced a deadly game of maneuvering between the two adversaries. So the Syrian military presence and its challenge to Christian control of Lebanon also coincided with a growing Palestinian armed presence there that threatened Israel's security along its Lebanese border. These developments had the makings of a crisis for Washington.

Reagan's First Foreign Policy Crisis

It was into this complicated and highly volatile quagmire that Ronald Reagan stumbled in May of 1981. Thirty-two difficult and often painful months later, he would withdraw the U.S. Marines from Beirut, in February 1984. In the interim, the president and his advisers would be called upon to make a series of hard decisions about Lebanon and to decrease their attention on the Soviet threat to the Gulf, contrary to the advice of the coalition led by Secretary Haig. Despite the fact that Lebanon was not its top priority, the Haig group took advantage of the escalating crisis in the eastern Mediterranean to enhance the fortunes of anti-Communists there. Siding with the Maronite rightists in Lebanon and opposing Syria, the Haig camp did not look unfavorably on the increasing tensions in the area.

The "Rightists Provoked Syria" School

The placement of Syrian missiles in Lebanon was the outcome of a game of escalating violence between Syria and the Lebanese rightists. Although Damascus and the Phalange jockeyed for strategic advantage during the winter of 1980, the conflict did not peak militarily until March 1981 when it became a serious problem for crisis managers in Washington. The Reagan administration split over the explanation for the growing violence. American intelligence analysts led one school of thought that later became the Habib group. It held that the Phalange rightists deliberately provoked a clash with Syria in order to force Israel into a confrontation with that nation and bring Israeli air power to bear on the side of the Christian militias.

These analysts based their inference on prior rightist provocation of Syria. In June 1978, a rightist Lebanese militia leader, Bashir Gemayel, incited Damascus by assassinating Syria's primary Christian ally in Lebanon, Tony Franjiyeh, thereby instigating a spiral of escalation that was difficult to quell.[10] Israeli military intelligence determined that the Phalange had initiated the crisis and alerted Prime Minister Begin of future provocations designed to pull Israel into a war with Syria. For example, two Israeli journalists, Schiff and Ya'ari, state that the director of military intelligence for the Israel Defense Forces suspected that a flare-up in the city of Zahle was essentially a Phalange plot to draw Israel into a clash with Syria. They also describe how the head of the Mossad, Israel's "CIA," came to suspect that the Phalangists must have received assurances from some high-ranking Israeli that Jerusalem would bail them out if they were trapped in Zahle.[11]

Consistent with the Mossad's interpretation, the Phalange picked Zahle, capital of the Bekaa Valley and due east of Beirut, as the site of its showdown with Syria. Damascus considered the Bekaa in Lebanon to be its first line of defense against Israeli air attack from the Mediterranean, and the Phalange therefore expected Syria to match and exceed the militia's moves in the valley. Consequently, proponents of the first school of thought concluded that Syria was a reluctant entrant into the Bekaa Valley.

The "Syria Provoked the Rightists" School

In contrast to the American intelligence analysts, policy officials aligned with Haig held that Syria enthusiastically seized the occasion of Phalange road-building activities to lay the groundwork for upgrading Syria's defenses against Israel in Lebanon. Proponents of this school of thought included State's Politico-Military Affairs, its Staff for Policy Planning, and some NSC staffers. According to their interpretation, Syria had lost aircraft over Lebanon in dogfights with Israel; as a result, Damascus had an incentive to clash with the Phalange and thereby obtain a pretext for missile deployment. These policy analysts concluded that Syria was a willing participant in the spiral of violence.

A third hypothesis, not seriously entertained in the administration, was that the Phalange move into Zahle had been coordinated with Israel and was part of a scheme to enable the Phalange and Israeli forces to link up after a thrust by Israel toward Zahle from southern Lebanon. Actually, there is little evidence regarding a Phalange-Israeli collusion to spark a crisis with Syria, but Israel had promised not to permit Syrian air power to be used against Phalange forces. Nonetheless, Jerusalem did not intend to be drawn into a war with Damascus on behalf of the Phalange.[12]

Syrian Missile Site Construction

Regardless of the explanation, the Phalange-Syrian conflict escalated during March 1981. The escalation drew the attention of officials in Washington concerned about the possibility of an outbreak of fighting between Syria and the friend of the Phalange forces in Lebanon--Israel. Meanwhile, Jerusalem's allies had moved into the slopes of Mount Sanin, begun to build a dirt road from Zahle to Christian areas aligned with Damascus, and then launched raids against Syrian positions along the Beirut-Damascus Highway.

Syria responded by imposing a siege around Zahle. It also proceeded to prepare missile sites near the Bekaa capital. Syrian construction crews dug four emplacements for stationing missiles, but by leaving them empty, Damascus may have been sending a signal that whether the missiles themselves would be deployed depended on what moves Jerusalem would make. A conciliatory gesture by Israel would mean a halt to construction; an escalatory move could induce Damascus to complete the missile deployment.

Schiff and Ya'ari believe that Damascus was using its missiles for political signaling.[13] Certainly, it makes little sense to telegraph in advance the location of a mobile weapons system. What actually followed was escalation. On April 28, 1981, Israeli aircraft shot down two Syrian helicopters that it initially thought were for the purpose of assaulting Phalange positions but later were confirmed to be transporting troops. The next day, Syria reacted by installing missiles in the prepared emplacements and deploying additional batteries of missiles with Soviet advisers on the Syrian side of the Lebanese border.

Syria viewed the Phalange move as a unilateral attempt to change the status quo in Lebanon, and Israel perceived Syria's missile deployment as a one-sided effort to alter the status quo between them. Consequently, Prime Minister Menachem Begin publicly threatened to destroy Syria's missiles if it refused to remove them from Lebanon. Israeli aircraft were poised to strike on the afternoon of April 30, 1981, but they delayed the attack because of poor weather conditions near Zahle.

With hindsight, it is clear that Syria had perceived a threat to its vital interests in the Phalange attempt to set up a political-military presence in Zahle. As Rabinovich states, "The move to Zahle and the effort to link it to the Maronite heartland by a direct road beyond Syria's control were interpreted by Syria as an attempt to change the status quo and to undermine Syria's position in the part of Lebanon most vital to its interests."[14]   Thus, the Phalange response to Syria's military presence in Lebanon placed Damascus and Jerusalem on a collision course that made war between the two a growing possibility.) That clash would come--but not for another year.

Escalation Without Warfare

The Missiles of May crisis did not result immediately or directly in warfare. Yet, a decade and a half earlier, another crisis in May did bring war the following month.   But when does a crisis culminate in war? The question of what links crisis and warfare is relevant to the present inquiry.[15]   Hence, it is instructive to compare the 1967 and 1981 cases.

During mid-May 1967, Egypt concentrated its forces in the Sinai Desert partly to deter threatened Israeli action against Syria. Egypt subsequently initiated a blockade of the Straits of Tiran on the Red Sea. Israel had asserted that a blockade was a *casus belli* or cause of war, and the credibility of its deterrent threat was at stake: Its ability to deter unacceptable activities would have been eroded if no action were taken to open the straits to Israeli shipping. Thus, Jerusalem decided on war in 1967 not just to open the straits, but to maintain its future deterrent capacity and rid itself of a threatening Egyptian troop concentration.

By contrast, Syria's 1981 missile deployment in Lebanon was not as threatening to Israel as the 1967 Egyptian troop buildup in the Sinai Desert had been. But if the missiles were deployed just over the Lebanese border within Syria, they could still be a threat to Israel's reconnaissance flights over Lebanon, even though that threat would be proportionately less than if they were actually in Lebanon.   The presence of two surface-to-air missile batteries in Lebanon induced Israel to divert its reconnaissance flights westwardly along the Mediterranean Coast. If these intelligence gathering operations could have continued over the Lebanese hinterland, they would have been more likely to detect both Syrian air and ground movements, as well as PLO troop deployments.

In effect, then, there was a decrease both in Israel's warning time in the event of a Syrian attack and in Jerusalem's capacity to detect PLO movements. Conversely, there was an increase in the cost of an Israeli attack via Lebanon. Although Syria obtained a substantial intelligence edge by moving the missiles across the Lebanese border, that disadvantage did not impair Israel as much as the Eygptian troop concentrations of 1967. Despite the fact that Damascus did not benefit as much as Cairo had fifteen years earlier, Syria nevertheless had much to gain by controlling the Bekaa Valley of Lebanon via missile deployment.

First, Syrian military planners would have multiple options for threatening Israel. (The Bekaa had strategic significance insofar as it could serve as a staging area for an attack across Israel's northern border that could cut off Jerusalem's forces in the Golan Heights and menace Israeli cities in the Galilee.) Second, Syrian control of the valley would complicate any Israeli attack to outflank Syria's prepared defenses between the Golan and Damascus by way of Lebanon. Third, Syria stood to receive enormous political benefit by taking and maintaining control of the Bekaa in the face of Israel's deterrent warnings. Syrian control of the valley via an air defense system actually violated a tacit understanding reached through the offices of the United States in the aftermath of the 1975-1976 civil war. In this implicit bargain, Israel had acknowledged Syria's ground combat presence in Lebanon north of the Litani River and Damascus had tacitly refrained from both air activity over Lebanon and installing missiles on Lebanese territory. Although it never explicitly acknowledged these implicit understandings, Damascus had acted as if it had accepted them.

Consequently, the missile deployment created a major dilemma for Israeli policymakers. On the one hand, unchallenged Syrian noncompliance threatened the credibility of Israel's deterrence and thus endangered its ability to deter other unacceptable Syrian actions in the future. On the other hand, an Israeli attack against Syria's missiles in Lebanon risked escalation. This dilemma of deterrence and escalation was also present in the 1967 case, yet the stakes in 1981 were far lower; hence, war was less likely.[16] Nonetheless, President Reagan's crisis managers were interested in how Jerusalem would resolve its conflict with Damascus.

The SAM-Site Game

Why Did Syria Place Surface-to-Air Missiles in Lebanon?

The sparring on the ground in Lebanon rang alarm bells in Washington, signaling an impending crisis. In the administration's debate over who had provoked whom, the Habib group's assessment had prevailed--the Phalange had incited Syria. The policy option that flowed from this assessment of Phalange culpability was to restrain Israel from unilaterally attacking Syria's missiles in Lebanon. (An assessment that Syria had been the "guilty party" would have bolstered those in the Haig coalition who wanted to give Israel a green light to attack Syria's missiles in Lebanon.) This close link between intelligence and policy suggests that intelligence led policy. In fact, however, officials (such as the president) who hoped to avoid the painful choice of giving Israel the go-ahead to attack actually adopted the intelligence estimate that would support their preferred option. It is only coincidental that this intelligence interpretation was proven correct.

There are two separate issues at hand. The first is: Who provoked whom? The second is: Who took advantage of whom? (Although the Phalange did incite Syria, Damascus took advantage of a third party provocation to serve its own strategic interests vis-a-vis Jerusalem.)

Washington's subsequent policy of restraining Jerusalem via diplomacy avoided an air battle between Israel and Syria in the short term. However, this red-light policy actually set the stage for a larger confrontation a year later. The fighting between the Syrians and the Phalange in Lebanon would develop into an even deadlier contest with far graver consequences for both Syria and Israel--the SAM-site game, which raised the question: Can a Syrian surface-to-air missile (SAM) take out an Israeli attack aircraft before that plane kills the missile?

Regionalists: Syrian Defense Against the Maronite Threat

From the first week of May 1981, the United States attempted to prevent the SAM-site game from escalating into a general war. Washington tried to restrain Jerusalem from attacking the missiles Damascus had placed in Lebanon. But the regionalists, led by Habib, and the globalists, such as Haig, were divided on the significance of the placement of Syria's missiles in Lebanon.

Regionalists are those officials who tend to see an issue from the perspective of local actors, rather than from a worldwide (e.g., an East/West) perspective, as globalists do. Regionalists also are reluctant to combine force with diplomacy because they believe that force is at best irrelevant and probably would make a bad situation worse. They contend that local conflicts primarily result from domestic political, economic, and social considerations and should not be unduly influenced by American military power.

Regionalists considered the missiles to be a way for Syria to defend its troops against the threat from Maronite militias, and they counseled restraint of Israel. In this regard, President Reagan met with his newly appointed envoy to the Middle East, Ambassador Philip Habib, on May 5, 1981. As former under secretary for political affairs at State, Habib also had been a negotiator with the American delegation at the Paris peace talks on Vietnam in the 1970s. A diplomat with a personal knowledge of the central players in the area, he was a consensus choice of officials intent on restraining Jerusalem and resolving the missile conflict without the use of force.

The goals for Habib's first mission to the Middle East were to restrain Israel in order to buy time for diplomacy, negotiate with Syria for the removal of its missiles, induce the Christians to negotiate with the Syrians, and help Lebanon extend central authority throughout the country.[17] According to the *Middle East Policy Survey* of May 8, 1981 (no. 31), State Department officials had said that Habib's primary aim was to negotiate Syrian withdrawal from the strategic mountain positions.

Although Reagan met with Habib in the presence of Haig and his allies, the president's preoccupation with American domestic economic affairs allowed regionalists to dominate the decisionmaking process. Reagan's inattention to the Syrian threat in Lebanon began a pattern of presidential noninvolvement that left American policy up for grabs among cabinet-level national security officials intent on pursuing bureaucratic, rather than presidential, goals for Lebanon. The outcome of these bargaining games left regionalists at State in control of the agenda for Habib's maiden mission to Lebanon.

The regionalists encouraged a compromise between Lebanese rightists and the Syrians. They wanted to bring about political changes on the ground and thereby reduce Syria's need for missiles that the regionalists thought were deployed in Lebanon simply because of rightist military activity. If the Lebanese rightists and the Syrians could strike a political compromise, there would be less need for these Lebanese to have military air support from Israel and thus less justification for Syria to have missiles in Lebanon.

The regionalists' approach was inherently contradictory for two reasons. First, to extend the authority of the minority Christian-dominated government, as Habib was charged to do, would conflict with the goal of striking a deal between Christian militia groups and Syria. Contrary to the American objective, (President Assad of Syria wanted to weaken the government of Lebanon's authority in areas relevant to Syria's security, such as the Bekaa Valley.) Second, expecting Damascus to withdraw its missiles after factional strife subsided mistakenly assumed that the missiles were placed in Lebanon because of the turmoil.

Globalists: Inter-Arab Conflict and Syrian Strategic Gain

In contrast to the regionalists, the globalists on the NSC staff hypothesized that Damascus took advantage of an unstable situation to place Soviet-supplied missiles in Lebanon. A traditional globalist position is that Soviet-origin weapons should not be used against America's friends. Consequently, what made the SAM-site game of particular interest to the globalists was the fact that the surface-to-air missiles were of Soviet-origin. Indeed, for globalists, the source of the missiles was as important as their targets. The globalists, therefore, disputed the regionalists' claim that Syria placed its missiles in Lebanon primarily to enhance its position relative to the Phalange.

Consistent with their focus on the Soviet origin of Syria's missiles, the globalists offered two complementary explanations for the missile deployment. The first is actually "regional" in that it concerns inter-Arab politics, while the second involves a strategic rationale for the missiles. The first hypothesis suggests a link between Palestinian jockeying for position in inter-Arab politics and Syria's militancy toward Israel.[18] Specifically, there may have been a connection between Palestinian political moves toward Jordan and Syria's deployment of its missiles in Lebanon.

During mid-April 1981, over 300 Palestinian delegates met in Damascus for the fifteenth session of the Palestinian National Council. They discussed difficulties involved with their situation in Lebanon and called for cooperation with all governments, including Jordan, which had opposed the Egypt-Israel peace treaty and autonomy negotiations. Less than two weeks after the council meeting, Damascus moved surface-to-air missiles forward from Syria into the Bekaa Valley. Although Palestinian political moves toward Jordan were followed by Syria's deployment of its missiles in Lebanon, it is doubtful that there is any causal connection between the two events.

While there is little validity for the inter-Arab explanation of missile deployment, there is considerable logic in favor of a strategic idea that turns on the deterrent power of missiles. Globalists reasoned that the missiles were a means of reinforcing Syria's forward defense line against Israel and emphasized that Damascus's first line of defense against Jerusalem's attack from the Mediterranean would be in Lebanon. The primary strategic aim of the missiles, then, was to deter a strike from Israel by raising its attack price (the expected cost of air operations via Lebanon). It also was important for Syria that its missiles in Lebanon increase the risk to Jerusalem in making any strike on Syria and jeopardize Israel's reconnaissance capability. The globalists therefore believed that the potential for Syria's missiles to diminish Israel's support for the Lebanese rightist militias was a secondary consideration relative to their ability to deter an Israeli attack on Syria via Lebanon. So, Syria's missile deployment in Lebanon contributed to its strategy of deterring an Israeli attack in the spring of 1981. Fourteen months earlier, in January 1980, Damascus had redeployed a brigade from Sidon to the Bekaa Valley. (As the map in Figure 1 shows, Sidon is on the coast south of Beirut--about halfway between it and Israel; the Bekaa Valley is in the lowland between the Christian-dominated mountains and Syria's border with Lebanon.) In deploying this brigade, Damascus had expressed concern about an attack by Israel via southeast Lebanon, bypassing Syria's strong defenses in the plains below the Golan Heights. In other words, by attacking Lebanon from the Mediterranean, Israel could isolate Syria's forces in Lebanon.

In Washington's eyes, Syria's redeployment of military forces from Sidon to the Bekaa left Israel with five options: (1) air strikes, (2) commando operations, (3) expanded military actions by Lebanese rightist militias supported by Israel's artillery, (4) intervention in Lebanon by Israeli combat units, and (5) reinforcement of Israel's forces on the Golan.

Syria's redeployment rang the "red-line bells" in Israel's Defense Ministry in January 1980. During the 1975-1976 Lebanon Civil War, Israeli officials had warned that they would not tolerate the introduction of Syrian forces below a certain "red line," generally thought to be the Litani River in southern Lebanon. And when Syria placed its missiles in Lebanon during May 1981, the bells in Tel Aviv rang again, echoing as far as the White House Situation Room, the State Department Operations Center, and the Pentagon war rooms.

The Interagency Process: A Premature Consensus for Peace

Within the U.S. Government, there is an interagency process designed to produce consensus for presidential decisionmaking. When foreign policy is at issue, the Department of State often has the lead in the discussions. When the problem involves defense or intelligence, the Department of Defense or the Central Intelligence Agency may take the lead, respectively. Regardless of the issue, the process generally includes officials from the State Department, the Office of the Secretary of Defense, the Executive Office of the President (e.g., the National Security Council staff), the Central Intelligence Agency, and the Organization of the Joint Chiefs of Staff.

With regionalists at State in the lead, the interagency process took up the issue of Lebanon as a situation that could escalate into a major crisis. A premature consensus developed that a major confrontation between Israel and Syria would have the following results: First, Syria would be defeated; second, Egypt's President Sadat would be placed in the position of having made a separate peace with a nation (Israel) that used force against another Arab state; third, the Camp David Palestinian autonomy talks would be delayed; and fourth, U.S.-Egyptian relations would be harmed. The president failed to have his staff challenge this consensus, which reinforced his propensity to avert war as it compromised Israel's red-line deterrence strategy on the Syrian presence in Lebanon.

Reflect upon an assumption implicit in the policy consensus in favor of a diplomatic deal enabling Syria to withdraw its missiles from Lebanon in the spring of 1981: The credentials of the United States to manage the Arab-Israeli peace process and provide security for the Gulf would be harmed if Israel used American-supplied arms to take out these Syrian weapons. Given the administration's gloomy forecast and the president's aversion toward Israel's use of force, it seemed to make sense for the Habib mission to seek a diplomatic bargain for solving the missile conflict. There is little indication that the president considered giving Israel a green light to use military means for taking out the missiles, as some globalists suggested.

Avoidance of Choice

Underlying American intelligence and the preferred diplomatic option was the perceived need to avoid making a choice between America's friends, such as Egypt and Israel. Any war between Israel and Syria might force Washington to choose between Jerusalem and Cairo because Egypt was likely to intervene on Syria's behalf in a lengthy war with Israel. But in the absence of such a war, the United Sates could avoid such a difficult choice. Thus, the green-light alternative of letting Israel remove the missiles received virtually no attention at the top. Globalists, however, felt that restraining Jerusalem from executing a quick surgical strike could actually lead to a prolonged conflict with widespread casualties later. Such an eventuality surely would harm U.S. objectives in the area, and ultimately the United States would need to choose between Israel and its antagonists.

Globalists at the Department of State's Bureau of Politico-Military Affairs, on the Staff for Policy Planning, and on the NSC staff anticipated that the risk of Soviet intervention on behalf of Syria grew the longer Israel delayed in removing Syria's missiles from Lebanon. However, regionalists at State's Bureau of Near Eastern and South Asian Affairs teamed up with political operatives from the White House and analysts from the Office of the Secretary of Defense, the Organization of the Joint Chiefs of Staff, and the Central Intelligence Agency to push for an active diplomatic effort to restrain Jerusalem--the red-light option.

Crisis Management: The SAM-Site Game Approaches

As the missile conflict intensified, the Department of State continued to take the lead and formed an interagency team dubbed the "Working Group." It met frequently at State from May 7-9, 1981, was staffed at just below the deputy assistant secretary level, and was cochaired by representatives of State's Politico-Military Affairs as well as Near Eastern and South Asian Affairs. After the Working Group's initial meeting on May 7, a small interagency planning group met.

According to former State Department officials, globalists from State's Politico-Military Bureau made the following strategic arguments in the Working Group. First, the worst outcome of the missile confrontation would be a war of attrition. In this case, Israel's military superiority could not end the conflict quickly or minimize damage to U.S. relations with the Arab world. (It is ironic to learn that a quick Israeli victory is the key to protecting U.S.-Arab relations.) One Politico-Military Affairs representative stated that, though a limited military engagement would be acceptable, there was reason to suspect that the fighting would escalate.

Although there was no direct challenge to this tacit argument in favor of giving Israel a green light, it did not become U.S. policy. Rather, State's Bureau of Near Eastern Affairs pushed for what became the consensus approach--restraint of Israel. Not doing so would have meant initiating the SAM-site game of guessing whether or not a Syrian surface-to-air missile could kill an Israeli aircraft before the plane could destroy the missile. The game assumed a failure for American policy--the use of force by either Israel or Syria--and the Bureau feared that the missiles could not be forcibly removed without unacceptable political damage to American goals elsewhere in the region.

The May meetings seriously considered the possibility that the SAM-site game would commence in earnest. Participants at the full Working Group session assumed without debate that the Syrian missiles in Lebanon were a legitimate *casus belli* for Israel--the missiles would justify the use of force if an alternative approach would not remove them. But the group advised that Israel should not resort to military action until U.S. diplomacy could act. American diplomats wanted to create a political climate that would reduce Syria's need to have its missiles in Lebanon. The consensus was to provide an incentive for Syria to withdraw its missiles voluntarily, without military action on the part of Israel.

Preliminary Contingency Planning: Resupplying Israel

At the May 7 Working Group meeting, participants next considered resupplying Israel in the event of a confrontation that escalated or expanded. According to former officials who took part in the session, there was no indication that American resupply would be used as a lever to punish or coerce Israel for attacking the SAMs. In previous situations similar to Lebanon, the resupply of Israel had been a contentious issue among American national security managers. Take, for example, the case of replenishing

Israel's arsenal during the 1973 war. Kissinger claims that he favored meeting Israel's request for immediate arms transfers in the early phases of the war, but that Defense Secretary James Schlesinger suggested delay in order to maintain the image of the United States as an honest broker.[19] Secondary sources highlight the controversy over resupply. They divide over whether Kissinger, indeed, did try to facilitate rearming Israel or whether he sought to delay arms shipments in hopes of finding a diplomatic solution with Soviet assistance.[20]

Globalists aligned with Haig dominated the May 1981 meeting when it came to the issue of resupplying Israel. They concluded that American action should be contingent on Soviet resupply of Syria. To that extent, most of the participants viewed a potential Israeli-Syrian confrontation from an East/West perspective. Even with such a common framework, however, there were different policy implications.

The Department of Defense (Office of the Secretary of Defense and the Organization of the Joint Chiefs of Staff) adopted a globalist approach regarding Soviet implications but firmly opposed an Israeli strike. Former officials of Defense recalled their rationale: Israeli air strikes with U.S.-supplied weapons would risk a U.S.-Soviet confrontation in the Mediterranean and place the United States at a disadvantage in the event of a Gulf war. Such air strikes would be particularly dangerous if host-nation support for an American defense of the Gulf was insufficient. Specifically, Defense officials worried that this Israeli action would diminish the likelihood that Gulf nations would allow the United States to pre-position supplies in the Gulf.

In addition, Defense feared that Israeli air strikes with American-origin weapons would complicate access rights negotiations with Gulf area states for use of their military facilities in Gulf contingencies. Officials in the department also worried that such air strikes would decrease the likelihood that the Gulf states would take part in joint military planning in preparation for a possible Southwest Asian military contingency--a Soviet invasion of Iran. Defense preferred a peacetime deterrence strategy involving a credible military presence in the Gulf area, access to improved Gulf facilities, and periodic deployment of American forces for combined exercises with host nations. Consequently, the department was reluctant for Israel to jeopardize this strategy with its air strikes against what the Pentagon viewed as a limited Syrian missile threat to Israel in Lebanon. Implicit in the Defense

Department's position is the traditional priority it gives the Gulf region over the Arab-Israeli zone.

Haig's allies in State's Politico-Military Affairs and Staff for Policy Planning also adopted a globalist approach but favored an Israeli strike. These officials reasoned that Israel's air strikes could take out the SAMs with minimal political damage to American goals elsewhere in the region. Such strikes also would demonstrate the superiority of Israel's American patronage and weapons over Syria's Soviet backing. Compared to Defense, State under Haig was less concerned that Israeli military actions would harm American relations with the Gulf states.

It is paradoxical that Defense would be more sensitive than State to political considerations in military contingency planning. State would allow for more military coordination and planning with Jerusalem than would Defense; State also had a higher tolerance for Israel's use of American-origin weapons. Ironically, Israeli air strikes using such equipment against an Arab state seemed politically unacceptable to the Department of Defense but politically acceptable to the Department of State. So, there was both a split within State and a conflict between it and Defense.

In the debate within and among the departments, the White House was a missing actor. As a result, the National Security Council was not used to infuse cabinet officials with a sense of White House priorities, other than the president's aversion to the risk that the use of force might entail. Thus, the NSC staff lacked the authority to harmonize disputes within the interagency process. The absence of coordination resulted in turf battles that diminished the chances for coherent policy formulation and facilitated the emergence of an unchallenged and premature policy consensus. Partly as a consequence, there was little synthesis of U.S. diplomacy with Israel's threat to use force.

Conclusions

Although the impending crisis was an opportunity for a combined diplomatic and military approach, Washington did not seize this occasion to formulate one. The actors in Lebanon were cast in such a complex system of relations that it was difficult for outside powers to anticipate the consequences of political/military intervention. Concerning the interagency debate within the administration, Habib and his allies dominated the policy process at the expense of the Haig coalition. The result was a policy calling for the restraint of Israel.

In short, the Department of State generally was less concerned than Defense with a possible ripple effect from action in the Arab-Israeli zone on the Gulf. Haig's global perspective tended to generate interagency accord on the issue of resupplying Israel in the event that Jerusalem used its air force to take out Syria's missiles in Lebanon. But that approach did not produce agreement about the air strikes themselves. Finally, the absence of White House leadership allowed policy to emerge from an unchallenged bureaucratic consensus and interagency bargaining that was neither guided by presidential priorities nor coordinated by the NSC staff. The SAM-site threat, however, did allow that staff to begin crisis contingency planning by specifying objectives on Lebanon under varying circumstances.

2

Contingency Planning

The Washington Game Plan: Syria Versus Israel

Leaks from State

When classified information leaks, bureaucratic warfare abounds. At issue here is whether the war was between the White House and the State Department or within State itself. The following leak appeared in the *Miami Herald* newspaper, among others:

> Washington--A White House "option paper" last spring [1981] seriously proposed that the United States declare war on Syria during the crisis over its moving of Soviet-made anti-aircraft missiles into Lebanon, State Department sources said.[1]

Someone at the State Department had leaked to syndicated columnist James McCartney the essence of NSC staff contingency planning for a possible war between Syria and Israel. The motivation may have been to force an overhaul in NSC staff personnel who dealt with the Middle East. Regardless, no one at the White House considered using American military force to remove Syria's missiles from Lebanon. Even McCartney admitted that "the proposal to use American jets to take out the Syrian missiles did not come from [National Security Adviser] Allen's staff...but emanated from the State Department's bureau of politico-military affairs."

State also was torn as Politico-Military Affairs and the Staff for Policy Planning competed with the Bureau of Near Eastern and South Asian Affairs for the ear of the secretary. In light of this, the Near Eastern bureau may have been the source of the leak; a more likely source, however, was State Department Counselor Robert McFarlane, who was in the process of departing from State to become deputy national security adviser. McFarlane wanted to

29

clean house when he arrived at the National Security Council, and the McCartney leak would have strengthened his hand in dismissing officials who were not loyal to him.

So, the issue of the locus of bureaucratic warfare can now be answered. The leaks from State indicate bureaucratic battles between the White House and the State Department, as well as within State itself. But despite the attempt by State to force personnel changes at the White House, the NSC staff was undaunted and weighed into the bureaucratic fray with a game plan for Lebanon.

U.S. Objectives

According to former officials at the White House, the NSC staff considered American objectives regarding Lebanon, as well as diplomatic and military contingencies. The staff divided objectives into short- and mid-term, diplomatic approaches into success or failure of the Habib mission, and military events into limited or expanded hostilities. The administration's short-term goals included:

1. preventing the outbreak of fighting between Israel and Syria, and
2. in the event of hostilities, limiting the scope and duration of fighting.

Mid-term objectives were:

1. to insulate the Camp David peace process (the Egypt-Israel Treaty and ongoing Sinai negotiations) from the effects of the Lebanese crisis;
2. to retain the confidence of moderate Arab states and thereby preserve U.S. ability to pursue the administration's Southwest Asian security strategy for the Gulf, Afghanistan, and Pakistan;
3. to retain Israel's confidence in American support for its fundamental security;
4. to deny the Soviets political benefits and focus blame for the failure of diplomatic efforts on them;
5. if fighting began, to bring it to an early halt in ways that reinforce the unique position of the United States in relation to the resolution of regional problems;

    6. to strengthen the government of Lebanon's hand throughout the country.

Although there was some consensus on this list of objectives, the administration gave little attention to the rank order or weight of each aim; therefore, it failed to calculate trade-offs. The president expressed interest in the short-term objectives of avoiding and limiting war but was silent on American goals concerning the Soviet Union and Israel. The secretary of state wanted to use the Lebanon crisis to accelerate the Camp David peace process, but he did not take into account the impact of such an approach on the administration's Southwest Asian security strategy. The secretary of defense stressed Southwest Asian security but opposed the use of Lebanon to enhance the success of the Arab-Israeli peace process.

Given the variety of goals advanced by key national security cabinet officers, it was important for the president to communicate his priorities and reconcile them with those of the other senior players. And in the absence of presidential leadership, the national security adviser and his staff did not attempt to harmonize priorities and suggest trade-offs among goals. In other words, the NSC adviser and staff lacked the political clout to coordinate the interagency process. Due to the president's desire to avoid or limit warfare, these two short-term goals became the guiding principles for the decisionmaking process.

Officials were reluctant to articulate differences in priorities across departments and focused instead upon alternative means for achieving their favored objective under various contingencies. Though there was considerable consensus to send Ambassador Habib to the Middle East, there was less agreement on which objectives he should emphasize in the field. In part because he was widely esteemed, there was little perceived need to specify priorities among objectives in his instructions. And because the ambassador had the confidence of the other principals, he had the opportunity to sort out priorities according to his own feel for contingencies as they unfolded.

Lebanon Contingencies

In addition to objectives, the NSC staff specified diplomatic contingencies and the options associated with them, as well as the expected benefits and costs of each option. One contingency was success of the Habib mission; it would not have entailed any immediate, follow-up American action. But in the event of an impasse, with an outbreak of hostilities appearing imminent, options required the synthesis of diplomatic and military factors. As an indication of the type of political/military reasoning that prevailed in the Reagan administration during the spring of 1981, consider the published accounts of another "war scare" over Lebanon, this time one year later. A theme underlying these accounts is that bureaucracy fluctuates between issuing red-light warnings to prevent Israel from taking military action against neighboring Arab states and giving it a green light to launch an attack.

Traditionally, Defense has advocated a red-light policy toward Israel. Such was the case during most of 1981-1982. For example, the *Middle East Policy Survey (MEPS)* of February 12 (no. 49) and March 12 (no. 51), 1982, told of the bureaucratic interplay on the prospective use of American force to support U.S. diplomatic objectives. *MEPS* stated that the Joint Chiefs of Staff wrote a contingency paper that recommended American-Soviet cooperation in Lebanon and anticipated the possibility of United States armed combat with Israel. The best estimate of U.S. military planners was that Israel would not be able to limit an attack to the PLO and would face major Syrian resistance. Accordingly, *MEPS* described the Chiefs' contingency plan as assuming a full-scale Arab-Israeli war and the need for the United States to distance itself from Israel and thereby avoid getting caught in an anticipated Arab backlash.

The red-light/green-light debate of 1981-1982 occurred within the context of the continuing presence of Syrian missiles in Lebanon and an extensive PLO buildup in the south of the country under the protection of this lethal missile umbrella. According to *MEPS* of May 8, 1981 (no. 31), a State Department official told this journal that "'Israel will eventually get a green light for military action.'" Another insider from State went even further in telling *MEPS* that the Habib mission would lay the diplomatic groundwork for a military strike against Syrian missiles in Lebanon. Beyond that, in the next edition of *MEPS* (May 22, 1981, no. 32), a key U.S. official was quoted as saying that "'whatever the method, it is 100 per cent certain that those missiles will be removed.'"

When Israel finally invaded Lebanon in June 1982, there was a charge that Washington had "authorized" the invasion. At issue is whether or not Secretary Alexander Haig had given Israel any such go-ahead; he has denied this. In meetings and communications with Israelis prior to the invasion, he insisted, he had repeatedly stated his formula that the United States would consider an Israeli attack justified only in strictly proportional response to "'an internationally recognized provocation.'"[2] Despite Haig's denial, even critics of the invasion contend that the government of Israel had reason to believe that Washington, in fact, had bestowed its tacit approval for a limited military action in Lebanon.[3] Indeed, Israel perceived a green light for one operation--a limited action in the south of Lebanon in response to a terrorist provocation--but pursued another--an all-out invasion of Lebanon, including a siege of Beirut.

Washington game planning linked objectives, contingencies, and options into more or less plausible scenarios of future states of affairs. The planning manifested an explicit intention on the part of the White House to approach the Missiles of May crisis in as rational a fashion as possible. Such planning, however, was only a guide to action for a select few who, in fact, did not have the action; State, rather than the White House, had the responsibility for originating the paperwork to begin the decisionmaking process. Thus, White House planning was by no means an actual description of the policymaking process itself but more of a prescriptive planning tool. That process was not nearly as organized as the planning would imply, and objectives were not cast in stone. Rather, goals floated in a fluid bargaining process among departments.

From Bureaucratic Warfare to Inconsistent Consensus

The White House, State, and Defense all had their own set of priorities. Within each of these organizations, moreover, there were differences of opinion between high-level officials and bureaucrats concerning America's objectives in Lebanon. And the unwillingness of the White House to impose its priorities allowed bureaucratic warfare to reign. President Reagan's laid-back management style assumed that logically coherent priorities would flow from bargaining among the principals. In fact, however, what emerged was a contradictory consensus. Thus, logical incoherence was the result of the president's failure to compel his national security cabinet officials to follow a presidential agenda.

The inconsistent consensus of the Reagan administration confused both friend and foe alike. For example, there was interagency concurrence on the need to prevent a war between Israel and Syria. But the different factions also agreed that Israel had the right to use force if American diplomacy failed to induce

Syria to withdraw its missiles from Lebanon: Syria's deployment of its missiles in Lebanon gave Israel a *casus belli*. Implicit in this contradiction were two messages for Israel--a public call for restraint and a private acknowledgement of its legitimate right to use force. In effect, then, the Reagan administration inadvertently had provided Israel with mixed signals: Do not take actions that would lead to war with Damascus, but, if diplomacy fails, use whatever force is necessary to remove the Syrian missiles in Lebanon. Such inconsistent consensus bedeviled Washington's approach toward Syria's missiles in Lebanon, but contradictory national security decision rules are not unique to the Reagan administration.

An analogous set of conflicting propositions faced U.S. presidents during the Vietnam era. Former Pentagon adviser Daniel Ellsberg suggests that the presidents in office between 1961 and 1975 made policy decisions on the basis of two rules: (1) do not lose the rest of Vietnam to Communist control before the next election, and (2) do not commit U.S. ground troops to a land war in Asia.[4] Ellsberg believes that presidents were more likely to break the second rule because they feared the domestic political risks of losing land to Communists after the "loss" of China in 1949 more than they feared incurring the costs of committing troops to a land war after having fought China in Korea during the early 1950s. Viewed in the long history of contradictory decision rules in the United States, President Reagan's inconsistent consensus over Lebanon was yet another chapter chronicling the tendency of chief executives to follow conflicting propositions.

The problem in transmitting dual messages is that the sender cannot be sure which signal the target and third parties will take as a basis for action.[5] In the case of the May 1981 crisis over Syria's missiles in Lebanon, Israel's preferred option was to use force; consequently, there was a risk that it would heed the U.S. message that supported this action. But, in fact, Jerusalem chose not to use force against Syrian missiles during the May 1981 crisis.

The difficulty caused by dual American messages also applied to Syria. However, unlike Israel, Syria chose the message that was compatible with its preferred option--retaining its missiles in Lebanon. That is, Damascus paid attention to the American message to Israel that cautioned Jerusalem not to take action against Syria. Nevertheless, the conflicting signals sent to Israel also confused Syria. Both countries understood America's role as a traffic signaler in a region packed with tanks and warplanes always threatening to collide. Neither antagonist, however, knew when the American signal would turn from red to green, giving a go-ahead for Israel to attack Syria's missiles in Lebanon. Yet, at the core of Washington game planning was a one-man diplomatic traffic cop working for restraint--Habib, who designed a program either to avoid war entirely or to limit its intensity and duration in the event of hostilities.

Strategic planning was a tool that the White House could have used to shape the interagency process and evaluate proposals from the bureaucracy. But the White House failed to assert itself. As a consequence, State retained the action, and its Bureau of Near Eastern and South Asian Affairs continued as the lead unit in the department. Under State's direction, a small executive committee of the Working Group came to be known as the Lebanon Task Force.

"Neutralization" of the Palestine Liberation Organization

One of the first activities of the Lebanon Task Force was a meeting on May 8, 1981. Proposals voiced by State at this session indicated how far its perception of the missile crisis diverged from that of the White House. Whereas 1600 Pennsylvania Avenue was concerned with preventing the outbreak of hostilities or at least bringing any fighting to a speedy halt, Foggy Bottom under Haig was thinking strategically--of using prospective hostilities to achieve broad American goals in the region. According to the recollection of officials who participated in the May 8 meeting, a high-ranking State Department official with undisputed authority to speak for the secretary suggested that the political neutrality of Lebanon ought to be the overall American objective. And to achieve this goal, U.S. policy had to help bring about the "neutralization" of the Palestinian resistance movement in Lebanon.

It is important to recognize the gravity of the statement about neutralization. In the context of Lebanon itself, neutrality implied moving it away from the Moslem core of the Arab world toward a more moderate position reflecting the Christian rightist view of the Arab-Israeli conflict; neutralizing the PLO, however, is a euphemism for destroying that organization. It is incredible that this statement was made by a regional specialist whose bureau was known for its long-standing belief that the Palestinian issue was the core of the Arab-Israeli conflict and that the PLO was the legitimate representative of the Palestinian people.

Ironically, State's circumlocution on neutralizing the PLO mirrored Israeli Defense Minister Ariel Sharon's concept of the 1982 war. He envisioned destroying the PLO as an organization in Lebanon to create a new strategic situation in the region. First, he believed, destruction of the PLO would weaken its control over the West Bank and Gaza Strip and enhance the likelihood that the Israeli idea of Palestinian autonomy could be imposed on these areas. Second, Sharon anticipated that Syria either would have to withdraw from Lebanon or face defeat of its army there. Israel's rightist allies then would assume control over the whole of Beirut and become the primary local political force among the competing factions. Under these conditions, Sharon hoped that his man in Lebanon, Bashir Gemayel, would assume power and sign a peace treaty with Israel.

Because State Department officials were not known to agree with Sharon's goal of destroying the PLO, one can surmise that the neutralization statement was an expression of the views of Secretary Haig himself. And though individuals generally are not as dominant as the roles they occupy in shaping foreign policy, especially imposing personalities can impress their particular world views on their subordinates. Hence, the regionalists at State uncomfortably wore the views of the secretary; indeed, he had outfitted the entire sixth floor of State in his ideological attire. But, upon Haig's abrupt departure, they shed this global garb in favor of tighter fitting, regional raiment.

A Green Light for Israel?

The May 8 Task Force meeting also was important because it considered the idea that the United States provide Israel with a green light to stamp out the PLO. Although the regional representative implied that destroying the PLO may have been a prerequisite for an ultimate U.S. objective of bringing neutrality to Lebanon, the exchange emphasized prospective Israeli military action in Lebanon aimed at removing Syria's missiles. As a result, the future of the PLO merited only secondary consideration. In a year's time and after a PLO military buildup, the priorities would be reversed.

The question of whether Washington had given a go-ahead signal to Jerusalem was significant in May 1981 because newspapers in Israel began adopting the line that the Habib mission was going to fail and that the United States expected Israel to launch a strike. These news accounts were known to the participants, and the reports therefore added a sense of urgency to the May 8 meeting. According to former officials who were present at that session, there was an exchange concerning what President Reagan should say in a letter to Prime Minister Begin. The consensus was that if Reagan's letter did not explicitly call for Israel to limit its military forces, Jerusalem would interpret it as at least an amber signal and, therefore, would use force in Lebanon.

Contrary to the consensus, the president's letter to Begin did not seek to restrain Israel except through the promise of a successful Habib mission. According to one public account, Reagan was said to have expressed understanding and support for Israel's insistence that Syria withdraw its surface-to-air missiles.[6] Indeed, the letter granted Israel's argument that Syria had no right to deploy missiles in Lebanon and called for a return to the status quo ante. By predicating Israeli restraint on the success of Habib's efforts, the letter's drafters implicitly and perhaps intentionally gave Israel a justification for military action in the event of Habib's failure. Indeed, *New York Times* reporter John Kifner wrote that, although Begin was willing to allow additional time for American diplomacy to resolve the crisis, Israel would remove the missiles militarily if they were not withdrawn.[7]

Neglecting to make an explicit American call for restraint constituted an ambiguous message that Israel exploited. And the uncertainty regarding the message would explode in 1982 amid charges and denials of an American nod to Israel for an invasion of Lebanon. Although the Habib mission succeeded in checking Israel during 1981, the administration's diplomacy failed in its efforts at rocket removal. And the ambiguities in presidential and other ministerial communications to Israel created a loophole through which the Israeli armed forces could roll into Lebanon.

It is a standard operating assumption in the United States Government that Israeli officials have a penchant for reading vagueness and ambiguity in American communications as a sign of informed consent to some preferred Israeli action. An American nod acknowledging that an Israeli suggestion has been heard and understood could be reported not only as an agreement to the substance of the idea but as a Washington proposal. Certainly, diplomatic ambiguity is a time-honored practice of most states, but Washington officials charged with the conduct of U.S.-Israel relations must play by explicit rules of the road lest they leave an opening through which Israeli tanks might rumble.

Explicit warnings from Washington, therefore, are necessary to secure Jerusalem's restraint. The relatively successful attempt of President Lyndon Johnson to keep Israel from using force is a case in point. On May 26, 1967, he proclaimed that "I must emphasize the necessity for Israel not to make itself responsible for the initiation of hostilities. Israel will not be alone unless it decides to do it alone. We cannot imagine that Israel will make this decision."[8] Johnson's call for restraint helped delay military action by Israel, but Jerusalem interpreted a follow-up message on June 3 as an amber light.

The degree of threat Israel faced in 1967 was far greater than that during 1981, and a lesson may be drawn from the two cases. Even in the more hostile environment of 1967, Johnson's explicit call for restraint only succeeded in delaying Israeli military action; thus, Reagan's implicit call for the same had little chance for success in 1981.

American Diplomacy and Israel's Threats

In addition to the question of what the president should say to Prime Minister Begin, there was a discussion at the May 8, 1981, meeting as to whether the threat of Israel's military action should be used to reinforce Habib's diplomacy. But officials did not reach a consensus on whether diplomacy and force should be coupled. Globalists argued in favor of combining the threat of force with diplomacy because of Syrian ties to the Soviet Union. They suggested that the United States should set some sort of implicit deadline by which time diplomacy should be able to remove the missiles, implying that Israel would be free to act if Syria did not meet the deadline. This group reasoned that, if Syria believed the United States would continue to counsel restraint to Israel, there would be less of an incentive for Syria to withdraw its missiles. The group also believed that the problem of a dual message to Israel had begun to complicate Habib's efforts. And because Damascus preferred to hear the restraint-of-Jerusalem message, the threat of Israeli military action against the missiles lacked credibility.

Despite the fact that the United States would have been blamed for Israel's actions in any event, regionalists argued that Washington should not be placed in a position of having given an implicit green light to Jerusalem and then suffering an anti-American backlash in both the Arab-Israeli and Gulf zones. In the end, the regionalists carried the day as the United States not only advised restraint but also failed to employ the threat of Israel's use of force as a lever to motivate Syria to withdraw its missiles through negotiations.

During the siege of Beirut in August 1982, this debate was played out once again.   At that time, Israel had surrounded Palestinian fighters in West Beirut.   Officials within the Reagan administration disagreed on the extent to which the Habib mission should use the threat of Israel's attack on the PLO in West Beirut as a lever to motivate its withdrawal from Beirut.   In both the May 1981 and the August 1982 cases, regionalists who recommended restraint and were unwilling to couple diplomacy with force dominated the policy process, to the detriment of American national security.

In a broader perspective, whether regionalists or globalists prevail depends upon American officials' perception of the Soviet role in a given conflict situation.   If decisionmakers see the Soviets as the main instigators or beneficiaries of a conflict involving third parties, globalists tend to win out over regionalists.   On the one hand, policyforcing events in the Gulf favor American globalists due in part to the proximity of the Soviet Union to that area and the concern over possible Soviet involvement in an unfolding conflict. On the other hand, such events in the Arab-Israeli zone favor American regionalists because the Soviet factor seems less important there.

The dispute between those who counsel restraint and those who advocate the threat and/or judicious use of force is a characteristic split within the policy elite.   For example, there were differences within the Nixon cabinet between Secretary of State Rogers and Assistant to the President for National Security Affairs Kissinger during the Jordanian crisis of 1970.   According to Kissinger's memoirs, Rogers believed that it was desirable to reassure nervous adversaries that the United States intended them no harm; in contrast, Kissinger felt that, once embarked on a confrontation course, implacability was both the better and safer course.[9] Although Rogers thought calming the atmosphere would contribute to conflict resolution, Kissinger believed that the incentive for rapid settlement was the danger that a situation might escalate.

During the 1981-1982 conflicts over Lebanon, there was a repeat of the Rogers/Kissinger dispute in the fierce battles between Secretary Haig and Judge William Clark, formerly Haig's deputy and subsequently assistant to the president for national security affairs. Haig followed the risk-taking approach, but Clark pursued the reassurance path. Contrary to the expectation of role theorists, however, individuals are able to transcend the limitations of their particular roles in the policy elite, as evidenced by the Rogers/Kissinger and Haig/Clark battles. If role factors are as important as the literature suggests, there would be more similarity over time among individuals occupying the same position than is demonstrated here.

U.S. Strategy in the Event of War: Blame Moscow

Another item on the agenda of the May 1981 meetings on Lebanon was what American objectives should be if hostilities between Israel and Syria seemed imminent. And once those objectives were established, what should the U.S. response be if Israel unilaterally decided to use force? No explicit decision was made on the options issue, but sentiment seemed to fall somewhere between all-out support for Israel and a straddling between Israel and Syria.

One conclusion that did emerge was that if Israel did strike Syria's missiles, the United States should set the stage to blame the Soviet Union for not reining in its client and for failing to persuade Syria to withdraw its missiles. In other words, the United States was prepared to accuse the Soviet Union for not preventing Syria from deploying missiles in the first place and for not inducing Syria to withdraw those missiles afterward. Although regionalists advocated restraint, even they were prepared to engage in "Soviet bashing" for the purpose of damage control vis-a-vis the moderate Arab countries. Both globalists and regionalists alike were ready to condemn the Soviets in the event that Israel jumped the gun, the former because it is the name of their game and the latter in order to protect America's image in the region by deflecting attention and anger from the American-Israeli side to the Soviet-Syrian team.

Compare American decisionmaking during the 1981-1982 crisis in Lebanon and that in three other cases--Lebanon in 1958, Jordan in 1970, and the 1973 Arab-Israeli war. Foreign policy specialist Alan Dowty notes an American tendency to blame the Soviets for the behavior of one of their local clients.[10] Even if the assumption of Soviet complicity is false, censuring the USSR may be the best policy because Washington's impact on Moscow may be greater than on a Soviet client. If American efforts were unable to persuade Syria to withdraw its missiles, the Dowty analysis would suggest that Washington should play its Moscow card so that the Soviets would exercise influence over their local client. No one at the May 1981 meetings at State, however, felt that the Soviet Union represented much of an option because it did not have diplomatic relations with Syria and Israel. Indeed, Syria probably would have viewed a Soviet attempt to mediate the missile conflict as meddling. At least as far as the 1981 case is concerned, Dowty's formula presupposed a greater amount of Soviet influence on the Syrians than American decisionmakers believed existed.

Evacuation of American Nationals from Lebanon

There was an intense discussion at the May 1981 meetings concerning evacuation of American nationals from Lebanon. One idea was to dissuade rightist militias from shelling the Beirut airport area while persuading the PLO to protect U.S. personnel. The Lebanese civil war of 1975-1976 served as precedent for the PLO to provide security for American personnel in evacuation contingencies. Participants also discussed the dilemma posed by evacuation. On the one hand, if the United States waited until there was a war to evacuate American citizens, it might be too late to get them out safely; on the other hand, if the administration withdrew American citizens prior to hostilities, evacuation might be interpreted as a signal of escalation and could lead to a self-fulfilling prophecy. (The United States believed that the United Kingdom already had stirred up British citizens in Beirut with talk of an impending evacuation.) The evacuation plan that the session finally accepted took advantage of a change of U.S. ambassadors in Lebanon as an excuse to draw down the staff. This policy actually had very little effect on the American community at large in Lebanon because it directly affected only U.S. government officials and their dependents. The administration adopted the drawdown plan on May 9, 1981, at a meeting of the Working Group especially convened to deal with this issue.

American Force Deployment

Several decisions on U.S. force deployment were on the agenda of the May 1981 meetings. At issue was the movement of U.S. naval vessels into the area around Lebanon. A specific concern was whether the aircraft carrier *Independence* should be moved from the Indian Ocean to the Mediterranean as a political signal of American intentions regarding the use of force. One of the problems with changing the carrier's movement was that it might appear the United States was acting in coordination with Israel in the event that nation chose to use force. Furthermore, the Pentagon had scheduled a destroyer and a frigate of the U.S. Navy to make a routine port call in Haifa during May. Reflect upon a situation where American ships made a port call as the *Independence* moved from the Indian Ocean to the Mediterranean. Under these circumstances, if there were a strike by Israel against the missiles in Lebanon, Arab leaders, with good justification, might accuse the United States of collusion with Israel.

The carrier *Forrestal* was already in the eastern Mediterranean. Hence, had the United States also brought the *Independence* into the area, it could well have been interpreted as a sign that Washington expected round-the-clock military activity. Typically, to conduct continuous carrier-based air operations, the navy prefers to have at least two of these vessels in a given area. But a major problem with this strategy in this case was that the *Independence* was an East Coast aircraft carrier--that is, its home port was on the eastern seaboard of the continental United States. As a result, the Soviet Union would have expected it to go through the Suez Canal from the Indian Ocean on the way to its home port. Thus, any political message intended by moving the *Independence* would be diluted if the Soviets indicated to the Syrians that the carrier was on a routine run from the Indian Ocean to the Mediterranean.

U.S. Force Deployment and American Diplomacy

The dispute within the bureaucracy concerning the movement of naval vessels highlights the relationship between force and diplomacy. Globalists in the Bureau of Politico-Military Affairs and Staff for Policy Planning at State, as well as those on the NSC staff, held that the ships should be moved as a political signal to reinforce Israel's threat to use military power. But the Office of the Secretary of Defense and the Organization of the Joint Chiefs of Staff took the position that there should be no changes in the operations of the aircraft carriers in support of Israel's threat to use military action. This recommendation comported with the Department of Defense's traditional view that military force should be used only in rare instances and that force deployment decisions should be subject only to military requirements, not to diplomatic needs. Implicit in the discussion were the issues of whether and how the United States should threaten to use force and if it should be identified with Israel in that regard. Two schools of thought characterized the debate, both of which drew their positions in May 1981 from an earlier situation--the case of Jordan during 1970.

The globalist position in the May meetings was based upon an inference that Syria had failed to commit its air force against Jordan during 1970 and then had withdrawn its tanks because the Israeli Air Force was primed to attack and the United States had a menacing presence in the eastern Mediterranean that neutralized Soviet forces there. Kissinger, then assistant to the president for national security affairs, managed American decisionmaking during the Jordan crisis of 1970. He attributes the withdrawal of Syrian armor and the withholding of Soviet forces during Jordan's civil war to American augmentation of its forces in the eastern Mediterranean and to Israeli mobilization.[11] Kissinger acknowledged the failure by General Hafez Assad, head of the Syrian Air Force and subsequently president, to commit his forces and provide cover for Syrian tanks in Jordan. However, Kissinger also implied that Assad's actions were more a result of the coordinated American-Israeli threat than a response to internal divisions within Syria.

The regionalist school during the May meetings held to its traditional viewpoint. It criticized the assumption that the Washington-Jerusalem threat of force was the factor most responsible for the Syrian failure to commit its air force and ultimately withdraw. This school drew its rationale from Kissinger's former NSC aide William Quandt, a regionalist in this context.[12] He argued against the globalist interpretation prevailing in the 1970s White House when he wrote that Kissinger misread the Syrian invasion of Jordan when he overemphasized the American and Soviet role and minimized domestic Syrian politics. Moreover, when Damascus ordered Syrian forces to withdraw from Jordan, the pullout may have had less to do with pressure from Washington and Moscow than the refusal of General Assad to commit the Syrian Air Force to an incursion planned by one of his rivals--Salah Jadid.

Similarly, former *New York Times* journalist Seymour Hersh grants that American and Israeli military threats played a role in the Syrian turnabout but maintains that these maneuvers were not the only factors in Syria's decisionmaking process. Like Quandt, Hersh believes an equally significant influence was rivalry between the military and civilian wings of the ruling Baath party in

Damascus--a dispute that recurred with the Syrian invasion of Jordan. Hersh attributes Assad's refusal to commit the air force to this domestic Syrian rivalry.[13] Because regionalists paid close attention to local events and domestic rivalries, they downplayed the Soviet role in the area and placed less credence in the efficacy of American military force as a factor in determining local outcomes. Consequently, regionalists were less likely to advocate the threat of American military force as a device to bring about a favorable political resolution to what they perceived as a local conflict.

Intelligence and the Policy Process

In addition to globalist and regionalist policy analysts, members of the intelligence community were also important in the decisionmaking process of May 1981. According to former officials, the intelligence bureaucracy did not expect the Soviet Union to take any military action during this crisis, beyond resupplying Syria in the event of an Israeli air strike. Although it gave considerable attention to the Soviet role in the missile crisis, intelligence considered the role to encompass only resupply of Syria--that is, few officials believed the Soviets would take military action against Israel. Some in the bureaucracy held that the Soviets might contemplate sending ground combat forces to Syria only if President Assad was about to be toppled. Thus, the Soviet factor offered little constraint on American management of the missile crisis. And the perceived lack of an operational Soviet threat against Israel reinforced the views of those policy analysts who wished to give maximum latitude to Israel. "Green lighters" temporarily had the right of way as the traffic in violence picked up speed.

Despite the assessment that the Soviets were unlikely to intervene if the missile crisis escalated, officials discussed the U.S.-Soviet military balance in relation to the possibility of an Israeli air strike. A high-ranking representative of Politico-Military Affairs at State pointed out that several military balances had changed since the Jordan crisis. First, there was an improvement in the Soviet capability to insert forces rapidly into a sensitive area. Second, there were changes at the global level, meaning in the nuclear balance. The United States was superior to the Soviet Union on both scales until 1973. Thereafter, approximate parity in strategic and power projection capability characterized U.S.-Soviet relations. Because the global military balance cast a shadow on regional politics, the change gave Moscow enhanced influence in the Middle East.

On the regional level, the "correlation of forces," (military balance), was favorable to the United States. In 1972, Cairo withdrew from the Soviet camp when President Sadat expelled Moscow's military advisers from Egypt. Although Iran left the West's side following the fall of the Shah in 1978, this American loss was partially offset when Iraq distanced itself from the Soviets after they failed to increase military assistance after the Iraq-Iran war began in September 1980.

The net assessment of changes at both the global and regional levels reinforced the intelligence estimate that Damascus could not expect help from the Soviet Union if Jerusalem launched air strikes against Syria's missiles in Lebanon. Some Middle East experts did believe that the Soviet Union would send ground combat forces to save President Assad of Syria, but Soviet specialists felt that Moscow would let Assad fall.

Globalists felt that, if there were an Israeli-Syrian war, Soviet troops should not remain in Damascus at war's end. When Moscow had threatened to send its troops into Egypt during the waning days of the 1973 war, globalists of that time were as alarmed by the prospect of that war ending with an enhanced Soviet presence in Egypt as with the fighting itself. The introduction of Soviet ground combat forces into an Arab-Israeli conflict would mean that the United States would have to choose between going to war to remove the Soviets or acquiescing to a direct Soviet combat presence in an Arab country. One of Kissinger's principles was that local conflicts should not end with a greater Soviet presence in the region than existed prior to that conflict. Although he was not physically present during the discussions at the various meetings in the first week of May 1981, Kissinger's ideas loomed large in the debates.

The Missile Crisis and the Arab-Israeli Peace Process

The May 1981 discussions also featured a split between globalists and regionalists over which American goals were at issue if the missile crisis escalated. Globalists viewed Lebanon from the perspective of East/West concerns, but regionalists interpreted the situation in terms of the Arab-Israeli conflict. Regionalists worried about the impact of the missile crisis on the peace process, especially the implications of events in Lebanon for Jerusalem's prospective withdrawal from the Sinai as required by the Egypt-

Israel Treaty of 1979. Because regionalists dominated policy, an overview of their position is enlightening.

First, regionalists believed that Egypt would accuse Israel and the United States of collusion if Jerusalem launched a military operation against the Syrian missiles in Lebanon. Second, there was concern that such an Egyptian charge against Israel and the United States would unravel the Camp David peace process by fueling Jerusalem's doubts about the reliability of Cairo's peace pledges. One nightmare scenario making the rounds was that an Israeli refusal to withdraw would lead to harsh statements by Cairo followed by an even tougher line by Jerusalem on the multinational force that was being negotiated between Egypt and Israel. Thereafter, Israeli politicians might succumb to the temptation of "Egypt-bashing" during the forthcoming elections in Israel. Jerusalem then might try to postpone its withdrawal from Sinai by refusing to accept the multinational force that was to monitor the situation after the Israelis had departed. Such a scenario could culminate in the demise of the Egypt-Israel Peace Treaty and the Camp David peace process.

Syrian Brinkmanship

Even as American decisionmakers met to "round-table" a United States strategy in the face of the missile problem, policyforcing events in the Middle East were overtaking both Washington game planning and actual decisions. In a televised address on May 3, 1981, Assad defended the emplacement of surface-to-air missiles in Lebanon, in the wake of Israel's shooting down two of his helicopters in Syrian-Phalange sparring. He falsely accused Israel and the United States of plotting against Syria and planning to partition Lebanon. Contrary to Assad's inflammatory rhetoric, the U.S. ambassador to Israel delivered a note from President Reagan to Prime Minister Begin on May 4, asking him to hold off military action against the Syrian missiles and allow time for diplomatic efforts to persuade Syria to remove them. As stated earlier, Begin already had informed the United States that Israel would strike at the missiles unless they were removed by a specified date.[14] But in response to the president's letter, the prime minister allowed additional time for U.S. diplomacy to resolve the Syrian missile issue. As Begin's letter was being delivered, however, Israeli planes streaked over the Bekaa Valley in eastern Lebanon on May 6 in the first reconnaissance mission since Syria deployed missiles in the area.

Two days later, the Syrian Defense Ministry issued a statement angrily rejecting Israeli demands for withdrawal of the missiles. According to SANA, the official Syrian news agency, the Defense Ministry announced that air defense systems, including missiles, were a part of the Syrian Armed Forces and would be present in the future anywhere Syrian soldiers needed them.[15] Subsequently, the Task Force on Lebanon, led by the Department of State, met in Washington early Saturday and Sunday mornings (May 9 and 10), while events in the Middle East propelled the situation into a full-blown crisis. Although political/military contingency planning for the outbreak of hostilities continued, American policy still focused on the Habib mission and a diplomatic resolution to the crisis.

Presidential Envoys Abroad in Times of Crisis

Sending a senior official abroad to engage in personal diplomacy on behalf of an administration in times of crisis is a long-standing tradition in American foreign policy. According to the literature on the area, the road to the Middle East historically has been an indirect route through the colonial capitals of London and Paris. For example, in response to Egyptian nationalization of the Suez Canal during 1956, President Dwight Eisenhower's secretary of state, John Foster Dulles, and his under secretary, Robert Murphy, made several trips to London to help cut a deal between the British and the French, on the one side, and the Egyptians, on the other. Deputy Under Secretary of State Loy Henderson accompanied an international delegation that traveled to Egypt to present President Nasser with the agreement. Within the year, Henderson also visited a number of Arab capitals, trying to coordinate policy concerning domestic instability in Syria and its prospective realignment toward the Soviet Union. The role of a direct Middle East emissary was formalized by Murphy's trips to Lebanon, Baghdad, and Cairo during the 1958 crisis in Lebanon.

Quandt notes that, in the late 1950s, the Murphy mission was the most important way to clarify U.S. objectives to the main actors in the region.[16] It also established the precedent, which the Habib mission could draw on later, for American mediation at the local level once the Soviet Union had been checked. Kissinger elevated America's role as broker to new heights of prominence with his renowned shuttle diplomacy among Jerusalem, Cairo, and

Damascus during 1974-1975. Finally, President Carter engaged the services of Robert Strauss and, later, Sol Linowitz as special envoys for the Palestinian autonomy talks between Israel and Egypt, as called for by the Camp David accords.

In terms of this American tradition of sending presidential envoys abroad in times of crisis, consider a study by national security affairs analysts Barry Blechman and Stephen Kaplan. They find that in the short and longer terms, the results were less frequently positive when administrations used personal diplomacy. Blechman and Kaplan pose these questions: "Did the envoys bungle their missions and thereby make positive outcomes less likely than if they had not gone at all? Or were special missions made only in the most difficult situations, those least likely to end positively in any case?" The authors conclude that although instances of bungling may exist, the difficulty of the personal envoy's assignment makes it hard to achieve a favorable outcome.[17]

The Habib Mission to Mediate Between Israel and Syria

Despite the long odds against success, the Habib mission did prevent an Israeli-Syrian armed clash over the missiles in the short term. The mission failed to remove the missiles, but at least it succeeded in restraining Jerusalem from initiating armed conflict during 1981. This accomplishment was obscured, however, by the fact that Israel invaded Lebanon a year later and destroyed the missiles as a by-product of its war against the Palestine Liberation Organization. Habib later would negotiate an end to the Israeli siege of Beirut and evacuation of the PLO from Lebanon.

Appointed by President Reagan as special envoy on May 5, 1981, in response to Syria's deployment of missiles in Lebanon on April 30, Habib arrived in Beirut for talks designed to elicit Lebanese input to a resolution of the missile crisis. It was of symbolic value for him to visit Lebanon first--a signal that the territorial integrity of that torn land was a high priority of the American government. Visiting Beirut first was consistent with the U.S. approach of seeking a solution on the ground among the warring factions. This method promised to undercut Syria's argument that its missiles were a necessary response to Israeli-abetted, right-wing Christian challenges to other Lebanese factions supported by Syria.

After talks in Beirut, Habib went to Damascus. He delivered a message from Reagan to Assad on May 10 and met with Begin in

Jerusalem the following day. On May 12, the Israel Defense Forces announced that missiles were fired unsuccessfully from Syrian territory at Israeli reconnaissance aircraft over Lebanon. Habib returned to Beirut, then went on to Damascus when a Syrian missile shot down one of several pilotless Israeli reconnaissance planes over the Bekaa Valley in Lebanon. With Israel's use of drones for gathering intelligence, the SAM-site game now became a down-a-drone-a-day game for Syria. Meanwhile, the Habib shuttle took off for Saudi Arabia for talks on the missile crisis. After the Israeli cabinet voted on May 17 to allow time for diplomatic efforts before resorting to military action against the missiles, Habib worked frantically to nail down an agreement with hurried talks in Damascus, Tel Aviv, and Beirut.

Despite the fact that a third pilotless Israeli aircraft was downed by Syrian missiles, Habib returned to Washington for consultation and won praise from the president and the secretary of state for his "successful" shuttle diplomacy. Although the Syrian missiles were still in Lebanon and Syria was still firing on Israel's drones, the special envoy had presided over an apparent lessening of tensions within Lebanon. But though his efforts may have succeeded in lowering the likelihood of general war in the short term, this proved to be a Pyrrhic victory. From mid-1981 to mid-1982, the PLO was able to take advantage of both the Habib-negotiated Israeli restraint regarding Syria's missiles in Lebanon and the Habib-arranged cease-fire between Israel and the PLO.

The confrontation between Syria and the right-wing Lebanese (Phalange) around the town of Zahle, Lebanon, which had precipitated the Missiles of May crisis, came to an end when the right-wing militia leader and later president, Bashir Gemayel, capitulated and pulled his forces out of the city.[18] This turn of events strengthened the convictions of those analysts who had argued that the Zahle incident was, from the first, a Maronite plot to draw Jerusalem and Damascus into a conflict in which the Phalange's Israeli patron would defeat its Syrian foe. These analysts believed such an outcome would reduce Syrian constraints on Phalange activities. The missiles were a major irritant to the Israelis, but despite Syrian control of Zahle and neighboring Mt. Sannin, no tragedy came to surrounding Maronite towns. There also was no sign of a "panicked flight" of Maronites from the Mount Lebanon fortress.[19] In the absence of a Syrian onslaught against the Christian rightists--which the Phalange had forecast and on which Israel had predicated its strident response--the need for

Israeli action against the missiles seemed less immediate. The missiles remained a smoldering source of concern for Israel but no longer consumed as much attention and energy either in Jerusalem or in Washington.

Habib's successful efforts to restrain Israel postponed the day of reckoning regarding war for Damascus and Jerusalem. Although the NSC staff sought to integrate diplomacy and force, the administration failed to achieve such a synthesis. As State continued its diplomacy-first strategy, Defense remained reluctant to contemplate the use of Israeli force. The White House, meanwhile, impatiently waited for the conflict to intensify before seizing the action from State. Because the president had failed to utilize the interagency process to develop agreement on priorities and trade-offs among goals, an inconsistent consensus was the result. Hence, logical incoherence was the order of the day in Washington as the cast of characters shifted in the Middle East.

Israel Versus the PLO

The PLO Military Buildup

With the apparent denouement of the Missiles of May drama, two key actors switched roles: The PLO replaced Syria. In the interim, however, the PLO was no longer a mouse that roared. Israeli compliance with American requests for time to allow for diplomacy to work its magic had sent an inadvertent signal to PLO Chairman Yasir Arafat--he could risk a further buildup of Palestinian forces. Israeli restraint also may have had the unintended consequence of signaling that Arafat could continue to turn Palestinian guerrilla fighters into a conventional army with greatly reduced fear of an Israeli attack. Seen in this light, Jerusalem's patience concerning the missiles while the PLO enhanced its military capabilities was the first of several major blunders that prefigured the 1982 invasion.

The PLO buildup included such qualitative gains as the integration of heavy weapons, for example, long-range artillery and multiple rocket launchers on trucks, into the Palestinian arsenal. This increased capacity became an unacceptable threat to Israeli settlements in the north. The growing Palestinian military infrastructure and Begin's desire to impress the Israeli public with restraint vis-a-vis Syria in an election year continued to create an incentive for renewed Israeli military action against the armed Palestinian presence in Lebanon.

A dramatic shift in attention from the Syrian missiles in Lebanon to the PLO was manifested when Israel stated on May 29 that its air force had destroyed Libyan antiaircraft missile batteries guarding Palestinian positions in southern Lebanon.   Two days later, the United States reported that it had requested the secretary general of the United Nations to convey to all parties, including the PLO, the need for restraint. This announcement signaled the start of indirect contacts between the United States and the PLO over Lebanon through the United Nations, Saudi Arabia, France, and Tunisia. The declaration also indicated a reorientation of American attention away from the sole preoccupation with the Missiles of May crisis between Israel and Syria to traditional warring between Israel and the Palestine Liberation Organization.   On June 2, Jerusalem resumed its air raids in the south, striking at a village north of Tyre that was said to be the regional headquarters of Fatah--the largest and most dominant group within the Palestinian resistance.   In addition, Israeli vessels bombarded a Palestinian refugee camp north of Tripoli, Lebanon.[20]

On June 6, 1981, Israeli-piloted and American-origin F-16 bombers gave the Palestinians in Lebanon a welcome, though temporary, respite as they streaked eastward over Jordan and Saudi Arabia to destroy a nuclear reactor in Baghdad, Iraq. The United States promptly condemned the raid yet only slapped Israel on the wrist with the announcement of a delay in scheduled shipment of four additional F-16 aircraft. The rationale for the temporary suspension was that the Israeli raid on Iraq may have violated a 1952 arms agreement between Israel and the United States concerning the uses of American-supplied equipment. Coincidentally, on the same day as the raid, Habib returned to the Middle East. He met with Lebanese leaders on June 9 and with Saudi officials four days later in Riyadh.

American Diplomacy

Despite the shift of escalating hostilities from the Jerusalem-Damascus pole to the Israeli-Palestinian axis, the United States continued to address the Syrian missiles indirectly by trying to bring about a political compromise within Lebanon. Following instructions from the Department of State, Habib resumed his mission in a futile attempt to effect a compromise among the factions in Lebanon. Washington's thinking was that a reduction in factional conflict would decrease Syria's incentives for keeping its missiles in Lebanon. This reasoning was based on the rather innocent assumption that factional strife, not strategic deterrence, was the reason for the missile deployment.

Habib then attempted to broker a deal between Jerusalem and Damascus. When proposals to trade Syria's removal of its missiles for a cessation of Israeli reconnaissance missions over Lebanon failed, Habib, as a last resort, shifted his attention to Saudi Arabia. According to the *Middle East Policy Survey* of June 5, 1981 (no. 33), administration officials said that the United States was relying on the Saudis to present a three-point plan to resolve the missile confrontation, calling for: (1) additional Saudi assistance, (2) Arabization of international peacekeeping forces in Lebanon, and (3) step-by-step de-escalation. Habib took note of the fact that, on May 20, Saudi Arabia and Kuwait had resumed their contributions to the Arab Deterrent Force (ADF) in Lebanon. This force consisted primarily of Syrian troops left over from the 1975-1976 civil war. Habib believed that, if Saudi Arabia would weigh in with Syria and help mediate disputes among Lebanese factions, there might be an incentive for Syria to withdraw its missiles. By the end of July 1981, the Saudi plan had become the Habib approach, and there was considerable optimism about the potential success of this approach at State.[21] However, the Saudi strategy failed, as had Habib's previous attempts to induce other Arab players to take actions that would result in the removal of the Syrian missiles from Lebanon.

Habib had succeeded only in persuading Jerusalem to hold its fire at least long enough for events themselves to convince the Israelis that the missiles were not so threatening as to warrant unilateral and immediate military action. But though Habib failed to get the missiles out of Lebanon, he succeeded in mediating a cease-fire between Israel and the PLO during July 1981. This truce meant that the sparring was not called off but merely delayed. During this reprieve, PLO arms acquisitions shot up as Israel laid down diplomatic markers of intent to take action against that organization.

Although the cease-fire caused the PLO strategy to shift from military to political targets of opportunity, the temporary truce failed to prevent the organization from continuing to transform itself from a guerrilla force into a conventional army. According to the *Middle East Policy Survey* of July 31, 1981 (no. 37), the Defense

Intelligence Agency confirmed Israeli estimates of a "massive" PLO buildup in recent months. The DIA also had detected growing PLO operations in Syria and Jordan. During January and February 1982, the PLO received a steady stream of long-range guns, rockets, and mortars in its arsenals in southern Lebanon. Those weapons had a range of fifteen miles and included about one hundred 130-millimeter guns, some sixty 122-millimeter rockets and their launchers, and numerous 120- and 160-millimeter mortars. At this point, there were some 15,000 armed Palestinians, and about one-third of these combatants operated in the area south of the Litani River near Israel's northern border with Lebanon. Along with the torrent of heavy weapons, there was a continuous stream of reinforcements to PLO combatants in Lebanon. These additional troops included expeditionary forces from Libya, Iraq, and the People's Democratic Republic of [South] Yemen. The PLO also enhanced its infrastructure with a major buildup in stocks of ammunition, gasoline, and food at strategic sites in southern Lebanon.

Ironically, the PLO buildup may have had Jerusalem's inadvertent blessing. Israel may have consented to an armistice without a PLO pledge not to repair its infrastructure or replenish its arsenal because key players in Israel were convinced that war was inevitable. If so, the loose terms of a cease-fire agreement could have paved the way for large-scale ground combat operations by Israeli forces. In this respect, Schiff and Ya'ari contend that the July 1981 cease-fire agreement was a harmful one, because it contained the "seeds of war."[22] The PLO was not constrained from building up its inventory; consequently, it could be expected to repair and augment the Palestinian military infrastructure. So, rather than serving as a cooling-off period in which diplomacy could work its magic, the suspension was merely a breathing spell between escalating rounds of combat.

Instead of focusing on the issue of the PLO military buildup during the cease-fire, the United States emphasized the rather odd priority of how to bolster the United Nations Interim Force in Lebanon (UNIFIL). In fact, the *Washington Post* of August 1, 1981, quoted a senior State Department official as saying that the immediate priority in Lebanon was to strengthen UNIFIL. Out in the field, however, Habib appeared to pay little attention to UNIFIL, as he addressed the PLO buildup, if not its general armed presence in Lebanon. During September 1981, he proposed that the PLO withdraw its heavy weapons in exchange for an Israeli commitment to refrain from low-level flights over southern Lebanon and remove Israel's military staff from that area. The *Middle East Policy Survey* of September 11, 1981 (no. 39), reported that President Reagan had "signed off" on a State Department plan designed to build upon the July 1981 Israel-PLO cease-fire in southern Lebanon. Initial stages of the State plan called for a pullback of heavy military equipment from southern Lebanon by both Israel and the Palestinian forces.

With the major exception of Habib's diplomacy, Washington paid scant attention to Lebanon as its focus shifted to the president's crowded legislative calendar in the fall of 1981. Easing its way to the top of that agenda was the controversial proposal to sell U.S. Airborne Warning and Control System (AWACS) reconnaissance planes to Saudi Arabia. The Saudi air defense enhancement package, including AWACS, was the central Middle East issue for the White House during September 1981 because of the apparent trade-off between foreign policy (Saudi Arabia) and domestic political considerations (the pro-Israel lobby).

Other events that pushed Lebanon off Washington's policy docket were Prime Minister Begin's visit of September 8-14, President Anwar Sadat's assassination on October 6, King Hussein's visit of November 2-4, the Soviet-ordered Polish crackdown on trade unionists (Solidarity) on December 12, Israel's annexation of the Golan Heights two days later, and the replacement of National Security Adviser Richard Allen by Deputy Secretary of State William Clark at year's end. Despite the crush of other business, Lebanon still managed to squeeze onto the calendar.

Jerusalem Comes to Washington

In preparation for Begin's September 1981 visit, State emphasized the need to maintain the July 1981 cessation of hostilities. Almost as an afterthought, the department acknowledged that Begin should be told that the United States had not forgotten about the problem of Syria's missiles in Lebanon. But by treating the Syrian missiles as something of a footnote, State implicitly edged toward a policy of conciliation with Syria. Consistent with the State Department approach of downplaying the missiles, according to the *Middle East Policy Survey* of November 6, 1981 (no. 43), the Department of Defense did the same: "While senior Pentagon officials acknowledge the damage the Israeli military has suffered in Lebanon to its deterrent image, they argue that Israeli security is not threatened by Syrian or PLO military activities in southern Lebanon."

With respect to the Begin visit of September 1981, Defense Minister Sharon began to lay down the first of his verbal markers at one of the plenary sessions. He indicated that Lebanon's strategic significance for Israel gave a strong justification for taking military action. Based upon the reports of Israeli participants at the session, Sharon asserted that his nation's intelligence collection facilities had been eroded by Syria's missiles in Lebanon. This degradation in intelligence capabilities on Syrian military movements occurred because of the increased risk to Israeli information-gathering efforts via the Lebanon platform. The erosion, in turn, reduced the amount of "early warning" time available to effect a general mobilization and troop deployment in the event of hostilities. Israel's withdrawal from part of Sinai in 1975 and its scheduled pullout from the remainder in April 1982 reduced its strategic depth and thereby shortened the amount of time between warning and an Arab attack. Sharon's marker concerning Lebanon took on added significance in light of the U.S. decision to sell an air defense enhancement package to Saudi Arabia. Israel argued that the proposed sale was a threat to its security because of the great intelligence value of that equipment.

The technique of laying down markers is used to condition the other party through subtle hints that a certain course of action is inevitable in view of unavoidable circumstances. The "drip method" of conditioning the United States to the inevitability of large-scale Israeli action was one of Sharon's favorite techniques.[23] In addition to making the PLO a target, Israel periodically laid down markers to demonstrate its continued unwillingness to accept Syrian missiles in Lebanon. The *Washington Post* of September 28, 1981, reported that Begin said Israel would not tolerate the missiles forever and therefore would welcome a resumption of Habib's mission to seek their removal. Furthermore, in mid-November, Sharon asserted that Israel would take military action to destroy both the Syrian missiles and Palestinian weapons in Lebanon if diplomatic efforts failed.

Israel's markers were indications that it had strategic designs on Lebanon in the near future. These verbal signs were reinforced by changes in capability measures. Additionally, Israeli sources indicated that in mid-November, Jerusalem had begun to increase the number of observation points along the border with Lebanon and to improve roads in the security zone controlled by its Lebanese surrogate in southern Lebanon, Major Haddad. If Israel were preparing to launch a major invasion, the capacity to move large numbers of forces would need to be enhanced, for example, by increasing the number of observation points and improving the roads that would be used during an attack.

Despite the lingering problem of the missiles and the emerging topic of Palestinian arms accumulation, State awaited a propitious moment to resume the Habib mission. That time came as the attenuated Arab League summit closed in Fez, Morocco, on November 25, 1981. Subsequently, Habib met with Syrian President Assad on December 2 and on following days with Jordan's King Hussein, Israeli Foreign Minister Shamir and Defense Minister Sharon, as well as Saudi Crown Prince Fahd. Upon his return to the United States on December 11, Habib reported on a general desire to maintain the cease-fire in Lebanon.[24]

Jerusalem's Strategic Designs

During Habib's visit to Israel on December 5, Sharon laid down another marker that was a virtual bombshell when it landed. According to a report in the December 5, 1981, *Washington Post*, an Israeli participant in the Habib talks said that there had been an emphasis on PLO deployments in South Lebanon since the July 24, 1981, cease-fire between Israel and the PLO. Moreover, the Israeli press held that Sharon expected the cease-fire to be broken by the Palestine Liberation Organization.[25] He outlined to Habib an ambitious plan concerning Lebanon and specified in great detail the concept for what ultimately became known as "Big Pines," the code name for the Sharon plan to drive the PLO out of Lebanon altogether and to install a pro-Israel rightist regime in Beirut.

Although generally thought to be Sharon's idea, the plan actually came from a document approved by the Israel Defense Forces two years earlier, that is, in 1979. There was dissatisfaction in the military with the aftermath of Jerusalem's incursion into southern Lebanon during 1978 because the action was restricted to an area up to the Litani River (only about fifteen miles from their common border). According to Sharon's memoirs, the lesson drawn a year following the Litani Operation by Israeli Defense Minister Ezer Weizman and Chief of Staff Motta Gur was that dealing effectively with the PLO in southern Lebanon required something more than a local operation; in fact, it would be necessary to target the entire PLO military and political infrastructure in Lebanon.[26] Israeli troops would come into armed conflict with Syrian occupation forces in the southern Bekaa Valley of Lebanon and in West Beirut. Sharon quotes from the 1979 plan written by the Israel Defense Forces' General Headquarters under the guidance of Weizman: "The IDF will occupy south Lebanon up to the Junia-Zahle line [that is, to the Christian enclave north of Beirut], will destroy terrorist forces so as to create a new situation in the area [and] will destroy Syrian and Lebanese forces as may be necessary in executing the mission."[27]   Thus, the so-called Sharon plan for the Israeli invasion of Lebanon and destruction of the PLO seems to have had widespread support within the military establishment, according to Sharon himself.

To appreciate the broader underpinnings for Israeli military contingency planning, consider the speech Sharon prepared for a December 14, 1981, conference at the Institute for Strategic Studies at Tel Aviv University.[28]   In conjunction with the General Headquarters plan, the Sharon speech presents the strategic concept for Israel's invasion of Lebanon.

Sharon held that radical Arab regimes such as Syria, Libya, Iraq, and South Yemen had a political/military strategy for the liquidation of Israel. Their approach included a military buildup, Soviet support, the oil weapon, and the use of the PLO as an instrument of violence against Israel. Not surprisingly, Sharon held that the PLO posed a political threat to the very existence of Israel.[29] He contended that the purposes of that organization were to undermine the stability and security of Israel, drag the confrontation states into war against Israel, and deter Arab countries as well as the moderate Palestinians from negotiations with Israel on the basis of the Camp David peace process. Sharon saw the PLO as an element in a Soviet strategy that required political upheaval to shift the region toward Soviet political/military patronage.

Sharon defined the Soviet goals: to obtain a sea-control capability in the Mediterranean, the Indian Ocean, the Gulf, and the Red Sea; to penetrate key countries in the Middle East and the Gulf from the direction of Afghanistan, Iraq, South Yemen, and Syria; to outflank NATO's eastern tier (Turkey) through Iran, Iraq, Syria, and Lebanon; to outflank NATO's southern tier in the Mediterranean via Libya, Syria, and Algeria; and to gain control over critical states in Africa from the direction of Libya, Algeria,

South Yemen, Ethiopia, Mozambique, Angola, and Congo-Brazzaville. Finally, Sharon defined these areas of Soviet interests as "the strategic hinterland of Israel."

With such a vision in mind, the "Big Pines" operation to drive the PLO from Lebanon and install a pro-Israel rightist regime in Beirut was simply a first step in securing Jerusalem's strategic hinterland. What was to Sharon a relatively small increment in a grand design appeared to Washington as a dangerous plan with no redeeming value. The *Middle East Policy Survey* of February 12, 1982 (no. 49), reported that State Department officials interpreted the Sharon plan for Lebanon as a call for a massive Israeli incursion north of the Litani River. Shocked by the audacity of the plan, Habib made it clear to Sharon that it was an unthinkable idea as far as the United States was concerned. But what was a nonstarter to Washington was a serious proposal in Jerusalem. According to Schiff and Ya'ari, Sharon had just briefed Israel's General Staff in October that destruction of the PLO would mean going to Beirut.[30] Begin followed up on Sharon's remarks to Habib in December 1981 by outlining a plan to the Israeli cabinet for a large-scale ground operation. Sharon, however, told the cabinet that Israeli units would not go into Beirut as a part of this plan. Nevertheless, Sharon did want to "clean up" Lebanon, that is, to push the PLO out of the country, make the Syrians withdraw, and create a pro-Israel, Christian-dominated Lebanon.

Conclusions

The consensus that emerged from Reagan administration planning during December 1981 was that Habib's quiet diplomacy would stand a greater chance of persuading Syria to remove its missiles if Israel were to decrease its public rhetoric. There was a dissenting view to the idea that Syria was susceptible to such persuasion, that is, that Damascus derived strategic benefits from having its missiles in Lebanon. The dissenters held that, in this connection, the missiles reduced Jerusalem's early warning of a Syrian attack because of a decrease in the operation of piloted Israeli aircraft over Lebanon. In addition, the missiles increased the costs that would be associated with an Israeli preemptive strike. Therefore, Syria would be unlikely to remove the missiles even if Israel were to tone down its rhetoric, according to the minority view.

Washington's strategic planning provided a framework in which the White House could monitor the ebb and flow of tensions between Israel and Syria. With the emergence of a consensus led by the State Department, American diplomacy seemed to be successful in lowering the likelihood of war without threats of U.S. force. Thus, the administration could turn its attention to the confrontation between Israel and the Palestine Liberation Organization with the same diplomatic approach. In so doing, it appeared to achieve yet another success in the form of an American-sponsored cease-fire during July 1981. The achievements of U.S. diplomacy quite reasonably created a strong sense of confidence in the administration's ability to produce results. Palestinian arms acquisitions had prompted a flurry of diplomatic markers from Israel to indicate its strong intent to destroy the PLO in Lebanon. The actors in the arms-up/markers-down political theater switched roles at year's end: Jerusalem began its own arms and troop buildup where the borders of Israel, Lebanon, and Syria converge. Ostensibly, Israel did so in anticipation of a military response by Syria to the de facto annexation of the Golan Heights by Israel in mid-December 1981. In reaction to Jeruslaem's arms acquisitions and troop concentrations, the PLO began to lay down its own diplomatic markers, warning of an Israeli invasion of Lebanon. To avoid providing Jerusalem with a pretext to invade, the PLO mainstream movement scrupulously adhered to the cease-fire along the Israel-Lebanon border.

While Jerusalem searched for an internationally recognized provocation to justify its invasion, Israeli troop concentrations in the north provided the capacity to act without mobilization and deployment delays. As 1982 began, the potentially deadly quarrel between Damascus and Jerusalem had been eclipsed by hostilities between Israel and the Beirut-based Palestine Liberation Organization. Because this familiar skirmishing seemed to be of lesser consequence than a war between Israel and Syria, the United States was less sensitive to growing diplomatic and military storm clouds on the horizon.

3

Diplomacy Sans Force

Military Capabilities and Political Intentions

Capabilities

The diplomacy of the United States helped to block a prospective confrontation between Damascus and Jerusalem. And with an increasing likelihood of hostilities between Israel and the PLO on the horizon, Washington began to bring its diplomatic tools to bear on their conflict. With the shift in diplomatic attention away from Syria there was a corresponding reorientation of intelligence toward the Palestinian aspect of the Arab-Israeli conflict. Thus, intelligence documents about Israeli-Palestinian military capabilities and political intentions were increasingly in demand among Washington officials. Because discovering intentions is so difficult, intelligence agencies often focus on capabilities. And one primary purpose of analyzing changes in capabilities is to estimate the likelihood of warfare.

With Israel and the PLO augmenting their arms, Washington detected an increase in the speed at which the fuse burned between Tel Aviv war rooms and Palestinian bunkers in Beirut. But despite agreement on the growing likelihood of war, the administration divided over the significance of the military buildup on both sides. Officials inclined to support Israel focused on the increase in Palestinian capabilities and inferred from it an offensive intent against Israel. Conversely, those less supportive of Jerusalem emphasized the enhancement of Israeli capabilities and deduced from this an offensive intent against the PLO in Lebanon.

The PLO's military buildup in Lebanon included qualitative gains, such as the incorporation of heavy weapons into its arsenal. The inventory consisted, inter alia, of long-range artillery, light arms, multiple rocket launchers, and a few dozen antiquated T-34 tanks. In light of previous shelling by Palestinian forces, American officials who favored Jerusalem feared that such an enhanced

61

artillery capability would pose an unacceptable threat to northern Israeli settlements along the Lebanese border.

Those less supportive of Jerusalem stressed the buildup of Israeli military forces along the border with Lebanon. Leaks to the press about Israel's growing capabilities reflected this group's attempt to thwart an attack by Jerusalem. *New York Times* correspondent, Marvine Howe, wrote that Israel stepped up its patrols, increased reconnaissance flights, and set up a new military camp at the base of the Golan Heights.[1] The mid-December 1981 estimate in Washington centered on a major buildup of the Israel Defense Forces (IDF) to between 12,000 and 25,000 troops in northern Israel following de facto annexation of the Golan Heights (actually, an extension of Israeli civilian law to Syrian territory). This augmentation of forces significantly improved Israel's ability to move its troops into Lebanon and led to the following conclusion. If the PLO were to resume artillery shelling on northern Israeli towns or to launch raids, Israel most likely would respond with a major attack to clean out the PLO south of the Litani River and, at the same time, destroy Syria's missiles in Lebanon.

There was sentiment within the American group that sought to prevent an Israeli attack that Jerusalem's troop concentrations might have been designed to lull the PLO into accepting a large-scale Israeli force near the Lebanon border. In other words, a large deployment of Israeli troops over an extended period of time would condition the PLO to the presence of such numbers without necessarily signaling an attack. Once the PLO was so deceived, Israeli forces could more easily begin an invasion of Lebanon and destroy that organization.

Those in the Administration who were inclined to pressure Israel not to attack split into factions. One side wanted to highlight Israel's military buildup via leaks to the press in order to delay or stop Jerusalem from mounting an invasion of Lebanon. The other side downplayed Israel's enhanced capabilities and hoped to impose sanctions on Jerusalem for annexing the Golan Heights mountains of Syria. Such sanctions would serve the dual purposes of punishing Jerusalem for prior misbehavior and warning it not to invade Lebanon in order to destroy PLO forces there.

Rather than address the arms and troop buildups, high-level American officials began a round of meetings to decide upon sanctions in response to Israel's annexation. By focusing on Israeli misbehavior and trying to formulate sanctions against Jerusalem, Washington's attention was deflected from Israel's arms race with the Palestinians. One reason for paying so much attention to the Golan Heights annexation was because Damascus claimed that it had "canceled" the de facto cease-fire that had been in effect between Syria and Israel since 1973, although it had not taken military action to back up its rhetoric.

At the White House, the National Security Council met formally on January 5, 1982, to consider Israel's refusal to rescind legislation annexing the Golan Heights.[2] Four days later, State announced that the United States remained unwilling to reopen the strategic cooperation agreement with Israel. This was yet another slap on Jerusalem's wrist. As reported in the *Middle East Policy Survey* of December 18, 1981 (no. 46), the administration acknowledged that it faced a dilemma: "'If we punish Israel severely, it is likely to react by moving into Lebanon. On the other hand, if we do nothing, Israel will interpret that as a green light for further provocative acts.'" Washington tried in vain to resolve its dilemma by adopting a policy of limited sanctions against Israel for its annexation of Syria's Golan Heights. By focusing on the Golan issue, however, Washington paid too little attention to the increasing capabilities of Israel and the PLO as well as to the meaning of such enhanced capabilities for an intent to fight a war in Lebanon.

Intentions

As the United States policy elite addressed the wrong issue--sanctions for prior misconduct by Israel--Jerusalem continued to "drip" explicit warnings of an intention to invade Lebanon. In the *Middle East Policy Survey* of January 15, 1982 (no. 47), a well-connected Israeli official told *MEPS* that Begin was waiting for a pretext to invade Lebanon. He would take action if even one rocket were fired on Israeli development towns along the border with Lebanon. So, as 1981 came to a close, the issue became when, not if, Israel would launch an invasion of Lebanon.

Just as Israel may have been lulling the PLO into an acceptance of a large-scale troop presence in the north, Jerusalem was conditioning Washington to accept an invasion when launched. On the one hand, the United States did not want to be surprised by an Israeli operation in Lebanon, and some in the administration were receptive to information from Israel regarding its intentions there. On the other hand, Washington wanted to distance itself from an Israeli invasion to avoid the charge of collusion with Jerusalem.

The *Middle East Policy Survey* of April 23, 1982 (no. 54), reported State Department sources as saying that the United States made it clear that it did not wish to have advance warning of any Israeli move against Lebanon. By declining to receive prior notice of Jerusalem's intent to attack, the department hoped to undercut the argument that Israel and the United States were planning a joint invasion of an Arab state.

Jerusalem was attempting to acclimate the PLO to a new and large-scale Israeli presence on the Lebanese border without giving that organization an indication of whether or when an invasion might occur. Meanwhile, the PLO was laying down markers via statements designed to alert the world to Israel's growing capacity and its stated intention to invade. Israeli correspondent David Landau reported that the PLO had been preparing for a large Israeli assault in southern Lebanon.[3] Moreover, Salah Khalaf, Arafat's second-in-command, said in an interview with United Press International that Israel had only delayed plans for a major operation in Lebanon. Because Lebanese rightists had been strengthening their positions in East Beirut, Khalaf had anticipated a large Israeli assault, which, he believed, had been postponed.

Meanwhile, an unauthorized disclosure of Washington's assessment of Israel's intentions appeared in the news. The information came in the form of a list of dangerous events that might occur in the region and surprise the United States. Officers of the American embassy in Tel Aviv compiled the events and forwarded them to Washington. Richard Straus published them in his *Middle East Policy Survey* of January 15, 1982 (no. 47). That edition also included a report on a possible Israeli invasion of southern Lebanon. There was, however, no suggestion that the military operation might involve Beirut.

Although American Ambassador to Israel Samuel Lewis had attended a December 5, 1981, meeting between Special Envoy Habib and Defense Minister Sharon when the latter discussed marching on Beirut, Lewis did not include in his list of events that the Israel Defense Forces might plan to take the Beirut headquarters of the Palestine Liberation Organization. One reason for the failure to alert Washington about the Beirut option was that Sharon had couched his warning of that prospect in such personal terms that both Habib and Lewis discounted it. Lewis, for one, felt that Sharon's plan was characterized by such a high degree of "megalomania" that Washington would take it with a grain of salt.

Even though perturbed by the leak of sensitive messages to Washington, Lewis, the consummate professional, continued to call the shots as he saw them. In mid-January 1982, former officials recalled that he perceived considerable dismay among high-level Israelis concerning Lebanon, and he felt that they wanted increased coordination between Jerusalem and Washington. A first topic for bilateral consultation would have been a definition of the kind of act by armed Palestinians that would warrant Israeli military action.

Lewis believed that Prime Minister Begin, Foreign Minister Shamir, and Defense Minister Sharon were highly disturbed by developments in Lebanon. They saw Ambassador Habib's December 1981 trip as a failure because the Syrian missiles were still in place, heavy weapons continued to flow into PLO armories, and the Syrian military presence in Lebanon remained. Additionally, there was no movement toward Lebanese national political "unity." Indeed, the Saudis, who were to lead reconciliation, had dropped out of the picture, and the work of the Arab Follow-Up Committee (AFUC) had stalled. Israeli leaders feared the worst for the forthcoming Lebanese presidential elections as their Phalange rightist allies increasingly were pressed to the wall.

In addition to the U.S. embassy in Tel Aviv, the American press evidenced foreknowledge of Israeli military planning. The *New York Times* Jerusalem correspondent, David Shipler, wrote in such great detail about Israeli military planning as to suggest that he received a leak from the "big dripper" himself, Israeli Defense Minister Sharon.[4] The irony was that a caption introduced the essay stating, "This article was subjected to military censorship." The heading instead might have read: "This article was dictated by the military censor." Whether manipulated or not, Shipler wrote that Israel had been considering plans for a large-scale invasion of southern Lebanon. The purpose of the operation would be to clear out Palestinian military reinforcements that had been introduced since the de facto cease-fire of July 1981. The article also reported that Israel had said it would invade if there were further cases of infiltration and terrorist attacks within Israel by armed Palestinians. Consider the following passage from Shipler's article as an indication that Sharon might have been the leaker:

As described here, Mr. Sharon's plan would be directed against the PLO in an effort to deal a decisive crippling blow to its military deployment in southern Lebanon. Ground troops would be used extensively, but without any intention of holding or occupying Lebanese territory.[5]

Retrospectively, Sharon may have engaged in an information/disinformation campaign. On the enlightenment side, he communicated Israel's intent to invade Lebanon contingent upon a Palestinian provocation. On the deception side, he was insincere at best when he claimed that Israeli ground troops would not hold Lebanese territory and implied that the operation would be confined to southern Lebanon. Even in the plan outlined to Habib and Lewis during December, Sharon had mentioned Beirut. Moreover, in the third week of February 1982, Habib had acknowledged that Sharon wanted to clean out the Palestinians "up north," that is, in the Beirut area.

By examining changes in military capabilities and diplomatic communications, intelligence analysts, embassy personnel, and the press made inferences regarding the intent of the principal actors and the likelihood of war in Lebanon. As was the case a year earlier concerning the Lebanese Maronite militias and Syrian forces in Lebanon, the issue was again the relationship among provocation, proportionality, and retaliation.

Israel Versus the Palestinians in Lebanon

Provocation and Proportionality

Jerusalem wanted to preclude any additional accusation that Washington was surprised when armed Palestinian incursions became so clearly provocative as to justify a proportionate Israeli response, such as an invasion of Lebanon. By involving the United States in the process of delineating a clear line on what could trigger an Israeli move into Lebanon, Israel hoped to deflect any official American criticism of its military action. Thus, Jerusalem sent its director of military intelligence, Major General Yehoshua Saguy, to meet with Secretary Haig in Washington on February 3, 1982. In discussing the Saguy visit, the *Middle East Policy Survey* on February 12, 1982 (no. 49), stated that: "US officials have told the *Survey* that they believe that the Israeli government is attempting to build a record of warnings over PLO activity that could be used to justify a major Israeli attack."

Although State viewed the Saguy trip primarily as an occasion to define an internationally recognized provocative action,

Jerusalem's leadership used the visit to secure Washington's tacit consent for a major ground operation in Lebanon. Unlike the Americans, the Israelis saw an obvious link between defining a provocation and obtaining American approval to invade. Approaching the linkage issue with diplomatic finesse, Saguy told Haig that if the PLO continued to violate the cessation of hostilities on any front, Israel would retaliate with a limited military operation in Lebanon, while avoiding a war with Syria. Haig responded that only a significant violation of the truce would justify such retaliation.[6] Saguy considered PLO actions against Israeli targets outside the Middle East as a significant violation; Haig did not.

The Haig-Saguy meeting ended without either side defining precisely what would constitute a significant violation of the cessation of hostilities. But though there was no agreed upon interpretation of the de facto cease-fire, the session widened its scope to include infiltration across the Jordanian border into Israel. On the one side, the PLO was maintaining the cease-fire on the Lebanon-Israel border and keeping open its option to target Israeli interests elsewhere. On the other side, Israel also respected the cease-fire on the border and demanded that the truce be applied globally. State may have been unaware of the fact that broadening the scope of the cease-fire simply enlarged the diplomatic opening through which Israeli tanks would ultimately roll.

Saguy's reference to "any front" contradicted the terms of the July 24, 1981, cease-fire. It prohibited military activity on the Israel-Lebanon border and failed to mention other frontiers, such as the Jordan-Israel boundary. The truce had been holding on the Israel-Lebanon border, as was generally expected. In other places, such as on the boundary with Jordan, sporadic military activity continued. In short, an outcome of the Haig-Saguy meeting was the secretary's acknowledgment that infiltration over *any* of Israel's borders was a cease-fire violation. The bottom line of the Haig-Saguy session is that it lowered the threshold for an Israeli invasion of Lebanon to destroy Palestinian combatants.

From Military Defeat to Political Victory

Israel's enhanced military capabilities, its drip method of signaling an intent to invade, and PLO expressions of apprehension were inputs to U.S. assessments of both the likelihood of warfare and the Palestinian goals in the event of an Israeli attack. In early February 1982, a question arose regarding what the PLO objective would be under the contingency of an Israeli invasion.   One prophetic prediction was that the PLO would seek to transform a regional war, which it could not win, into an international diplomatic competition, where it stood a better chance of prevailing.

Isolating Israel in the global community would compel the United States to reevaluate its position and withhold diplomatic support from that nation.   The PLO strategy was to turn military defeat into political victory, following the precedent established by President Anwar Sadat in the 1973 war.   During that conflict, Sadat guided Egypt into the peace process with American mediation--a diplomatic victory--on the ashes of Egypt's battlefield defeats at the hands of Israel.   And just as Cairo had to experience a semblance of military success to achieve its diplomatic triumph, the PLO needed to make at least one stand where it could claim parity as a beleaguered Palestinian "David" holding off the mighty "Goliath."

American intelligence reasonably believed that the southern Lebanon towns of Nabitiya (just north of the Litani River and inland from the Mediterranean coast) and/or Tyre (just south of the Litani River) would be possible sites for a PLO resistance.   One purpose of making such stands would be to stall the fighting until negotiations could result in a truce imposed by the outside powers. The PLO strategy would seek to portray Israel as engaging in the genocide of the Palestinian people by refusing to accept a cease-fire. Therefore, they would emerge as the wronged party that the international community would compensate for the harm they suffered at the hands of Israel.   Their inclusion in a peace conference to negotiate an overall political settlement would be a down payment on a mortgage to build a Palestinian homeland. Recall that U.S. intelligence believed the PLO would make its stand in southern Lebanon sites (rather than in Beirut bunkers).   This belief was prescient.

The White House Organizes for Force and Diplomacy

Special Situations Group and Crisis Pre-Planning Group

During the winter of 1982, diplomatic markers laid down by Israel, together with its enhanced military capabilities, suggested an increasing likelihood of war.   The growing prospect that Jerusalem might authorize the use of force made it imperative in Washington that diplomatic activities be coordinated with military planning. Only the White House could effect such a synthesis of diplomacy and force. And in the reports from the American embassy in Tel Aviv, the intelligence community, and the press, the staff at 1600 Pennsylvania Avenue saw an opening for managing both Foggy Bottom and the Pentagon.

National Security Adviser Clark had moved to the White House in January 1982 from State, where he was deputy secretary. Clark brought with him Robert (Bud) McFarlane, who had served as counselor at State. Although Clark (called "the judge" because of his background as a California supreme court justice), was circumspect in weighing sides of opposing arguments and had the president's ear, he initially lacked expertise in foreign affairs. Ex-marine Bud McFarlane was reputed to be an experienced national security bureaucratic infighter from his days on the staff of the Senate Committee on Armed Services and as military assistant to Henry Kissinger when the latter was at the White House during the 1970s. McFarlane became special envoy to the Middle East in July 1983, national security adviser in October of that year, and resigned two years later. Admiral John Poindexter rounded out the national security management team as military assistant to Allen and Clark, later as McFarlane's deputy, and as national security adviser himself upon McFarlane's departure. (Poindexter resigned in 1987 and was convicted in 1990 for his activities in the Iran affair.)

On February 9, 1982, McFarlane called for a meeting of the Crisis Pre-Planning Group (CPPG), comprised of his NSC staffers, Special Assistants to the President Thomas Reed and Norman Bailey, as well as Assistant to the Vice President for National Security Affairs Nancy Bearg Dyke. Reed was a businessman and friend of the president from California who later departed from the White House staff under allegations of inside business trading activities. Bailey, a scholar-diplomat, was in charge of planning. Dyke, another policy planner, was initially at Defense and became the vice president's liaison to the national security bureaucracy.

These three met to discuss preliminary procedures for crisis management. Given their bureaucratic interests, it was not at all surprising that their suggestions involved strengthening the White House relative to State and Defense. The tool for seizing the action from these two departments was the Special Situations Group (SSG). It was the administration's main interagency body for handling crises. Created by the president upon entering the Oval Office in 1981, the SSG was the White House answer to the challenge posed by Secretary Haig. By entrusting crisis management in the hands of Vice President George Bush, Haig's adversaries at the White House sought to diminish his authority and control his actions.

After coordinating with McFarlane and Poindexter, Reed, Bailey, and Dyke decided that Judge Clark should ask Bush to call a meeting of the SSG to discuss crisis pre-planning. The SSG included Vice President Bush, Secretary of State Haig, Secretary of Defense Caspar Weinberger, Assistant to the President Clark, Chairman of the Joint Chiefs of Staff Admiral James Watkins, Director of Central Intelligence William Casey, White House Chief of Staff James Baker, Counselor to the President Edwin Meese, Deputy White House Chief of Staff Michael Deaver, and Chief of Staff to the Vice President Admiral Daniel Murphy.

The Crisis Pre-Planning Group recommended the formation of SSG panels at the assistant secretary level to begin planning for crisis situations. Each panel was to be chaired by the NSC staff, which would have the action for preparing the initial discussion paper. Actually, the CPPG suggestions were in the pipeline prior to the impending crisis over Lebanon; the White House simply seized the occasion that the Lebanon crisis afforded to enhance its role to the detriment of State. Not only was the administration responding directly to security threats, it was being driven to reorganize by bureaucratic ambitions. Given the uncertainty of the security threat and the transparency of the grab for power, White House proposals that had enhanced its influence were sidetracked as State held on to the action for Lebanon.

Contingency Group on Lebanon

Although the White House was attempting to reorganize the government at the top, with itself at the pinnacle, State retained the responsibility for initiating paperwork for the crisis by maintaining control at a lower level of the interagency process. State asserted itself via the Contingency Group on Lebanon--a small senior group that convened on February 8, 1982. Its purpose was to "task" contingency papers on the fast-breaking developments concerning Lebanon. Attendees from State were Group Chairman and Deputy Secretary Walter Stoessel, Director of the Staff for Policy Planning Paul Wolfowitz, Deputy Assistant Secretary Draper, and Deputy Director of Politico-Military Affairs Arnold Kanter. Representing the NSC staff was Geoffrey Kemp, Director of its Near Eastern and South Asian office. The CIA was represented by John McMahon,

deputy director for operations and later the deputy at the "Agency."
Participants from the Office of the Secretary of Defense included
Principal Deputy Assistant Secretary for International Security
Affairs Noel Koch and his aide, David Ransom. The Organization
of the Joint Chiefs of Staff (OJCS) representative was General Paul
Gorman, an assistant to the chairman.

According to former officials who attended the meeting, Deputy
Assistant Secretary Draper briefed the Contingency Group on
Lebanon concerning Ambassador Habib's diplomatic contacts and on
the Sharon plan of December 1981. Representatives from State,
the CIA, and the OJCS agreed to contribute to a cable message to
Secretary Haig, who was abroad at the time. This communication
would summarize U.S. measures aimed at preventing or containing
the crisis over Lebanon. The group tasked the CIA to provide an
intelligence assessment of Soviet moves and possible involvement in
a regional crisis about Lebanon. It tasked the OJCS to provide a
description of the U.S. force posture in the area, including assets
available to support an evacuation of American citizens and to
reinforce the U.S. posture in the region. State assumed the duties
of first integrating CIA and OJCS papers with the department's
evaluation of diplomatic options in Europe and in the Middle East,
then summarizing the package for the cable to Haig.

The bottom line was that State had retained the action because
the White House attempt to seize it was premature in the absence
of an ongoing war. One effect of the State Department's continued
domination of policy was to make it difficult to coordinate American
diplomacy with Israel's threats to use force; State simply could not
orchestrate its diplomatic efforts with Jerusalem's military threats.
Although Haig himself was inclined to combine diplomacy and force,
he was unable to get his department to develop a consensus in the
interagency community for this idea. Because State was split,
moreover, this had the effect of diminishing Haig's influence in the
administration and left it with an apparently risk-free diplomacy-
first approach.

The Toothless Tiger

Washington game planning and its organizational maneuvering
in crisis management shared the elusive goal of effecting a
synthesis of diplomatic and military tools. Only the president,
however, had the political clout to interrelate State, Defense, and
the National Security Council staff, as well as the interagency

groups to which they belong, such as the Lebanon Task Force, the Working Group, and the Contingency Group on Lebanon. Perhaps one of the reasons the president failed to exercise leadership was because of the reluctance of Weinberger to follow Haig's lead in seeking to harmonize United States diplomacy with Israel's threats.

With Haig's influence on the wane, those opposed to him found willing allies in other departments, most notably at Defense. Because the Department of Defense discourages the use of force except in carefully designed and limited circumstances, it was pleased to support the diplomacy-first approach of Haig's opponents at State. A State-Defense consensus developed (with Haig increasingly on the sidelines) in favor of a diplomacy sans force policy toward Lebanon, dubbed the "toothless tiger" approach. This diplomacy-only approach consisted initially of imploring Saudi Arabia and conciliating Syria.

The administration's position in mid-February 1982 was indicative of the failure to integrate diplomacy with force. Discussions in Washington focused primarily on the need for another diplomatic mission of reassurance to the region rather than on the possibility of augmenting Israel's threats to compel a Syrian withdrawal of its missiles from Lebanon. Because the situation had calmed but was still unpredictable, it appeared to be a good moment for Habib to visit the area. In advance of Israel's final withdrawal from the Sinai scheduled for April, another diplomatic mission might be timely. Such a mission would have had a twofold purpose: (1) to consolidate the cease-fire between Israel and the PLO in Lebanon; and (2) to seek first-hand clarification from all parties concerning where they stood and where they were headed. Habib planned to visit Lebanon, Jordan, Israel, Saudi Arabia, and Syria. A brief overview of the administration's plans for Habib's trip as of mid-February 1982 follows.

In Lebanon: Habib would take a reading on the forthcoming presidential elections and the Arab Follow-Up Committee regarding reconciliation among the factions. He would reiterate the need to maintain the cease-fire and encourage support for the central government of Lebanon. Indeed, during Habib's visit to Lebanon on March 9, he told Prime Minister Shafiq al-Wazzan that his main concern was to maintain the cease-fire between Israel and the Palestine Liberation Organization.[7] Furthermore, in a meeting with Chamber of Deputies Speaker Kamil al-As'ad on March 10, Habib explained that one of his goals was to stabilize the situation in Lebanon.

In Jordan: Habib would brief King Hussein on the results of meetings elsewhere and underscore the hope that the king would continue to help minimize the chance of further military actions via Jordan by armed Palestinians, because these activities could endanger the cessation of hostilities. According to the Jordanian press of March 5, Habib conducted the briefings as planned.[8] Israeli radio, moreover, reported on March 4 that the king continued in his resolve to prevent infiltration of armed Palestinians from Jordan into Israel.[9]

In Israel: Habib would obtain Jerusalem's latest thinking on Lebanon, emphasize the need for forbearance in the face of minor provocative incidents, and probe Israel's intentions.

In Saudi Arabia: Habib would discover if the Saudis were still determined to remain engaged in Lebanon and in what ways. He would solicit their thoughts on the possibilities for further efforts to stem the flow of heavy weaponry into Lebanon and to gain Syrian cooperation in at least some troop withdrawals. Habib was to explore whether some movement on the issue of Syrian missiles was possible. Although State believed that it appeared hopeless at that moment, Washington vainly implored Riyadh to induce Damascus to remove its missiles from Lebanon.

In Syria: Habib would probe President Assad's intentions about maintaining a dialogue on Lebanon. He also would express a desire for Syrian cooperation and flexibility in the Arab Follow-Up Committee and the need to avoid PLO or Syrian provocation of Israel. Habib's trip to Syria raised the issue of whether or not Washington pursued a policy of "buying off" Damascus.

Appeasement

American Appeasement of Syria

Appeasement is a conciliatory policy designed to buy off a potential protagonist at the sacrifice of principles. Syria's placement of missiles in Lebanon violated a tacit accord between Damascus and Jerusalem. Brokered by Washington, the accord followed the 1975-1976 civil war in Lebanon. In addition to maintaining a state of war with Israel, the presence of Syria's missiles in Lebanon might have placed Damascus on a confrontation course with both Jerusalem and Washington. Assuming that one principle of American foreign policy is to honor commitments and implement accords it helps to broker, there was some obligation for the United States to support the terms of that implicit agreement. Washington sought to induce Damascus to remove its missiles from Lebanon by way of a diplomatic method of persuasion without including negative incentives in a strategy of coercive diplomacy. And when diplomatic persuasion failed, furthermore, the regionalists who dominated the interagency process were reluctant to reinforce Jerusalem's coercive diplomacy vis-a-vis Damascus with a comparable American strategy.

American policy regarding Syria sought: (1) to avert a confrontation on Syrian noncompliance with the 1976 tacit understanding on missile deployment, (2) to refrain from confronting Syria for its thinly disguised attempts to foment Palestinian infiltration and raids from Jordan into Israel, (3) to avoid linking Syria to the massive buildup of PLO arms in Lebanon, and (4) to avoid mention of the Syrian armed presence in Lebanon.

Ignoring divisive subjects, American policy focused on topics Syria desired, such as electing a president of Lebanon who would not oppose the Syrian armed presence there.   State's policy of overlooking Syrian delicts and addressing points of mutual interest was undertaken even though there was no evidence that a "dovish" U.S. position would bring reciprocity from Damascus.   It was innocent at best to imagine either that a conciliatory American policy would induce reciprocal Syrian behavior or that Saudi Arabia was willing or able to influence Damascus.   By appeasing the Syrian military dictator and acting like a supplicant before the Saudi princes, the United States weakened its image as leader of the free world.

The administration's approach in mid-February 1982 was symptomatic of the quality of American diplomacy at that time. U.S. policy never even attempted to integrate diplomacy with force. In Syria, Habib was not supposed to bring up, much less criticize, either the Syrian missiles or the flood of PLO arms pouring into Lebanon. Instructing Habib to ask for Syrian assistance in avoiding a Palestinian provocation of Israel, moreover, overlooked hard evidence of Syrian complicity in the infiltration of armed Palestinians from Jordan coming into Israel for the very purpose of inciting Jerusalem.   And though PLO arms and infiltration, as well as Syria's missiles, were not to be discussed with Damascus (the only actor that had some control over them), they ironically *were* to be mentioned in Riyadh, which at best had only indirect influence on these crucial elements.

Not surprisingly, American diplomacy in 1982 did not persuade Syria to cooperate in the removal of its missiles from Lebanon or curtailment of its support for Palestinian arms shipments and infiltration via Jordan. One reason was because this diplomacy was not orchestrated with force, for example, by exacerbating domestic unrest already underway in Syria. As leader of the Alawite minority that controlled Syria, President Assad was able to crush his internal opposition--the underground Sunni fundamentalist Muslim Brotherhood--with a minimum of fear that the dissidents had American support. He ordered tank and artillery fire to level the ancient city of Hamma, located in northwestern Syria, in 1982, resulting in thousands of casualties.

But despite Assad's repression, domestic turmoil erupted anew four years later. On March 13, 1986, a refrigerator truck exploded in the midst of Damascus, killing 50 persons, and a month later, on April 16, seven bombs exploded in public trains and buses in northern Syria, resulting in about 300 casualties. Damascus accused Iraq of supporting the Muslim Brotherhood with funds and explosives smuggled into Syria via Turkey.[10] If true, Baghdad simply was playing the game of "subversion"--a traditional method of inter-Arab politics. Although there are notable exceptions, for example, American subversion of Iran during the 1950s, the United States did not have as strong a tradition of using subversion as a tool of foreign policy in the Middle East and thus had been reluctant to combine the threat of subversion with diplomatic incentives four years earlier.

During February 1982, a few American officials were more inclined to treat President Assad as his Arab brothers might have, that is, with a hint or even a healthy dose of subversion to encourage compliance. As reported in the *Middle East Policy Survey* of February 12, 1982 (no. 49): "A surprising number of US officials and independent observers subscribed to the position that the usefulness of Habib's efforts may be at an end. Some officials fault Habib for dealing only with 'marginal issues' and argue that the US could have been tougher with Syrian President Assad." On the NSC staff, for instance, there were those who were critical of the diplomacy without force policy and sought, without success, to synthesize these key elements of national security policy.

Whatever small leverage the United States had over Assad lay more in the threat to destabilize Syria than in entreaties for Syria to practice restraint. Why should Assad preach limits to a PLO mainstream leadership he actively was trying to subvert? By sponsoring raids into Israel via Jordan by dissident Palestinian groups, Assad hoped that these attacks would be blamed on the PLO centrists and Jordan, both of which then would have to bear the brunt of Israel's retaliation.

So, with respect to Syria, the NSC minority position would have promoted the use of U.S. leverage over Damascus tied to President Assad's suspicion that the United States and Israel were working in concert to destabilize his rule. According to official Syrian radio of March 3, Damascus viewed the United States as the foremost enemy of the Arab nation.[11] Furthermore, the broadcast stated that Syria was confronting an assault led by a Zionist-imperialist (Israel and the United States) coalition headed by the Muslim Brotherhood of Syrian oppositionists. On that same day, former officials revealed that Assad even queried Habib as to whether Washington conducted covert operations in Syria. Assad's query was echoed on March 4 in Syria's official radio commentary on the Habib visit, accusing the United States of inciting remnants of the Muslim Brotherhood against his regime.[12]

When Habib supposedly denied that the United States supported destabilization of Syria, Assad asked if Habib was in a position to know, and Habib replied that he would take it to President Reagan for a definitive reply. When the special envoy brought Assad's suspicions to the attention of the president, there reportedly was a humorous exchange among the principals, implying that they were not sure whether or not there was a clandestine American role in Syria's unrest. The implicit consensus among the president's aides, however, was that Washington was not involved.

Despite Habib's denials, Assad nevertheless was concerned about the role of outside powers in Syria's unrest and believed that the United States had authorized Jordan and/or Israel to instigate trouble within Syria. Contrary to Assad's line of reasoning, some Israelis believed that Syrian instability might provide Assad with an incentive for war with Israel in Lebanon. The *Middle East Policy Survey* of February 12, 1982 (no. 49), reported: "Israeli sources speculate that a conflict with Israel over Lebanon could become the means by which Assad forestalls a full-scale civil war." Because there was no attempt to exploit his apprehensions, diplomacy and force were not as tightly coupled as they might have been. The looseness of this linkage would come to haunt American policymakers as the fuse continued to burn to the powder keg in

Beirut. While the cord sizzled, Habib's diplomacy vis-a-vis Syria failed, perhaps because it was not reinforced by even subtle hints of American involvement in the attempts to unsettle Syria. Rather than encouraging Habib to deny American participation in the Muslim Brotherhood's destabilization efforts, State could have instructed him to be less vehement in his denial, leaving open the possibility of using the threat of force to complement American diplomacy.

It is surprising that Habib declined to exploit Assad's fears regarding American involvement in Syrian turmoil in light of his comments that implied otherwise on February 23, 1982, during a meeting at State. Attending the session with Ambassador Habib were three NSC staffers: Norman Bailey, director of policy planning; Geoffrey Kemp, director of the Near Eastern and South Asian office; and the author, senior staff member of that office. Habib's apparent willingness to use domestic unrest in Syria as a lever to obtain concessions from Damascus on its missiles in Lebanon, as well as support for the PLO infiltration of Israel via Jordan received little backing from the State Department's Bureau of Near Eastern and South Asian Affairs.

In contrast to the prevailing policy line toward Syria in mid-1982, there have been officials at the Department of State and on the NSC staff who have expressed an understanding of Syria's vulnerability to external pressure, given its internal problems. Between tours of government service, Dennis Ross, a member of the Department of State Staff for Policy Planning during 1981 and subsequently head of that office in the Bush administration in 1989, wrote that the Assad regime would be constrained internationally by internal factors that would continue to absorb Syrian attention, energy, and resources and were likely to limit Assad's coercive potential in the rest of the region. Moreover, the Syrian president has demonstrated a willingness to accept tacit or indirect international constraints if he himself believes there is some internal danger.[13] The Ross approach to Syria, however, was not adopted in 1982 by the Reagan administration, so there was a reluctance to pressure Damascus.

An American appeasement policy toward Syria was bound to fail in light of that nation's history of provoking Israel to score points in the Arab cold war. For example, Syria purposefully incited large-scale Israeli retaliatory raids on Jordan in November 1966 as part of tensions between Damascus and Amman.

Responding to additional provocations from Damascus, Jerusalem ordered attacks on Syria itself during April 1967. These raids and further threats of retaliation during May 1967 started the parties on a slippery slope toward warfare. As part of a process that Damascus and the PLO initiated, Egypt deployed combat forces in the Sinai, requested the withdrawal of the United Nations Emergency Force there, and ordered that the Straits of Tiran on the Red Sea be closed to Israeli shipping.

One goal of Damascus in 1967 was to instigate a cycle of violence that would force a reluctant Cairo into a war with Jerusalem. The intent was to compel Egypt into an entente with revolutionary nations, such as Syria, and against moderate states, such as Jordan and Saudi Arabia. Cairo, indeed, signed a defense treaty with Damascus during November 1966, not only to deter Israel from striking Syria but also, and primarily, to restrain Damascus. Formal alignment would bind Damascus to conduct advance consultation with Cairo. The Egyptian alignment strategy to avoid war paradoxically enhanced the threat perceived by Israel and gave Jerusalem added incentive to launch a preemptive strike against both Egypt and Syria in June 1967.[14]

Given prior Syrian behavior, the administration's policy of sending Habib to Damascus during February 1982 was based upon wishful thinking instead of consideration of such historical facts as the Syrian role in provoking the 1966-1967 escalation. Only the credulous could imagine that Syria would cease to act according to its pattern of using Palestinians to incite Israel and gain advantages in inter-Arab rivalries. The irony was that the State Department regionalists who favored the policy of appeasing Damascus were supposedly experts on Syrian history. So, the NSC staffers' preference for a tough policy--combining the threat to destabilize Syria with positive incentives in order to compel Damascus to exercise restraint vis-a-vis Jerusalem, Amman, and Beirut--lost out to the administration's more moderate policy.

In short, the absence of effective White House leadership in the interagency process allowed State's views of mid-February 1982 to dominate policymaking. Consequently, Habib followed State's guidelines when he met with President Assad on March 3. According to Syrian sources, Habib said that the United States wished to maintain a dialogue, and that it was important to sustain the cease-fire in Lebanon.[15] The Syrian reports are consistent with Habib's denial that America was involved in an attempt to destabilize Syria.

Leverage

American Pressure on Israel

The unwillingness to use implied threats to exercise American leverage over Syria contrasted sharply with U.S. readiness to exert diplomatic pressure on Israel for military restraint. According to Jerusalem radio, during Ambassador Habib's meeting with Prime Minister Begin on March 1 and at a subsequent meeting of March 8, Begin took exception to President Reagan's comments concerning Israel and Lebanon.[16] He believed that Reagan wanted Israel to produce evidence of its peaceful intent regarding Lebanon. The prime minister, however, felt that the burden rested on the PLO to demonstrate its peaceful intentions toward Israel. He charged that organization with enhancing its military infrastructure, while Israel's qualitative edge was eroding with the buildup of its adversaries. In addition, Begin was concerned about the American sale of an air defense package, including sophisticated surveillance aircraft, to Saudi Arabia in the fall of 1981. Begin cited the president's message of May 3 of that year to the effect that the status quo ante (before the Syrian missiles were placed in Lebanon) must be restored.[17]

According to *New York Times* journalist Bernard Gwertzman, President Reagan sent a message to Prime Minister Begin praising Israel for showing restraint and urging additional time for American diplomatic efforts to bear fruit before Israel used military force against Syria's missiles in Lebanon.[18] The prime minister also referred to his own message of January 18, 1982, regarding the Syrian deployment. As reported in the *Middle East Policy Survey* of February 12, 1982 (no. 49), Prime Minister Begin stated that Israel would not move against the PLO unless there was a "clear provocation." Regarding Syria, Begin's letter stressed that (1) Syrian troops should be withdrawn from strategic positions they had seized in the fighting during spring 1981 near Zahle, Lebanon, (2) together with Syria's missiles in Lebanon, missiles on the Syrian side of the border also were unacceptable, and (3) Syrian missiles must not be used against Israeli reconnaissance overflights within Lebanon.

Contrast the prime minister's comments concerning both the permitted Israeli action in Lebanon and the PLO buildup there with the July 1981 cease-fire between that organization and Israel. Although the term "hostile military actions" used in the accord did not explicitly identify Israeli overflights, neither did the terms specifically exclude such activities. Furthermore, the cease-fire agreement did not preclude a PLO arms buildup in Lebanon. Nevertheless, Begin complained to Habib that the accord was incompatible with the movement of heavy weapons by the PLO into southern Lebanon.

A *Middle East Policy Survey* on February 12, 1982 (no. 49), stated that according to U.S. intelligence sources, the PLO gradually had built up its activities in Lebanon. In addition to trying to purchase surface-to-surface missiles, *MEPS* reported the PLO was in the process of buying T-54 and T-55 tanks. By winter 1981-1982, that organization had placed in Lebanon some three hundred artillery pieces, two hundred mortars, several of which were 130-millimeter guns with a 27-kilometer range. In addition, it also had sixty to seventy tanks in Lebanon--including T-54s, as contrasted with the thirty to forty less sophisticated T-34s that were there before the cessation of hostilities.

Despite the defiant rhetoric in opposition to the PLO buildup, Begin seemed to welcome the temporary truce with the Palestine Liberation Organization. Indeed, Israeli Foreign Minister Shamir met with Ambassador Habib on March 8 and expressed great interest in his optimistic assessment that the cease-fire would hold. Israel's enthusiastic response to Habib's analysis was apparent in subsequent Israeli press commentary. Moreover, Israeli television news reported that Habib had received indications in Syria, Saudi Arabia, and Jordan that those nations also were interested in maintaining stability and avoiding a resumption of hostilities.[19]

In addition to the Shamir-Habib session on March 8, there was a meeting between Begin and Habib. A dispute regarding the scope of the 1981 cease-fire occurred at that meeting.[20] The issue was whether the accord applied worldwide. Begin argued it did; Habib claimed it did not. The day before, Sharon had given an interview on Israeli radio that undercut Begin's view that the cease-fire was applicable globally.[21] In answer to a question of what would constitute a provocation that would warrant an Israeli attack against the PLO in Lebanon, Sharon said that a clear provocation exists when the killing of Jews in Israel is authorized. Thus, while the prime minister privately claimed that the cease-fire applied worldwide, the minister of defense publicly implied that it held only within Israel. There was agreement, however, that the point of origin of an attack was the criterion for judging whether there was a violation. If a gunboat sailed from Israel into international waters and then shelled Damour in Lebanon, Israel would be in noncompliance with the accord. Similarly, if the PLO sent a unit from Lebanon into Israel via Jordan, that also would be a violation.

Even the Kingdom of Jordan implicitly recognized the Begin-Habib consensus on the scope of the cease-fire terms. For instance, Israeli radio reported on March 4 that the Kingdom's minister of foreign affairs said in an interview with a Kuwaiti newspaper, *As-Siyasah*, that Amman would not allow PLO combatants to infiltrate Israel from Jordan; such an infiltration would provide Israel with a pretext to attack Jordan.[22] A PLO unit had originated in Lebanon during late January 1982, had infiltrated Israel from Jordan, and was apprehended within Israel with forty-nine hand grenades and ten kilograms of explosives. Rather than condemning this apparent violation of the temporary truce, the State Department later merely issued a statement one month later that the United States did not condone violence from any quarter.

At the March 8 meeting of Begin and Habib, the government of Israel gave mixed signals regarding the expectation of hostilities. According to Israeli sources, the session started going downhill when Defense Minister Sharon said that he opposed consultations between the United States and Israel over southern Lebanon contingencies because such meetings would tie Israel's hands. Coordination, he believed, could be an instrument for applying pressure on Israel to exercise restraint. In contrast to Sharon, Begin had expressed a great deal of interest in joint planning with the United States in the event the Syrians attacked or threatened Lebanese rightists. As a result of Begin's request, Habib later recommended the creation of an interagency team to be led by Deputy Assistant Secretary Draper for regular, systematic consultations with the Israelis, beginning in April 1982 and continuing at approximately two-month intervals.

Begin proposed the establishment of a formal U.S.-Israel Commission on Lebanon Contingencies, but Habib favored only close consultations over prospective military activities for fear that the inevitable leak of a formal arrangement would damage the U.S. role as mediator. Regarding the defense minister, moreover, Sharon was correct. The Habib formula of consultations was, in fact, a means for the United States to exercise control over Israel. Ironically, Begin also may have been using the mechanism of formal consultations as a tool to restrain his own defense minister.

Saudi Arabia as a Fulcrum for Syria

After Habib departed from the Middle East, he briefed the French in Paris on March 12. The French connection would prove to be significant as an indirect channel to the PLO and for setting up a multinational force to oversee the withdrawal of Palestinian combatants during September 1982. The bottom line of Habib's two-and-a-half-week trip to Lebanon, Israel, Syria, Jordan, and Saudi Arabia was the need for an Arab fulcrum with which to apply leverage on the Syrians, who remained unyielding when it came to Lebanon. Ambassador Habib felt that the Saudis could circumvent Syrian roadblocks and draw out the Lebanese genius for compromise to produce a political outcome for Lebanon that was satisfactory to American interests.

Why did Habib elect the Kingdom of Saudi Arabia to exercise leverage over Syria? Former U.S. officials confirmed that Crown Prince Fahd had assured Habib that Saudi Arabia would continue to play a role in Lebanon in the context of working toward Syrian withdrawal, assist in Lebanese presidential elections, and strengthen the cease-fire. Habib also inferred from a meeting between Fahd and PLO Chairman Yasir Arafat on March 7 that the Saudis could be influential not only with the Syrians but also with the Palestinians, or at least with the centrist politicians in their movement.

Evidence supporting Saudi willingness to exercise influence due to Habib's encouragement was found in the press. Israeli journalist David Landau wrote that the Fahd-Arafat meeting sparked speculation in Israel that Habib may have induced the Saudis to use their influence over the PLO to reinforce the cease-fire in southern Lebanon.[23] In short, a core issue of U.S. diplomacy regarding Lebanon was the extent to which Saudi Arabia could (1) serve as interlocutor in defusing the missile crisis between Israel and Syria, (2) provide the political context for national reconciliation among Lebanese factions, and (3) arrange and maintain a cease-fire between Israel and the Palestine Liberation Organization.

As early as the May 7, 1981, Working Group meeting on Lebanon, there was a discussion of the potential for a Saudi role. Washington game planning also anticipated that Habib would visit Riyadh at the end of his Middle East trip to explain U.S. intentions to the Saudis. The goal was to lower the likelihood that the Saudis would fall into Syria's lap by default. Also during the spring of 1981, the Saudis requested that the United States restrain Israel from acting unilaterally to remove Syria's missiles from Lebanon.

This request received serious consideration at the highest levels of the White House. In conversations with the Saudis, however, globalists adroitly sidestepped the Saudi request. They seized upon Damascus-Moscow links as a pretext for shifting the blame for any hostilities away from Israel and the United States, redirecting it, instead, toward the Soviet Union and its radical surrogates in the area.

There is some justification for the belief that the Saudis could be an effective fulcrum vis-a-vis Syria, but, on balance, this idea is a nonstarter. Damascus and Riyadh have had relatively good bilateral relations that go back many years. These links manifest themselves on a personal level by the historically close ties of President Assad's brother (often at odds with the president) with one of the high-ranking members of the Saudi royal family. Furthermore, Middle East specialist John Devlin claims that Saudi Arabia has been helpful to Syria for problemsolving concerning Lebanon and in defusing crises with Jordan, in addition to being a source of money.[24] It was State's intent to take advantage of this perception of Saudi influence in order to induce Syrian restraint.

However, the overwhelming weight of policy and academic opinion contrasts with Devlin's expectations. Kissinger, for one, emphasizes the conservative, risk-averse nature of the Saudi leadership.[25] He illustrates this tendency to avoid risk by referring to Saudi leaders as following, rather than leading, policy. The Kingdom, he says, always has wanted the protection of an inter-Arab consensus before acting, a passive Saudi policy that stems from a perennial desire to avoid confrontation. In view of this situation, Kissinger concludes, it is not surprising that the Saudis do not see themselves in a leadership role. One of Kissinger's former NSC aides, William Quandt, notes that militarily and demographically Saudi Arabia is not in the same league as Egypt, Iraq, or Syria.[26] Despite massive arms acquisitions from the United States, Saudi Arabia remains a relatively weak military power.

In addition to its military weakness, the Kingdom of Saudi Arabia has historically been reluctant to take the lead in diplomatic initiatives. This hesitancy was evident in the aftermath of the Camp David peace negotiations. Regardless of their general advocacy of peace, the Saudis probably had no intention to back the Camp David accords, and, indeed, they did not publicly support them. In fact, they even aligned with anti-Egyptian forces during November 1978. Writing along the same lines after he left the presidency, Jimmy Carter expressed disappointment that the Saudis were not fulfilling American expectations.[27] Given these precedents, State should not have placed as much responsibility on the Saudis as it did during 1982.

Within the U.S. Government, one would have expected regional experts, who ostensibly were sensitive to Saudi risk aversity, to have blown the whistle. It not only would have been a formidable task for the Saudis to sustain a complex diplomatic initiative on the Syrian missiles, but adding Lebanese reconciliation and the armed Palestinians in Lebanon to the agenda would have entailed even greater difficulties. Even at State, however, there were critics who were cognizant of the mistaken belief that Saudi Arabia neither could exert enough pressure nor provide enough money to induce a Syrian withdrawal from Lebanon.[28]

Regionalists dominated the policy process that unrealistically assumed Saudi risk-taking behavior; in contrast, globalists had a more valid view of Saudi risk aversity, but they did not prevail. One of the planners in 1982 was Dennis Ross. Again, writing between tours in the government, Ross states that the United States needs:

> to face up to the limits of Saudi power and lower...[United States] expectations about what the Saudis can and will do. For too long...[the U.S. has] exaggerated Saudi power, counting on them to moderate the PLO, support Jordan and Egypt, and deliver the Syrians. Policies based on this premise were bound to fail even while they put the Saudis more on the spot. Thus, apart from guaranteeing failure, these policies further reduced Saudi willingness to run risks.[29]

If globalists at the State Department were sensitive to Saudi risk aversity, the intelligence community apparently was not. Intelligence analysts provided little warning that the Saudis would be unable to sustain a diplomatic initiative of such enormity given their propensity for avoiding choices and their proclivity to split differences among those who implore the Kingdom. Thus, the regionalists at State not only prevailed in bureaucratic politics but also created a diplomacy with minimal threat of force for Syria, as well as one based upon false assumptions of Saudi risk-taking. For Damascus, there was a diplomacy without force; for Riyadh, a diplomacy without intelligence.

Intelligence in the War for Washington

State's dominance spelled victory for that department in the Foggy Bottom section of Washington and defeat for the White House in McFarlane's premature attempt to seize the reins of policy. The success of a bureaucratic coup d'etat by 1600 Pennsylvania Avenue was dependent on how many other departments and agencies could be attracted to its side in the battle against State for supremacy. One such agency up for grabs in the war for Washington was the Central Intelligence Agency in Langley, Virginia--the Agency. The White House, in the person of the Deputy National Security Adviser McFarlane, gained Langley's support, reinforcing the view that an impending crisis required reorganization, with 1600 Pennsylvania Avenue rather than Foggy Bottom as the site of the action. The White House approach to coalition-building was to alter the regular schedule of intelligence reporting. The CIA is the lead agency in routinely drafting National Intelligence Estimates (NIEs), for example, on Lebanon. McFarlane commissioned a Special National Intelligence Estimate (SNIE) in mid-February 1982, partly as a tool used in organizational maneuvering during the spring of that year. (See Chapter 9 for an elaboration of McFarlane's abuse of intelligence in bureaucratic warfare concerning both Lebanon and Iran.)

The Special National Intelligence Estimate had both bureaucratic and substantive implications. The estimate reinforced McFarlane's attempt to reorganize the interagency structure and give himself a dominant role. Indeed, McFarlane tasked the intelligence community to prepare the estimate outside its normal schedule of reports. His quest for power via intelligence tasking was checked partly by State, which took several blocking actions, such as promptly convening the Contingency Group on Lebanon on February 18, 1982.

The consensus in the administration as of mid-February was logically inconsistent concerning the scope of an expected invasion. On the one hand, Israel aimed to drive the PLO north of the Zahrani River (in southern Lebanon just to the north of the Litani River). Jerusalem's purpose here was to force the PLO beyond artillery range of Israel's northern border with Lebanon. On the other hand, Israel's goals also included destroying as much of the PLO leadership as possible. Because many of the leaders resided in Beirut or could be expected to flee there under fire, the Israel Defense Forces would need to take the fighting to Beirut--well beyond the Zahrani River. The consensus in the administration was inconsistent in concluding that Israel's goals would be both geographically limited and targeted at the Beirut-based PLO leadership. Moreover, the prevailing opinion in Washington failed to take into account Israeli Defense Minister Sharon's plan to restructure Lebanon's political system after the military defeat of the Palestine Liberation Organization.

Another deficiency in the administration's dominant attitude in the spring of 1982 was that it did not assess the impact of American diplomacy on the likelihood that certain events would transpire. Although the revised estimate contended that concern over a U.S. reaction was an external constraint on Israel's intent to attack, there was no attempt to assess the consequence of Habib's efforts on the prospect of war. But there probably was a relationship between American diplomacy and the likelihood of warfare when the revised estimate was issued in mid-February 1982. According to the *Middle East Policy Survey* of March 26, 1982 (no. 52), after Habib met with the president during the third week of March, the U.S. intelligence community contended that hostilities were less likely to surface. Similarly, the community's revised estimate one month earlier could have taken into account the impact of American diplomacy on the prospect of war.

In contrast to the intelligence agencies, the NSC staff did address the impact of policy on the likelihood of warfare. They concluded that Habib's diplomacy would raise slightly the threshold at which Israel would strike, given a PLO provocation; in light of his diplomacy, it would take a greater provocation for Israel to launch an invasion, absent Habib. It is not surprising that intelligence agencies are reluctant to discuss future states of affairs in terms of the options available to U.S. decisionmakers; these agencies generally attempt to keep intelligence apart from policy to avoid being biased by policy considerations. But though intelligence agencies traditionally seek to be free of potentially distorting effects of foreknowledge about policy options, a White House aide, McFarlane, displayed little reluctance to use those intelligence estimates that justified his personal policy preferences and bureaucratic political ambitions.

Conclusions

Military capabilities and political intentions indicated a growing likelihood of warfare during the winter and spring of 1982. Officials who were inclined to support Israel focused on the increase in Palestinian capabilities and inferred an offensive intent by the PLO against northern Israel. Those less supportive of Jerusalem emphasized Israel's enhanced military capabilities as indicative of its hostile intent toward the PLO in southern Lebanon. At issue was whether a Palestinian provocation would result in an Israeli response that was proportional or greater in intensity than the original act; in the event of an Israeli attack on the PLO in Lebanon, moreover, that organization was likely to attempt to turn military defeat into political victory.

U.S. policy toward Syrian missiles in Lebanon and the arms buildup between Israel and the PLO was formulated in the context of a gap between a premature grab for power by a White House staffer, McFarlane, via crisis management machinery, and State's continued role as the department with the action on a day-by-day basis. In the absence of a policyforcing event, it is unlikely that a White House aide could lead a coalition to seize the reins of the government. It takes a crisis for the balance of power to shift to the White House; without the justification of policyforcing events, the White House simply does not have the legitimate right or need to order departments and agencies to act in areas that are their traditional responsibilities. Notwithstanding the coalition of the White House and the intelligence community in sounding the alarm bells of impending crisis, McFarlane failed to expand his power. However, as conflict intensified and the need to synthesize diplomacy and force considerations finally became compelling, his role would grow.

An impotent policy toward Syria resulted from the regionalists' dominance at the State Department. But the interagency process failed to modify State's predilection for a diplomacy-only policy toward Syria. Although rumors flew about town concerning a possible American ultimatum to Syria, there was no serious consideration given to this alternative within the policy elite as it pursued an appeasement approach toward Syria. Relative to the "wildcats" of the Middle East, such as Iraq and Syria, that were periodically baring their teeth to bolster their diplomacy, the United States was more like a toothless tiger. Whereas Syria regularly mixed force with diplomacy, the Department of State failed to find a formula to blend these two components of national security policy.

One possible explanation for this failure lies in the difficulties of trying to manage a crisis with a single department (State) rather than an interagency process led by the White House. With the president at the helm in a crisis, the interagency process might be able to effect a consistent policy that combines force with diplomacy. If the main purpose of an interagency process is to produce policies that integrate competing values, that approach is more likely to produce a consistent or coherent policy in response to a policyforcing event than a system dominated by a single organization. So, one conclusion is that White House management of the interagency process is appropriate and desirable in the context of policyforcing events; in routine situations, however, coordination of the interagency process should remain in the department or agency most relevant to the issue at hand.

In the meantime, the regionalists at the State Department prevailed and the question arose: Would State, acting largely alone, seek to blend diplomacy with force? In brief, the answer was no. American diplomacy succeeded in avoiding war between Israel and Syria during the spring of 1981 and achieved a cease-fire between Israel and the PLO that summer. But it was tested once more a year later and was found wanting. The spring of 1982 produced an interlude in which American diplomacy failed to capitalize on the opportunity to prevent the guns of June.

4

The Lull Before the Storm

The Reagan Initiative

Reassuring Jordan and Placating the PLO

The administration's policy of restraining Israel, appeasing Syria, and imploring Saudi Arabia was a program of diplomacy without force. Although this policy was failing to slow down the burning fuse to Beirut, regionalists advocated even more of the same but with new targets for American entreaties--the Palestine Liberation Organization and Jordan. There is a paradox in Israel's threats to invade Lebanon in order to rid it of the Palestinian armed presence: Jerusalem's diplomatic markers and military buildup actually shifted the Palestinian issue from the back to the front burner in U.S. policymaking. Contrary to Israel's wishes, its threats placed the PLO in a position to benefit from American willingness to make concessions in the name of peace. Jerusalem's threat of war had the unintended consequence of planting the seeds of peace in Washington; thus, it conceived the Reagan peace initiative.

Of seminal importance in the conception of the Reagan initiative was the Kingdom of Jordan. King Hussein's response to the threat of an Israeli invasion of Lebanon was to make a plea for a solution to the "Palestine" problem. He reasoned that Israel's long-term strategy was "to create new facts" in the region. The Lebanese phase of that stratagem was a step toward achieving Israeli Defense Minister Sharon's dream of turning Jordan into the Palestinian homeland. He first wanted to destroy the PLO in Lebanon and impose a friendly regime there; secondly, Sharon hoped to force King Hussein to abdicate in favor of Chairman Arafat, thereby making Jordan the Palestinian state. This scenario implies that Israel would retain the West Bank of the Jordan River and that Palestinians there would be expelled to the East Bank, that is, to Jordan. Sharon's dream, however, was Hussein's nightmare. Hence, the king charged that the United States would have made an historic error if it allowed the Palestinians to take over the Hashemite Kingdom of Jordan.

King Hussein foresaw devastating consequences for the Kingdom if the United States placed the Palestinian issue on the back burner while restructuring Lebanon. He insisted that a solution to the Lebanon problem must be coupled with an overall settlement of the Palestinian issue. In keeping with Hussein's preferences, Washington issued a series of public statements designed to reassure the king, and it also included him on Habib's itinerary during the envoy's visits to the region.

A theme underlying American pronouncements was that Jordan's "unique and enduring character" was a fact of political life in the region and something that the United States was committed to uphold. As a result, Jordan was not to become the Palestinian state as an outcome of the peace process. In addition, the administration revised its initial priorities so that the Arab-Israeli zone became a primary focus of attention at the expense of Soviet and Iranian threats to the Gulf area. In short, Washington supplemented its program of restraining Israel, appeasing Syria, and imploring Saudi Arabia with a policy of reassuring Jordan.

Regionalists Versus Globalists

The crisis over Lebanon intensified and then reached a plateau. This temporary lull provided an opening for regionalists to gain ground on globalists by proposing a major change in policy toward the Palestinians. In the hard soil of the Middle East, regionalists seized the opportunity to plant the Reagan initiative. Like gamblers in a diplomatic garden, they took the chance that the respite from the high-threat environment was a moment to develop a new policy. Their risk-taking paid off in the form of a secret policy change. But the initiative failed, and officials associated with it also suffered.

Press accounts of the Reagan initiative often trace its origins to the period immediately after the Senate confirmed George Shultz and he was sworn in as secretary of state--July 16, 1982.[1] The following day, Shultz did convene two high-level groups of advisers in "close hold" sessions at State. Globalists were led by Kissinger, who, one month earlier, had written publicly that the Israeli invasion had opened up extraordinary opportunities for a dynamic American diplomacy throughout the Middle East. Accordingly, he held that the United States must allow Jordan to take the lead on

West Bank negotiations.[2] Indeed, the defeat of the PLO in Lebanon and the demonstration of the limits of Syrian and Soviet willingness to run risks gave Jordan the chance to take charge of negotiations on the Palestinian problem. Kissinger's globalist approach was consistent with prior American policy, yet it provided the basis for what was perceived to be a new policy toward the Palestinian issue. The Reagan initiative assumed that the inhabitants of the West Bank and Gaza would be associated with the East Bank of the Jordan River, that is, with the Kingdom of Jordan.

A second group of professional diplomats, dominated by the regionalists, argued that Israel's invasion of Lebanon had harmed American interests in the Arab world. Because of an "illusion of collusion" between Israel and the United States, the invasion was a setback without any redeeming benefits. This group called for direct PLO participation in the peace process without reference to Jordan. There was also an apparent softening of the 1975 American terms for that organization's formal involvement in the negotiations. These U.S. conditions for PLO participation in the peace process had included a renunciation of terror, recognition of Israel's right to exist, and acceptance of United Nations Resolutions 242 and 338. (These resolutions call for negotiations among the parties based on the formula of Israeli withdrawal from land occupied during the 1967 war in exchange for peace from the Arab states.) However, after Israel's invasion of Lebanon, the regionalist call for PLO participation in the peace process downplayed these prior American conditions.

Although planning for a shift in policy peaked under Shultz between July 17 and August 19, 1982, paperwork had actually begun in the spring of that year under Haig, who resigned on June 25. Haig may not have pursued the Reagan initiative in the same manner as Shultz, but it is instructive to note that its origins, in fact, preceded Shultz. The first high-level discussion at the Reagan White House concerning a new Palestinian policy occurred during Habib's briefing after his March visit to the Middle East. The special envoy met with senior officials at the White House on March 18, including the president, Deputy Secretary Walter Stoessel, Counselor to the President Edwin Meese, Deputy Chief of Staff Michael Deaver, Deputy Assistant to the President for National Security Affairs Robert McFarlane, Assistant Secretary of State Nicholas Veliotes, myself as the National Security Council senior staff member, and Deputy Assistant Secretary of State Morris Draper.

The special envoy stated his belief that the likelihood of an early breakdown of the July 1981 cessation of hostilities had been reduced. According to Don Oberdorfer of the *Washington Post*, Habib reported that Israel, Lebanon, Syria, and Saudi Arabia all reaffirmed the desirability of maintaining the temporary truce.[3] On the basis of the mid-March discussions at the White House on the Palestinian issue, it was clear that the regionalists continued to hold the reins of power. Further, those who believed that U.S. interests in the Arab world would be gravely harmed by an Israeli invasion had increased their influence. Were it not for the group of Kissinger-led globalists who were brought in by Shultz as external advisers, the regionalists of the spring would have completely dominated policy in the fall of 1982. Though Haig was a globalist, his seventh-floor colleagues of the same stripe had let him down. The paperwork was in the hands of sixth-floor operatives, who headed the regional bureaus at Foggy Bottom. Paradoxically, the same professionals in the Near Eastern and South Asian Affairs Bureau who advocated "neutralizing" the PLO in May of 1981 now called for dramatic concessions to the Palestinians a year later. This policy change is all the more interesting because it occurred under the same secretary of state, Alexander Haig.

Haig had not changed his own global "pinstripes," so the explanation was that his control over the department had begun to wane. With the secretary's diminished influence, the regionalists added a new Palestinian dimension to the diplomacy-without-force policy of "restrain, appease, implore, and reassure." As regionalists gained over globalists, Soviet-bashing became passe and Arafat became the "great white hope" of *Le Maison Blanche*, a favorite restaurant near the White House staff offices. Pragmatists began to prevail over ideologues: Deals became more attractive than principles. Professional bureaucrats had an opening for their comprehensive plans to reach policy elites, and peace planning became a cottage industry at State. In the interlude before the storm, the regionalists planted the seeds of a new diplomatic scheme in fertile soil. Thus, the threat of war, warfare itself, and the lull in fighting had the unexpected result of facilitating the peace process in the autumn of 1982.

With the fall of a weakened Haig and the rise of an inexperienced Shultz, the new secretary wisely introduced globalists from without to check regionalists from within. Bargaining between these two contending groups for the new secretary's ear produced a plan that combined two elements: (1) a Jordan-first approach, and

(2) concessions to the Palestinians without recognizing the Palestine Liberation Organization. In spite of such innovative balancing, however, the seeds of September--the Reagan initiative--failed to flower. In addition to an increase in the pace of the peace process, the spring of 1982 was a time to sort through the complexities of policymaking as evidenced by overlapping dilemmas confronting the key participants.

Diplomacy and Force Dilemmas: The Quest for Peace

The Security Dilemma

The Middle East is a field of conflict where dilemmas continually emerge and converge. In this respect, the actors in the Lebanon conflict saw themselves as locked in a security dilemma--a situation in which the security of all is mutually exclusive: One party's efforts to gain security increased the net insecurity of the other actors. For example, the armed Palestinians' attempt to enhance their security in southern Lebanon decreased the Israelis' security in northern Israel. Perceptions of a security dilemma required choices between equally unsatisfactory alternatives. A basic security problem regarding the Middle East might appear at first glance as a choice between force and diplomacy--between augmenting and diminishing risks. In fact, however, the choice is not between these two extremes; rather, the issue is finding the appropriate balance between them. Force and diplomacy need not be given equal weight in every situation; consequently, the appropriate proportions of each must be determined on a case-by-case basis.

Complementarity is the key to unlocking security dilemmas in the Middle East. Although there is tension between using the threat of force to induce compliance and employing the diplomacy of reassurance to keep a situation under control, these measures should be used in concert. Given the difficulty in choosing between force and diplomacy, decisionmakers within Israel, the PLO, the United States, and the Soviet Union saw themselves on the horns of overlapping security dilemmas concerning the Middle East.

Overlapping Dilemmas: The PLO and Israel

While Prime Minister Begin was trying to force the PLO to choose between abandoning armed struggle or facing the consequences of an attack by Israel, PLO Chairman Yasir Arafat was facing a dilemma of his own with respect to the use of force. On the one side, Arafat had to authorize enough force to cover his flanks vis-a-vis internal Palestinian constituencies, particularly non-PLO hard-liners, such as Abu Nidal--with whom Arafat exchanged death threats.   Abu Nidal was involved in an attempted assassination of an Israeli diplomat in London, an act of violence designed to precipitate an Israeli invasion of Lebanon. As a result, he is a focal point of the discussion here.

On the other side, though Arafat had to use sufficient force against Israel to appease Palestinian rejectionists, he also had to limit that force to avoid provoking Israel. Such was the chairman's dilemma.   During the spring lull of 1982, military incidents had transpired between Israelis and armed Palestinians, but neither group wanted to accept blame for the breakdown of the temporary truce.   By saddling the other party with responsibility for the resumption of fighting, the protagonists would place themselves in a position to receive more international diplomatic support than they would otherwise get.   Such diplomatic backing was even more important for the Palestinians than for Israel.

Using limited force to avoid inciting Jerusalem, centrist Palestinians, led by Arafat, sought to quiet their "domestic" left-wing opposition with occasional forays into Israel. Arafat, however, was in an untenable position.   His opposition wanted to kill or simply oust him from power altogether. These oppositionists even would favor provoking Israel to invade Lebanon and destroy the majority of the armed Palestinian movement in order to eliminate Arafat.

Compared to Sharon, Begin was a moderate in Israeli national security affairs. Unlike Abu Nidal, who existed outside of Arafat's coalition, Sharon was a part of Begin's political constituency. Thus, Sharon had to be mollified. Begin was under pressure from the right wing to authorize enough force to satisfy his hard-liners but not so much force that the United States would be alarmed. He sought to resolve his dilemma by adopting proportionate responses to PLO provocations that would not upset the United States at the same time.   Like Arafat, Begin was in an untenable position. Sharon would be satisfied with nothing short of a major invasion of Lebanon and searched for any pretext to justify such an assault. Similarly, Abu Nidal would have been content only with an Israeli invasion of Lebanon, and he sought a provocation that would lead to such an attack.

Abu Nidal and Ariel Sharon shared a mutual interest in war, albeit from different perspectives. Certainly, these two men were not parallel: Abu Nidal violently opposed Arafat, but Sharon was a member of Begin's political party, in the government, and in many ways Begin's right-hand man. Nevertheless, Abu Nidal and Ariel Sharon served as firebrands who motivated Arafat and Begin, respectively, to use more force than either might have employed absent such pressure. Thus, Israel and the PLO straddled overlapping dilemmas: Each was trying to place the onus on the other side for the choices it wanted to make. After Sharon virtually hijacked the government of Israel, it was looking for a reason to invade southern Lebanon while averting a confrontation with the United States. Similarly, the PLO was using limited violence as a means to hold itself together while avoiding a provocation of Jerusalem.

With respect to the domestic constituencies of Arafat's Fatah group, the years 1967-1969 saw the growth of a variety of Palestinian guerrilla organizations, some of which fought the Fatah centrists for overall control. During 1968, Fatah decided to take other groups into the leadership. This expansion meant that this group could never exercise the kind of hegemony over the movement that other successful "liberation" groups enjoyed. As Helena Cobban states, Fatah had to learn to live with a variety of other guerrilla movements within the PLO's overall framework.[4] Hence, Arafat had to steer his ship of "state" through rocks deliberately placed by those who opposed his policies. The Palestinian helmsman needed to placate the oppositionists so frequently that it was difficult to distinguish his policies from those of more radical sailors, such as Abu Nidal.

British police had tied the June 3, 1982, assassination attempt on an Israeli diplomat in London to Abu Nidal. They identified the assailant as a young West Bank Palestinian under the control of an older accomplice who also was arrested. This man was an Iraqi "businessman," whom British authorities considered to be an operative of Baghdad's official intelligence service. Iraq most probably was the source of the contract given to Abu Nidal's organization. At one time, he was a confidant of Arafat, but the two had become bitter enemies, and Abu Nidal's Fatah Revolutionary Council in Baghdad claimed that it, rather than Arafat's accommodationist Fatah organization based in Beirut, was the soul of Palestinian nationalism. Schiff and Ya'ari confirm the Iraqi link, stating that at a secret camp near Baghdad, Abu Nidal, with the aid of Iraqi intelligence agents, trained his hit squads to ambush PLO activists.[5]

President Saddam Hussein of Iraq wanted to sponsor an attack on an Israeli diplomat to embarrass his fellow Ba'athist, President Assad of Syria. Baghdad sought to place Damascus on the horns of a dilemma in the event of an Israeli invasion of Lebanon. If Syria failed to rescue the PLO in Lebanon, it would be perceived as an unreliable backer of the Palestinian cause relative to Iraq. Conversely, if Syrian forces attempted to save the PLO, they would be soundly defeated by the Israelis. Although Abu Nidal generally sent death squads to make hits within the Palestinian family, an Israeli diplomat was picked on the occasion in question partly because he was associated with efforts to bring together PLO operatives in England with internationally known Jews.[6] (A paradox of the peace process is that intra-Palestinian violence may increase with a rise in activities that might result in a negotiated settlement of the Arab-Israeli conflict.)

The shelling of northern Israel on May 9, 1982, illustrates the PLO's attempt to employ a measured response that would satisfy its radicals without giving Israel an internationally recognized provocation. The PLO construed this attack as political, not military. The shellings avoided civilians and, therefore, did not constitute a "serious" violation of the cease-fire. The PLO also declared that no further response would be made to Jerusalem's air strikes, which had been prompted by the attempted assassination of an Israeli diplomat in Paris in early May 1982. Third parties assessed the PLO tactic as a rather civilized way to fight. Sharon, however, called the PLO shelling more than a clear provocation. That the cycle of violence began with an attempt to kill an Israeli in Paris suggests that Jerusalem's toleration of provocation worldwide had decreased its threshold for action in Lebanon. Increasingly severe Israeli air raids into Lebanon indicated that, by mid-May the threshold for action had been lowered. A major Israeli operation could be triggered by much less in June than in March or April because of the accumulation of incidents in the Near East, as well as in Europe.

A minority view in the Reagan administration assumed that Israel would act as it had during the spring 1978 Litani incursion into Lebanon, which took place before the Camp David accords were signed in the summer. Cairo, a signatory at Camp David, hardly blinked when Jerusalem acted against the armed Palestinians in Lebanon that spring. Similarly, as the April 25, 1982, date for

Israel's final withdrawal from Sinai approached, Cairo was in no position to rush to the Palestinians' defense for fear that Jerusalem would not adhere to the 1979 treaty that required Israeli withdrawal.

Although the minority position did not dominate the Reagan administration, that view reinforced a general uncertainty regarding Israel's intentions on the Sinai withdrawal. As a result of this uncertainty, Deputy Secretary of State Walter Stoessel visited Prime Minister Begin in Jerusalem on April 15, 1982. According to Israeli radio, Begin gave no hint that Israel might not pull out from the remaining portion of the Sinai as planned.[7] Israel was concerned about renewed Egyptian ties to the PLO and Palestinian arms smuggling from Lebanon into the Gaza Strip, but there was no evidence of a link between such ties and either PLO smuggling or Israel's Sinai withdrawal.

During the spring of 1982, the administration was divided over the extent to which Israel's Lebanon policy was contingent upon its Sinai withdrawal. A small group of analysts held that Jerusalem intended to authorize a massive operation against the PLO in southern Lebanon before the April 25 withdrawal deadline. This group reasoned that Israel's remaining presence in Sinai gave it a means to secure Egyptian and American tolerance for actions in Lebanon. An extreme version of this view held that Israeli leaders had a change of heart about the Camp David accords and calculated that a large-scale attack in Lebanon would cause Egypt to abrogate the agreement before recovering the rest of Sinai. Such an abrogation would relieve Israel of the onus of breaking an agreement that the United States had a strong interest in preserving.

The consensus view, led by the Defense Intelligence Agency, differed.[8] The agreed-upon estimate was that Israel, in fact, was planning a major operation designed to eliminate the armed Palestinian presence in southern Lebanon. There was considerable doubt, however, whether the timing of the invasion hinged upon the Sinai withdrawal. Proponents of this second school of thought correctly believed that Cairo was committed to holding up its end of the peace bargain of Camp David even after the deadline. They contended that Jerusalem felt Cairo's commitment was strong enough to survive a shock, such as a major incursion into Lebanon, and that the strategic advantages for Israel of continuing peace with Egypt would justify accepting the risks of returning the remaining portion of Sinai. Certainly, it would be politically painful to abolish Sinai settlements, and relinquishing the remainder of that desert would mean the loss of military advantages, such as strategic depth and, thereby, early warning time. Nevertheless, the consensus was that neither settlements nor depth would be decisive factors. In sum, they saw little connection between Israeli-Egyptian relations and Jerusalem's intent to attack the PLO in Lebanon before April 25. Israel, however, could act before that deadline if there were a major provocation.

Although the approaching Sinai withdrawal deadline eased Israel's predicament, it sharpened that of the Palestine Liberation Organization. The suspicion that Egypt's military weight had been neutralized by its incentive to see an uninterrupted Camp David peace process gave the PLO further reason for apprehension. In response to growing indications that Israel was about to use force, the PLO sought to enlist the diplomatic support of moderate Arab states. Arafat asked the prime minister of Tunisia to intervene with the White House and to explain that the PLO would like to negotiate. Because it could not recognize Israel, the PLO would allow others to negotiate tacitly on its behalf, thereby giving implicit recognition of the Jewish state. In proposing such a circuitous formula, the PLO was seeking negotiations in a way that took into account the constraints on that organization. Due to internal rivalries in the Palestinian movement, PLO bargaining generally needs to be indirect.

The struggle within the Palestinian movement worked to the detriment of the Arafat-led centrist coalition. It was possible that the oppositionists were trying to overthrow Arafat by provoking an Israeli invasion. The fact that the Abu Nidal faction of the Palestinian resistance most likely shot Israeli Ambassador Shlomo Argov in London in June of 1982 suggests that the oppositionists were trying to depose Arafat by inciting Jerusalem. In terms of the American connection, the PLO chairman managed his opposition in the Palestinian movement quite differently than Prime Minister Begin treated Defense Minister Sharon. Begin did not seek to extract the maximum out of Washington by having Sharon on his right demanding more militant action in Lebanon. Arafat, however, did attempt to extract an ultimate political bonus from the White House by the fact that Abu Nidal was the *enfant terrible* of the movement.

The terms of Arafat's opening bid to Washington included U.S. recognition of the PLO prior to that organization's renunciation of terrorism, recognition of Israel's right to exist, and acceptance of

United Nations Resolutions 242 and 338. Arafat's offer was actually a demand for a political windfall and hence a non-starter. It resisted the idea of simultaneous recognition of the PLO and Israel, a proposal that would have seized the diplomatic initiative. In search of a diplomatic premium for the Palestinians, Tunisian Prime Minister Mzali did Arafat's bidding at the White House on May 15, 1982.[9]

Paradoxically, Arafat's demarche to 1600 Pennsylvania Avenue strengthened both of the contending camps of Washington policymakers. Regionalists scored some points due to the heightened sense that the impending crisis could be resolved by placating the Palestine Liberation Organization. They seized upon Arafat's message and argued for trading off America's commitment to Israel not to negotiate with the PLO for the benefit of helping the Arafat wing within that organization. Arafat's bid coincided with the administration's desire to isolate the oppositionists among the armed Palestinians, and direct American contact with the PLO, in principle, appeared as a practical route for enhancing the status of the centrists. Such direct contact, however, could not be implemented without risking a storm of opprobrium from Jerusalem and the pro-Israel lobby in the States. Quite understandably, the president and his special envoy put this idea into cold storage. Washington's cool response strengthened globalists. They were incensed by the outrageous PLO demands, suspicious that Moscow would benefit if they were granted, and adamant that standing firm against Soviet surrogates was paramount.

The cross-cutting dilemmas regarding diplomacy and force were not resolved. The PLO's problem was not remedied by making an indirect approach to the White House; neither was Israel's predicament solved by blocking America's moves toward the Palestine Liberation Organization. In fact, the security dilemma facing Israel became more acute with each passing day in which Jerusalem failed to act.

Overlapping Dilemmas: The U.S. and the USSR

Choices for Washington and Moscow also became more pointed and interlocking as time wore on and Israeli restraint was matched by Syrian and PLO intransigence. The Americans and Soviets were trying to circumvent similar dilemmas concerning Israel and Syria, respectively. The United States hoped to avoid making a choice between giving Israel a green light to take out Syria's missiles and a red light not to do so. The color green implied risks because of the danger of escalation and expanded hostilities; red carried the risk of encouraging Syria to believe that it could successfully challenge Israeli deterrence, an idea that might lead to general war later. The United States eventually resolved this dilemma by choosing to restrain Jerusalem and appease Damascus, rather than opting for the riskier route of encouraging Israel to use force in the service of American diplomacy.

The Soviet Union sought to avoid a choice between supporting or restraining Syria. Support for Damascus carried with it the risk that the Syrians would make additional challenges to Jerusalem's deterrence, leading to a subsequent war; seeking to restrain Damascus might result in an ouster of Soviet advisers from Syria and increase its reliance on the West for arms, as well as for diplomatic assistance in reclaiming territory lost to Israel during 1967. Although Moscow preferred not to have a full-scale confrontation between Syria and Israel, the Kremlin did not want to see Damascus back down in the face of imperialist/Zionist pressure. The USSR managed its dilemma by giving Syria what amounted to an amber light to keep the missiles in Lebanon. Hence, in resolving their respective dilemmas, the superpowers chose different courses. The Kremlin favored its comrade's course of action, and the White House attempted to modify its partner's conduct.

The main actors in the key capitals sought to balance apparently conflicting objectives and speculated about the likelihood of warfare in the context of these overlapping dilemmas. Given the complexity of the predicaments, there was great uncertainty throughout the administration. Typically, the more complex a decision situation is, the more it is characterized by such uncertainty. To simplify complexity and reduce uncertainty, analysts drew upon the standard operating procedures of the intelligence discipline and highlighted the concepts of intent and capability.[10]

Combining Capability and Intent

Capability

As stated in Chapter 3, intent and capability are key components of the intelligence assessment craft.[11] To get a perspective on Israel's intent of attacking and its capability of assaulting the PLO in Lebanon, the following overview of the Syrian capacity to deter such an onslaught is instructive.

Syria had been engaged in a military buildup of great magnitude. After the Camp David accords of 1978, Damascus assumed that it would have to fight alone to regain the Golan Heights lost to and annexed by Jerusalem during 1967 and 1981, respectively. By mid-May of 1982, Syria's military was significantly stronger than it had been in 1973. According to *The Military Balance*, by the International Institute of Strategic Studies, the number of Syrian armored divisions had risen from two to four.[12] Syria had equipped many armored divisions with Soviet-supplied T-72 tanks and fully mechanized its two infantry divisions. In 1973, Syria had only six commando battalions, which had achieved some degree of success against Israel, but by 1982, Damascus had expanded its forces to over twenty-seven battalions.

If hostilities between Israel and Syria in Lebanon had spread to the Golan, Damascus still could use the T-72 tanks from its arsenal of over 800 to isolate Israeli forces there. Jerusalem may not have been able to use its ground-fired, antitank weapons effectively against the T-72s because of the tanks' heavy frontal armor. However, though Syria's overall strength had increased relative to that of Israel, Damascus could not deter Jerusalem from attacking Lebanon. Israel's localized capabilities for invading Lebanon, moreover, had been enhanced rapidly in the six months prior to the June 1982 invasion of Lebanon, further eroding Syria's deterrence capacity.

Capability and intent indicators provided mixed signals on the prospects for Israel to move its forces into Lebanon. One capability indicator showed an increased likelihood of attack. A May 9 meeting of the cabinet in Jerusalem approved air strikes in response to the April 3 assassination of an Israeli diplomat, Bar Simon Tov, in Paris. In these attacks directed at armed Palestinians in Lebanon, six civilians were reported killed and twenty wounded. The PLO retaliated with limited artillery fire into northern Israel, and both sides claimed violations of the July 1981 cease-fire. The May 9 meeting also authorized the mobilization of up to 5,000 reservists, including armored, mechanized infantry, and combat support units. These actions raised Israel's troop strength on its border with Lebanon and Syria to approximately 30,000, equaling or exceeding the level of April 10-12. In addition, a week after the authorization of the buildup, Israeli aircraft overflew Beirut and staged mock attacks, drawing heavy fire from Palestinian antiaircraft positions.

Although the military buildup of the May 10-17, 1982, period suggested an increasing capability for attack, a drawdown of Israel's military forces on the northern front began during the third week of May. This partial cutback implied a declining likelihood of a large-scale invasion. Some elements in the administration believed that the reduction in forces tended to rule out an attack on the PLO in Lebanon without another period of buildup. They offered several reasons to explain the drawdown, such as the expense of keeping larger-than-normal numbers of troops on the northern front.

It is interesting to note how expenses constrained extended military buildups in a prior case, fifteen years earlier. Israel mobilized partially on May 16, 1967, did so on a larger scale three days later, and launched a preemptive strike on June 5.[13] The 1967 and 1982 cases are comparable in that both included a call-up of reservists in a period prior to the outbreak of war. The cases differ, however, in that Israel required a considerably larger mobilization in 1967 than it did fifteen years later. Consider the economic effect of the 1967 mobilization as indicated in a statement by General Moshe Dayan, a former chief of staff and later Israeli defense minister:

> When Egyptian forces began moving into Sinai in mid-May [1967], and four days later mobilization was begun of Israeli army reservists, the immediate effect was a partial paralysis of the Israeli economy.[14]

An additional factor in 1982 was the likelihood that morale would suffer if reservists, who had been mobilized and deployed in the north, were not given an opportunity either to fight or return to their homes. Still another reason that explained the drawdown, and thereby pointed to a low likelihood of an Israeli attack, was an alleged attempt to create a better climate for Defense Minister Sharon's visit to Washington in late May and Prime Minister Begin's trip in mid-June. A final explanation is that the Syrians had pulled back some of their forces in the Bekaa Valley of Lebanon, thereby further decreasing tensions.

In the typical tradition of covering their flanks, the same analysts who believed that the drawdown of Israeli forces along the Lebanese border reduced the likelihood of attack cautioned that, in fact, Sharon may have had limited authority to launch a small-scale operation in the event of a provocation and would have to clear such an action only with Begin, rather than the entire cabinet. It makes little sense, however, to maintain major force deployments if the intent is to launch only limited retaliatory strikes. In short, the drawdown of these major forces was a capability indicator that signaled a diminished likelihood of an Israeli invasion of Lebanon, contrary to other capability indicators.

Intent

Intention indicators also sent divergent messages. According to Israeli sources, one of their diplomats in the Washington embassy met with Deputy Secretary of State Walter Stoessel in his capacity as acting secretary on May 17. The envoy conveyed an oral message from Prime Minister Begin about Lebanon; Israel did not want to surprise the United States. The message stated that it might well become imperative--even inevitable--that Israel take action to remove the threat because the Syrian missiles in Lebanon, along with the PLO armed presence there, comprised a stronger threat to Israel during 1982 than the Soviet missiles in Cuba had presented to the United States two decades earlier. The prime minister wanted to remind the secretary of the promise made by the president a year earlier: America would do whatever was necessary to restore the status quo ante and remove the Syrian surface-to-air missiles from Lebanon. Although Habib, in his quiet diplomacy, had made several visits to the area, the situation remained unresolved. State interpreted Israel's expressed desire to avoid surprising the United States as a final notification that the cease-fire was virtually dead and that a major conflict would break out soon in Lebanon.

Acting Secretary Stoessel briefed Assistant to the President for National Security Affairs Clark after meeting with the Israeli diplomat. He proposed and Clark agreed that it was now time for a presidential message to the prime minister. On the basis of reports from former officials, the core of that communication was a call for restraint. As drafted by State's Near East Bureau, the message declared that a large-scale Israeli operation in Lebanon would be considered throughout the world, including in the United States, as grossly disproportionate to the provocations and challenges Israel thus far had been handling with considerable success. State's draft also urged that Israel forswear a major assault into Lebanon because it would be difficult to explain this to the American people. A large-scale attack, furthermore, most likely would lead to close questioning of its legal implications.

Introducing the juridical consequences of an invasion is an implicit threat to withhold American arms. An Israeli invasion of Lebanon using American-origin equipment could be a violation of the end-use restriction specified in the Arms Export Control Act of 1976. The State Department draft added that a major Israeli military strike into Lebanon could raise serious questions that would have a great impact on the American-Israeli relationship. Almost as an aside, the draft called for the president to stand by all of his previous commitments concerning the situation in Lebanon. This latter statement had a limpness that would have gutted the president's strong message of a year earlier, which committed the United States to attempt a restoration of the status quo ante, that is, prior to the introduction of Syrian missiles in Lebanon.

The draft, formulated in Haig's absence and without his explicit authority, violated his principles of how to deal with Israel. Former associates of Secretary of State Haig reported that he generally opposed employing the threat of sanctions against Israel--he felt it would be self-defeating for the United States to threaten sanctions against Israel before an invasion of Lebanon had even occurred. Haig believed that the only thing that kept Israel from invading Lebanon in late May of 1982 was the U.S. commitment for a return to the status quo ante via diplomatic efforts to remove Syria's missiles from Lebanon. The secretary also found the language in the draft of the letter to be unacceptable. Never in the history of American-Israeli relations had such a strongly worded letter been dispatched. Haig declined to approve the letter, ostensibly because a communication from the president would not have been the correct mechanism at the time. But the underlying motivation for killing the message may have been that the secretary hoped to nip the growth of an anti-Haig cabal in the bud. Upon the secretary's return, he found a clique opposed to him, centered in his own sixth and seventh floors at Foggy Bottom (the Near East Bureau and the acting secretary), as well as in the West Wing basement at 1600 Pennsylvania Avenue where Judge Clark had his White House office.

Another "intention event" that was inconsistent with the drawdown capability signs occurred during the second week of May. The chief of staff of the Israel Defense Forces, Rafael Eitan, stated that Israel's response to a PLO action would not be proportionate to the strength of the provocation but to Jerusalem's own capability. According to the *Middle East Policy Survey* of September 25, 1981 (no. 40), more than half a year earlier, Eitan had warned that in the event of a PLO violation of the cease-fire, Israel would react "many times harder" than it did during the summer of 1981. In other words, Israel's response would not be proportionate to the action perpetrated against it, but commensurate to the power of the Israel Defense Forces vis-a-vis the Palestine Liberation Organization. Israeli sources, moreover, quoted Eitan as saying in the spring of the following year: "They step on our foot, we take off their whole head!" So much for the Old Testament eye-for-an-eye, tooth-for-a-tooth type of proportionality. Eitan's pungent remarks demonstrated a hardening of the government of Israel's attitudes concerning the PLO and fit with the Israeli diplomat's comments to Deputy Secretary Stoessel. Israel's chief of staff's statements suggest an increase in Jerusalem's intent to invade.

Conclusions

In sum, capability and intent indicators combined to provide mixed signals concerning the likelihood of warfare. There were three capability indicators that seemed to suggest an Israeli attack: (1) air strikes, (2) mobilization of forces, and (3) overflight of Beirut. Additionally, there were two intent indicators that supported the attack inference, namely: (1) the Israeli diplomat's meeting with Stoessel, and (2) Eitan's outright rejection of proportionality. On the other side of the ledger, there was only one--albeit major-- development that reduced the likelihood of warfare: the drawdown of Israeli forces. Despite the importance of this capability indicator, the consensus, on balance, remained that Israel's capacity to attack translated into an intention to do so in the near future.

It is paradoxical that Israel's diplomatic markers and military buildup facilitated a shift in the administration's attention from the security of the Gulf to the Arab-Israeli peace process, at the time when Jerusalem did not want Washington to focus on that process. It is also ironic that Israeli military actions led to an American diplomatic policy of reassuring the Jordanians and conciliating the Palestinians. Again, these are not policies Jerusalem desired.

The major external and regional actors saw themselves to be locked in overlapping dilemmas that limited their perceived choices to the use of either force or diplomacy. In fact, however, solutions need not have involved choices between these options but rather a proper balancing of the two.   Finally, in light of Jerusalem's augmented capability to use force and Washington's failing diplomacy of constraining Israel without restoring the status quo ante, the storm clouds rumbled with increased severity. Although a different American approach may not have averted the Lebanon War, the United States should have pursued an alternative strategy. It should have attempted tacit coordination of American diplomacy with Israel's threat to use force. There should have been an implication of American involvement in attempts to destabilize the Assad regime in Syria. Furthermore, the United States should not have implored Saudi Arabia to act beyond its capacity regarding Syria.   Such an alternative policy may have given diplomacy additional time to avert the war.

5

The Guns of June

Diplomatic Signaling

Crisis, Escalation, War?

Intent and capability indicators may suggest that war is on the horizon, yet hostilities do not necessarily follow. If crisis managers act to avert war and steer the protagonists on a path toward peace, escalation to armed conflict may be avoided. The Missiles of May crisis, for example, failed to produce a war in June. As a result of Habib's creative diplomacy, the year 1981 was war-free and even had a cease-fire as a bonus. Although Israel did attack the Syrian missiles during the invasion of Lebanon a year later, the principal motivation for that war was Jerusalem's desire to rid Lebanon of a Palestinian armed presence that was perceived as a threat to Israeli security.

Similarly, fighting between Syrian forces and Lebanese rightists did not escalate and expand into a war that included Israel, nor did hostilities between Israel and the PLO escalate and expand into a general war between Israel and Syria. Diplomacy that is not coordinated with force is bound to be only partly successful, but even a diplomacy coordinated with force could not have stilled the guns of June. There are two reasons why: Abu Nidal and Ariel Sharon. Nevertheless, diplomacy with force may have taken the ball away from this odd couple, thereby permitting some unexpected development to shift the focus from their regional fights to debates in international arenas. Accordingly, a traditional goal of diplomacy is to buy time before war occurs.

Ariel Sharon and Abu Nidal

Ariel Sharon, the Israeli defense minister, performed as a classical villain in the drama that unfolded in Lebanon. Abu Nidal, Palestinian general contractor for the intelligence services of Iraq,

Syria, and Libya, acted as a traditional agent provocateur in Israel's Lebanon War. As indicated in Chapter 4, these two actors play major parts in the Lebanon tragedy.

Abu Nidal is the nom de guerre of Sabry al Banna, whose Al Fatah Revolutionary Council broke away from Yasir Arafat's centrist movement in 1974. Although Abu Nidal was most likely responsible for the assassination attempt that provided a pretext for Israel to launch its invasion, Sharon played a more crucial and sustained role, especially in relation to the United States. Thus, Sharon receives more attention in this analysis than does Abu Nidal. Although both men are tacit allies in the Israeli invasion of Lebanon, the basic Israeli-Palestinian confrontation is still between the Government of Israel and Arafat's Palestine Liberation Organization.

Abu Nidal is actually a fringe player compared to Arafat in the long-term contest with the state of Israel. But because Abu Nidal pushed an unwilling PLO into a deadly confrontation with Israel in Lebanon, he warrants more attention than would otherwise be the case. If there were no "Abu Nidals" pressuring Arafat to take extremist actions against Israel, the centrist Palestinian organizations might be able to devise negotiating positions that would be acceptable to Israel and the United States. Similarly, in the absence of the "Sharons" of Israel, its government could take a more moderate stance in the peace process than it has in the past.

A week before hostilities commenced in Lebanon, Defense Minister Sharon paid a visit to the United States. In preparation for his May 1982 visit, the administration again assessed the situation in Lebanon. The consensus was that an Israeli invasion of Lebanon, particularly one that expanded to involve Syria, would be met with strong, negative reaction across the world. The Israeli Foreign Ministry, however, had obtained indications that some U.S. officials were favorably disposed to an Israeli military action that would drive Soviet-supported Syrian forces from Lebanon. Accordingly, one of the aims of Sharon's visit to Washington, from Jerusalem's viewpoint, was to ascertain the degree of support among American globalists for an Israeli invasion of Lebanon.

Inducements and Sanctions

From the perspective of American regionalists who opposed an Israeli invasion, one U.S. goal for Sharon's visit was to induce Jerusalem to exercise continued restraint on both the Syrian missiles and the PLO in Lebanon. The stated purposes of Sharon's trip were to iron out the differences between Washington and Jerusalem on Lebanon and smooth over disputes concerning the Memorandum of Understanding (MOU) that institutionalized security cooperation between the two allies. Although it had been signed November 30, 1981, the strategic cooperation accord had not been brought into force because Israel had extended its laws to (that is, annexed) the Golan Heights of Syria during December 1981.

The formal position of the U.S. government was that the Memorandum of Understanding had not been implemented by the time of Israel's December 14, 1981, annexation of the Golan. The government of Israel's position, however, was that signing the agreement brought it into force and that the United States had suspended it, thereby breaking an accord with Israel. (In 1985, the United States and Israel began to implement the contents of the agreement without publicly addressing the suspension issue that was in contention during 1981-1982.)

During Sharon's May 1982 meeting with Secretary of Defense Caspar Weinberger, the secretary failed to mention that the accord could be implemented. Weinberger declined to follow the interagency-approved "talking points" sent over from the White House by then Deputy Assistant to the President Robert McFarlane. Although he was at the White House, McFarlane was a bureaucratic lightweight compared to the president's friend, Weinberger. But McFarlane's talking points reflected an interagency consensus in which Department of Defense representatives had participated, and therefore Weinberger should have paid more attention to them. Nevertheless, he simply ignored McFarlane. Because the chief White House aide responsible for Lebanon policy lacked the clout to bring the secretary of defense into compliance with interagency guidance, this detracted from the potential effectiveness of the National Security Council staff headed by McFarlane. Again, the weakness of the NSC staff resulted in outcomes that reflected the preferences of a single department (in this case Defense) rather than an interagency consensus.

Instead of focusing on the bureaucratic warfare in Washington, Jerusalem Radio inferred from Weinberger's violation of the president's instructions how intent the secretary felt about Sharon's approach of threatening war in Lebanon.[1] Going well beyond the interagency consensus, Weinberger even alluded to the possibility of future American sanctions against Israel if it should harm "vital interests" of the United States; the secretary allegedly told the defense minister that the sanctions Sharon wanted canceled were imposed by Reagan and it would be the president who would decide when to lift them.

The *Middle East Policy Survey* of June 4, 1982 (no. 57), also discusses Weinberger's failure to follow the interagency script: "Some [administration] officials speculate that Weinberger was furious at Begin who had just attacked a statement by the Defense Secretary that advanced arms to Jordan would benefit the US and serve the cause of peace. Also, they believe that Weinberger wanted to avoid giving anything to Sharon, whose policy and style are anathema in Washington." In other words, press accounts in Jerusalem and Washington downplayed the interagency rivalry in the administration and highlighted the purposive intent of the United States as a unitary actor trying to keep a wayward ally in line.

By offering the stick of sanctions while holding back the carrot of strategic cooperation, Weinberger sought to punish Israel for prior misdeeds, but he may have strengthened Sharon's hand with Israelis who expressed less enthusiasm than he for invading Lebanon. In sending Sharon home empty-handed, Weinberger unintentionally may have boosted the stock of his Israeli counterpart and nemesis. Sharon could argue that the risk of invasion at least would not include suspension of the strategic cooperation accord for it remained in indefinite limbo.

Sharon seemed intent on involving Israel in a war to oust the PLO from Lebanon in the event that this organization broke the cease-fire.[2] In short, war would not have been averted or even delayed if Weinberger had been more forthcoming with strategic cooperation; Sharon's position in the Israeli cabinet, however, could have been undercut by a strategic cooperation accord. Because the only issue for Sharon was when, not whether, to attack, no amount of signaling with strategic cooperation carrots or even the sticks of negative sanctions could have stopped his mad dash for Beirut.

Signaling for Conflict Management

The Sharon-Weinberger debate reflects persistent differences between Israel and the United States, including how to reconcile their common and conflicting concerns. America's responsibilities to other states, particularly those within the Arab world that remain technically at war with Israel, clash with U.S. obligations to the Jewish state. Such conflicting American commitments inevitably lead to disputes between Washington and Jerusalem. These disagreements are likely when Israel's use of force against Arab states involves the use of American-origin equipment.

To minimize the damage to U.S. concerns within the Arab world when Israel may be contemplating the exercise of force, the United States has developed an elaborate diplomatic signaling system of primarily red and amber lights. Conflict management through such traffic signals does not rule out the use of force by Israel; it simply performs a damage limitation function for Washington. When Jerusalem has employed force, the United Sates has covered its flanks in the Arab world by opposing Israeli military action. Thus, the traffic signal approach reduces the effect of the dilemma posed to the United States by the Arab-Israeli conflict.

Weinberger's admonitions to Sharon are an extreme manifestation of the time-honored American practice of attempting to bring Jerusalem's policies in line with those of Washington. Unlike Weinberger, Haig was willing to harmonize Israel's use of force with America's diplomacy. His principal purpose in meeting with Sharon was to induce the defense minister to accept a formula that would calibrate force in proportion with provocation. The underlying assumption was that if there were a measure of proportionality in Israel's use of force, then it would be perceived as more legitimate and thereby less damaging to American concerns within the Arab world. It is clear that Haig provided Sharon with a go-ahead for a limited operation given a commensurate aggravation. There also is no doubt that Sharon had his forces speed through the green light before it could change colors. Uncertainty arises, however, over where in Lebanon the green light shaded into amber and finally into red.

Although the diplomacy of traffic signaling is unlikely to be effective, a superpower has little choice but to use this limited tool in its relations with allies. Accordingly, reflect upon Sharon's visit with Haig in late May 1982. The secretary felt that one more provocation by armed Palestinians and Israel would deliver a "knockout blow" to the PLO. He challenged Sharon's grandiose plan both to pacify southern Lebanon and rewrite the political map in favor of Israel's Lebanese rightist allies, forcibly stating that

> unless there was an internationally recognized provocation, and unless Israeli retaliation was proportionate to any such

provocation, an attack by Israel into Lebanon would have a devastating effect in the United States.[3]

Haig spoke in "legalese," but Sharon responded in emotional terms with echoes from the holocaust: "'How many Jews,'" he asked Haig, "'have to be killed for it to be a clear provocation? One Jew? Two Jews? Five? Six?'"[4] Although Haig had quashed his own department's draft of a presidential letter to Begin on the grounds that it was too strident, the statement to Sharon reiterated America's call for restraint, albeit in less forceful tones than those in the draft message.

According to the Israeli press, Haig warned Sharon against becoming entangled in Lebanon and stated that Washington's position toward Jerusalem's actions in Lebanon would depend upon the degree of provocation.[5] Sharon, however, reportedly told Haig that Israel would not accept an attempt to restrict its freedom of action in Lebanon; Jerusalem would exercise its right of self-defense whenever it saw fit to do so.

Haig believed that he had been clear in his call for restraint, and Defense Minister Sharon even acknowledged the force of Secretary Haig's position, stating that "Haig had been unequivocally opposed to the Peace for Galilee operation."[6] Nonetheless, Sharon came away from the meeting pleased. He felt that Haig had confirmed Israel's right to act in self-defense in response to provocative acts. As in the session with Director of Military Intelligence Saguy during February 1982, Washington again failed to define for Jerusalem what would constitute a significant violation of the July 1981 cease-fire.

Sharon emerged from the Washington meetings of May 1982 believing that he had received at least an agreement to conduct a limited military operation and tacit consent for more. Fearful of just such an interpretation, National Security Adviser Clark, acting on behalf of the president, ordered Haig to send a clarifying letter on May 28, 1982, to Prime Minister Begin. Although Haig's letter to Begin states that absolute restraint was necessary, it failed to change the impression Sharon had brought back from Washington, and the message may have vindicated Sharon.[7]

Despite the fact that some Israelis viewed Haig's letter to Begin as simply a way for the administration to cover itself, it had a profound impact on the prime minister.[8] It even caused him to quote in despair from the Bible (Proverbs 27:6): "Painful are the wounds inflicted by a friend." On the implicit idea that Israel should not respond with force if only a few of its citizens were killed at the hands of armed Palestinians--"proportionality"--Sharon quotes Begin as writing to Haig that "'the man has not been born who will ever obtain from me consent to let Jews be killed by a bloodthirsty enemy.'"[9]

Obviously, some American signal had been transmitted to Jerusalem, but what was its color? Haig sent amber for a limited operation, the White House wanted red, but Begin and Sharon only saw green. Thus, Schiff and Ya'ari suggest that it was clear that the Israeli government had grounds for believing that Washington had given its tacit approval on a limited military action in Lebanon.[10] As a result, diplomatic signaling had failed to manage the traffic in violence.

Palestinian Provocation -- Israeli Attack

As the rumblings of war grew louder, the noise ricocheted off the secure walls of the White House Situation Room. On June 4, Palestinian gunmen attempted to assassinate Israel's ambassador to Britain, Sholomo Argov. Although the PLO mainstream in Beirut denied responsibility for Abu Nidal's handiwork, Jerusalem nevertheless attributed the assault to that organization. On the next day, Israeli aircraft attacked the PLO in Beirut and its southern Lebanon positions in partial reprisal for the assassination attempt. Lebanese sources reported 45 killed and 150 wounded as the PLO continued to deny responsibility for Argov's shooting. Meanwhile, Israeli and PLO forces exchanged fire across the Lebanese border, and Israel's Air Force continued to attack Palestinian targets further north.

The United Nations Security Council convened an emergency session at Lebanon's request and unanimously approved Resolution 508, calling for a cease-fire commencing no later than midnight, Eastern Daylight Time, on June 6, 1982. A UN spokesman said that some Israeli tanks and artillery had crossed the border into Lebanon, and by June 6, Israel had begun a major invasion by land, sea, and air, with 25,000 troops and 250 planes. The stated goal of the operation was to push PLO forces and artillery 40 kilometers (25 miles) north, virtually out of range of Israel. The UN Security Council also approved Resolution 509, demanding that Israel withdraw its forces from Lebanon and requesting all parties to observe earlier cease-fire calls. After only one day of fighting, however, Israeli forces had captured key PLO positions in southern

Lebanon and advanced beyond the original objective of 25 miles. By the third day, Israeli troops advanced to within 15 miles of Beirut as heavy fighting continued along the Lebanese coast. Jerusalem's military successes in Lebanon then began to present Damascus with painful choices.

Syria on the Horns of a Dilemma

Israeli military units conducted operations aimed at cutting the Beirut-Damascus Highway, moves that caught the Syrians by surprise. Damascus reacted with limited air strikes against Israeli positions but then began to withdraw from the more vulnerable areas. The sudden push toward the highway threatened Syria's entire position in western Lebanon and therefore created a high risk of an all-out confrontation between Israel and Syria. Either Damascus had to commit additional forces or accept the new red line that Israel had established in central Lebanon. The administration believed that neither Israel nor Syria wanted war with each other on June 8 but felt that the likelihood of general hostilities between the two increased the longer the fighting continued in Lebanon. To make matters worse for Damascus, the Iraq-Iran war, Egypt-Israel peace treaty, and Syria's political isolation from the Arab majority made a unified Arab response in support of Syria difficult.

The Israeli invasion looked very threatening through the eyes of Syria's leadership. The dominant role Damascus played in Lebanon, Syria's claim as protector of the Palestinians, and its security interests in the Bekaa Valley were all jeopardized. As Iraq had anticipated in sponsoring Abu Nidal's provocation of Israel, Syria now sat on the horns of a dilemma: either fight and fail, or stay and sue for peace. Fighting undoubtedly would result in a Syrian military loss; not fighting would mean a political loss for Damascus--lowered prestige and credibility within the Arab world due to its failure to protect the Palestinians.

Syria attempted to resolve its dilemma by committing its First Armored Division and additional air defense units with surface-to-air (SAM) missiles to bolster its forces in the valley. Syrian defensive moves, such as adding another 15,000 troops to Lebanon, were bound to escalate and perhaps expand the fighting. Because the PLO had been cut off in the south and faced annihilation as Israeli forces progressed toward Beirut, Damascus faced increasing pressures to take active measures.

American Intelligence Assessments

The United States assumed that, as of June 8, Jerusalem counted on a quick military victory with few Israeli casualties. A rapid triumph would minimize domestic and American reactions, keep Syria out, and preempt a major Egyptian response. During these initial days of fighting, Washington believed that Jerusalem's goal was to keep the PLO north of the Zahrani River, out of range of northern Israel. Although Jerusalem had long desired to destroy the PLO, the risks of doing so were decisive in the past and were likely to be no less so at the beginning of the war. The principal factors limiting Israel's actions in Lebanon were the expected casualties, the danger of a wider war with Syria, and the risk of a negative American reaction. Thus, the administration concluded that the Israel Defense Forces were reluctant to take on the Syrians in the Bekaa Valley or march on Beirut.

In response to a hypothetical query about what Jerusalem would decide to do when the forty-kilometer band of Lebanese territory was cleared of the PLO armed presence, the June 8 consensus failed to anticipate an Israeli advance beyond the security zone. Rather, it anticipated that Israel would avoid a repetition of the post-Litani Operation period of 1978. At that time, Jerusalem had ordered the withdrawal of forces without a satisfactory solution to the problem of PLO attacks on northern Israel from southern Lebanon.

The United States, together with most of the Israeli cabinet, believed that Jerusalem had limited goals in Lebanon. This estimate coincided with the policy preferences of globalists in the administration. This contingent wanted to give their counterparts, who were thought to be a minority in the Israeli cabinet, more than enough leeway to accomplish virtually any goals they deemed appropriate as the fighting created new situations. An American estimate of modest Israeli goals would facilitate maximum military action by Jerusalem because there would be no need for Washington to call for restraint. However, contrary to the belief that Sharon was in the minority, he was, in fact, able to dupe a majority in the Israeli cabinet about developments on the ground and gained approval early in the fighting to destroy Syria's missiles in Lebanon. On June 9, Israeli aircraft downed twenty-two Syrian planes without a loss, forcing Damascus to sue for a cease-fire agreement two days later.

American Diplomatic Moves

The fighting in Lebanon prompted a series of American diplomatic moves. The president met with his special envoy on June 6, during the economic summit in Europe. Habib then departed for Jerusalem the next day for a meeting with Prime Minister Begin.[11] The envoy's main goal was to secure compliance with United Nations Security Council Resolution 509, which demanded that Israel withdraw its forces from Lebanon and requested that all parties observe earlier cease-fire calls. On the same day, State announced a new policy position in light of the war: A divided Lebanon must not be the outcome of the violence, Israel must withdraw, and the Palestinians must cease using Lebanon as a launching pad for attacks against Israel.

According to *New York Times* reporter Hedrick Smith, Secretary of State Haig said that Habib met with Prime Minister Begin and told him that the United States wanted Israel to comply with UN Resolution 509.[12] To reinforce Habib's efforts, Vice President Bush met at the White House with Israeli Ambassador to Washington Moshe Arens. The following day, the United States vetoed a Spanish draft that condemned noncompliance with Resolutions 508 (which called for a cease-fire no later than June 6, 1982) and 509; in the event of noncompliance, this Spanish draft ordered consideration of practical ways and means to induce compliance. There was an implication of sanctions against Israel under Chapter Seven of the United Nations Charter; in such situations, the United States generally vetoes resolutions in the Security Council by voting in the negative.

Following a Crisis Pre-Planning Group meeting, President Reagan placed a stern telephone call to Prime Minister Begin from Brussels at 2:00 A.M. Washington time, 9:00 A.M. in Jerusalem. Envoy Habib arrived in Damascus on June 9, and he delivered a letter from Reagan to President Assad calling for a cease-fire at 6:00 A.M., June 10.[13] In addition to carrying the Reagan communication, the *Middle East Policy Survey* of June 18, 1982 (no. 58), reported that Habib brought a message from Begin that Israel hoped to avert a clash with Syrian forces; at about the same time, Israeli jets were attacking Syrian missile sites in Lebanon. So, Habib now believed he was misused by the Israelis.

Also on June 9, President Reagan held a meeting on Lebanon with Saudi Foreign Minister Saud in Brussels. The vice president conferred at the White House with Egyptian Foreign Minister Ali, who then met with the president six days later. On June 10, the vice president held a meeting with a group of Arab ambassadors. Following an emergency session of the Israeli Cabinet at 4:00 A.M., American Ambassador to Israel Samuel Lewis conveyed a message from the President urging a cease-fire and immediate preparation for an Israeli withdrawal. According to Israel Defense Forces Radio, the message from the president was an unequivocal demand that Israel cease the hostilities in Lebanon.[14]

Meanwhile, Secretary Haig turned down an invitation to visit Jerusalem because the Israeli leadership had not shown enough flexibility. After a Special Situations Group (SSG) meeting on June 10, the United States decided to delay shipment of F-16 aircraft to Israel. The president and his party returned from Europe on June 11. The vice president met with Egyptian Ambassador Ashraf Ghorbal, and Special Envoy Habib returned to Jerusalem, before going to Beirut three days later. He conveyed Israeli proposals calling for a demilitarized, twenty-five-mile security belt and the withdrawal of Syrian forces.

On June 17, Habib asked Jerusalem to refrain from military actions for forty-eight hours to permit the disarming of the PLO and the departure of its leaders.[15] In the interim, the president sent a message to Prime Minister Begin expressing a deep commitment to Israel and stating that the United States was trying to forestall the danger of escalation and prevent a wider conflict between Israel and Syria. The president acknowledged that Syria must withdraw from Lebanon, but stated that Habib needed time to achieve such an objective. On the next day, Haig met Begin in New York as the United Nations passed Resolution 511, extending the mandate of the United Nations Interim Forces in Lebanon for two months.

The Interagency Process and American Policy

With the dramatic developments taking place in Lebanon, the fuse that was lit in May 1981 finally ignited the powder keg during June 1982. Washington's responses from June 6-18 emerged from an interagency process that was initially led by State but subsequently dominated by the White House, as Haig's influence over Lebanon policy steadily diminished. Although Haig's star was on the decline, he had the ear of the president while they were in Europe during the economic summit. According to the June 18, 1982 (no. 58), *Middle East Policy Survey* key U.S. policymakers suggested that while in Europe, Reagan was removed from a Washington bureaucracy hostile to Israel and was captive to the views of Haig. With respect to the bureaucratic politics of American decisionmaking, when Secretary Haig was away in Europe until mid-June, Lebanon was managed on an interagency basis. When Haig returned with the president, State, under Haig's immediate direction, tried to regain the action, but its influence had lessened as the White House finally was able to implement its crisis management reorganization plans. By then, 1600 Pennsylvania Avenue, rather than Foggy Bottom had become the site where the action began.

Meanwhile, a Middle East Working Group was created in the Operations Center at State. James Collins, a mid-level career foreign service officer who formerly dealt with the Middle East in the American Embassy in Moscow, provided staff support to Deputy Assistant Secretary Draper, head of the group that later became the Lebanon Task Force.

Prior to the outbreak of hostilities, analysts believed that retaliation by Israel for the assassination attempt would depend on whether the ambassador survived and on the identity of the assailants, as well as the sponsoring organization. Based on these factors, the interagency consensus on June 4 was that Jerusalem would not carry out a massive invasion of Lebanon. Moreover, globalists contended that, unless there was evidence that Israel was about to conduct a major military operation, a message of restraint from Washington would be misunderstood at such an emotional moment. The globalists also urged that, when limited military action occurred, the United States should be prepared to control the risks by urging maximum restraint not on the Israelis but on the Palestinians and Syrians, through the mechanism of an already scheduled trip to the region by Habib.

The administration was not unreasonable in assuming that the identity of the individual assailants and sponsoring state would be tied to Jerusalem's decision to launch a major invasion. Even Israel's own intelligence services were puzzled when Begin refused to hear their carefully prepared briefing on the likely sponsor--Abu Nidal. In fact, the prime minister held that all the armed Palestinians carrying out military operations against Israel were PLO.[16] Irrespective of the Israeli position on the identity issue, however, it was surprising that Washington was prepared to forgo cautioning Israel in favor of urging maximum restraint on the PLO and on Syria.

State's position from June 4 to June 25, when Haig was sacked, was that U.S. leverage over Israel stemmed from Jerusalem's own need to leave Lebanon, not from prospective negative sanctions. The United States had to stand firm against European and Arab pressure and not compel a precipitate Israeli withdrawal. Jerusalem's vulnerability in Lebanon offered Washington a chance to extract concessions in the form of enlightened occupation policies on the West Bank of the Jordan River and in the Gaza Strip along the Mediterranean Coast, as well as a freeze on Jewish settlements on the West Bank.

State considered the 1982 war in Lebanon as an opportunity for American diplomacy, just as the 1973 war involving Israel versus Egypt and Syria had been. Foggy Bottom wanted to use the crisis as an occasion for innovative actions that would achieve the following goals: secure Israel's northern border, end the civil war in Lebanon, and stimulate the Arab-Israeli peace process, that is, give new life to the Palestinian autonomy talks between Egypt and Israel.

To achieve such major objectives, State designed a policy on two fronts. First, facilitate a rapid withdrawal of Israeli forces but only under conditions that would reduce the potential for future conflict. Second, reconstitute and strengthen the government of Lebanon based upon a new social compact, reduced Syrian presence, and a revised modus vivendi for structuring relations between the Palestinians and Lebanese. Specific elements of American policy that could take advantage of the situation included: (1) public proposals to establish a buffer zone and a political process to avoid UN mischiefmaking while compelling Israel and others to heed the American agenda, and (2) understandings among the United States, Israel, France, Lebanese factions, Saudi Arabia, and Syria regarding, among other things, a strengthened peacekeeping force.

Peacekeeping Alternatives

There were three options regarding peacekeeping. The first was a blend of internal Lebanese forces under Israeli control. The second was a renewal of the United Nations Interim Force in Lebanon (UNIFIL) with an expanded geographical mandate. The third alternative was an international peacekeeping force outside of the United Nations. The first option--indigenous forces under the control of Israel--had the advantage of operating under the protection of Jerusalem's military umbrella. The paradox was that such a relatively leak-proof shield would have been too thin a veneer of Israeli rule and thus would lack legitimacy. The second option--an international force under the UN--would have had more legitimacy than Israeli rule, but it would have been subject to either Soviet opposition or leverage tied to the renewal of the mandate. The third option--an international force outside the UN--would have permitted American military participation. This involvement would have provided a dramatic illustration of Washington's concern, which in turn could have reassured Jerusalem.

The downside of U.S. participation in a peacekeeping force was that American troops could be vulnerable to attack if they were inserted into Lebanon before establishing a solid political framework among the contending factions. Direct American participation had to follow, or be associated with, political accommodation. Otherwise, U.S. troops would be perceived merely as one of the many factions, and thereby they would be as subject to armed attack as any other group. In the end, the third approach, an international force outside the UN and with American participation, emerged as the official U.S. policy.

Bureaucratic Warfare

State: Crisis as an Opportunity

Although the White House was gaining influence, State, as the lead department, had the action for designing a new policy in light of Israel's invasion. However, the department's major approach--viewing the Lebanon crisis as an opportunity for diplomacy--had little support within the interagency community. State Department proponents of this policy included Secretary Haig, the Staff for Policy Planning, and Politico-Military Affairs. Standing in opposition to this approach was the Bureau of Near Eastern and South Asian Affairs, which had better support within the interagency community than did the secretary and his departmental allies. The goal of changing the political map of the region through the insertion of U.S. forces in Lebanon had little support anywhere in the government. Prior to the invasion, diplomacy and force did not march in parallel; after the invasion, State attempted to blend the two but failed to develop the interagency consensus necessary to effect a synthesis.

Defense: No Political Benefits from Israeli Force

Even if State had worked to develop a consensus on a marketable package of diplomacy and force, Defense was an unwilling buyer. Always reluctant to see its own forces used for diplomatic purposes, this department was particularly opposed to taking advantage of a crisis initiated by Israel. Both the Office of the Secretary of Defense and the Organization of the Joint Chiefs of Staff accused State of rationalizing Israel's invasion to derive political benefits. In addition, Defense strongly opposed the introduction of U.S. forces as part of an international peacekeeping organization. In this instance, the United States had no political agreement as it had during American participation in the peacekeeping force between Egypt and Israel--the 1982 Multi-National Force and Observers (MFO) in the Sinai Desert.

Also, U.S. military involvement in an international force for Lebanon would have invited a corresponding Soviet presence in the area, thereby polarizing the region even further. Moreover, Defense contended that there was a lack of support in the American public for U.S. participation. Finally, almost as a throwaway line, Defense raised the old saw that U.S. military involvement in Lebanon would decrease the technical readiness of its military forces elsewhere.

What is notable about the Defense Department critique is its ratio of diplomatic to military criteria. Going well beyond its mandate on military matters, Defense held that it was unseemly to derive diplomatic benefits from Israel's use of force. The best that can be said for this critique is that it makes little sense. What is the Department of State supposed to do if not attempt to exploit difficult international situations in hopes of furthering American diplomatic goals? Indeed, State should be in the business of taking advantage of crises irrespective of their origin in order to advance U.S. objectives. Even though it was the wrong department to suggest it, Defense was on solid ground in underscoring the need for a political framework for the deployment of American forces as part of an international peacekeeping organization.

Although critical of State's approach, Defense failed to make any formal recommendations of its own. Alternative informal approaches that did emerge from discussion with Defense Department representatives included an odd, hands-off proposal to stand back and let Israel set up a minority rightist-dominated government in Lebanon that would be bound to fail. Such a collapse could lead to irreparable harm with little conceivable gain. Because a narrow, right-wing government could not possibly have endured, this proposal actually may have been a trial balloon floated by some Pentagon officials who wanted to gauge bureaucratic support for a program of punitive measures against Israel. Although there is no direct evidence to sustain this inference, those who made the suggestion were known to have preferred American sanctions against Israel.

Another informal idea floated by Defense was to buy time for the current policy by calling for a cease-fire and a new status quo. This option also had many liabilities because that approach had not prevented war and was rapidly being overtaken by events in the field. The favored alternative that Defense considered but did not endorse was to make a new effort for a so-called balanced peace, insist on Israeli withdrawal, and use such a pullout to compel the PLO to make concessions. "Balanced" in this context is a code word for a pro-Arab, if not anti-Israel policy. But forcing an Israeli withdrawal and then using the pullback to induce PLO concessions is illogical. That organization would have no incentive to make such concessions without Israeli forces in the area.

The White House: Crisis as an Occasion to Seize Power

The failure of Defense to play a serious part in the interagency process left the door open for State to continue its domination. At this point, however, the White House began to sense an opening for itself. Given a split between State and Defense, the White House role loomed larger than it would have if the two departments had concurred. Accordingly, the White House set up a process to moderate State's views into positions that attracted wide support within the bureaucracy.

Deputy Assistant to the President McFarlane began the process by calling a meeting of the Crisis Pre-Planning Group led by his National Security Council staff. Procedurally, the CPPG was a National Security Council body at the under-secretary level that fed the Special Situations Group, which is at the secretary (cabinet) level. The Special Situations Group tasked the CPPG, which in turn tasked the Middle East Working Group. During the first weekend of fighting, there were face-to-face meetings, along with conference telephone calls. Finally, the National Security Planning Group (NSPG)--a third body--was comprised of cabinet-level statutory members of, and at times advisers to, the National Security

Council; the NSPG generally had no staff aides so that it could consider the most sensitive subjects on a close-hold basis.

McFarlane appointed Colonel Oliver North of the NSC staff as secretary to the crisis group. North had successive bureaucratic triumphs during the mid-1980s concerning Lebanon, the U.S. invasion of Grenada, American interception of an Egyptian aircraft over the Mediterranean carrying the Palestinian leader of the *Achille Lauro* cruise ship hijacking, and the U.S. bombing of Libya, until he fell from grace over the Iran-contra affair in 1986. Together with McFarlane and Poindexter, North achieved public notoriety during November 1986. He played a critical role in the covert sale of American arms to Iran and the diversion of profits from those sales to American-supported opposition forces (contras) fighting against the Sandinista regime in Nicaragua.

Because of the simultaneous escalation of the Lebanon crisis and the Iraq-Iran war during mid-year 1982, there was some initial confusion, abetted by North's humorous asides, over which crisis was to be the focus of attention at the meeting. Concluding that Lebanon was at issue, the Crisis Pre-Planning Group recommended a meeting of the Special Situations Group (SSG), also under White House leadership. Those attending the SSG meeting on June 5 were the vice president, Secretary of Defense Weinberger, Acting Secretary of State Stoessel, Director of Central Intelligence William Casey, Chairman of the Joint Chiefs of Staff David Jones, Counselor to the President Edwin Meese, and Deputy Assistant to the President McFarlane. Two subsequent SSG meetings occurred via secure telephone hookup during that weekend.

The White House as Balancer Between State and Defense

From these heated meetings, former officials recalled their consensus of June 6. The bottom line was that Jerusalem had to be made aware that its behavior was unacceptable and that the United States was unwilling to acquiesce in it. Israel had to understand from the outset that Washington did not approve of the invasion, that the fighting was harmful to U.S. interests, and that the American people would not support Israel, especially if engagements with Syrian forces drew in the Soviets. Further, Washington would have to take firm measures with Jerusalem if Prime Minister Begin remained unresponsive to Ambassador Habib's call for restraint. High-level officials from the White House, the Office of the Secretary of Defense, and the Joint Chiefs of Staff led this consensus.   State was a dissenter, advocating flexibility in the American position until it was clear how Ambassador Habib's efforts were proceeding.

State's guiding principle was to keep U.S. options open by refraining from actions that could later complicate Habib's efforts with Begin.   Because the prime minister was the key to U.S. conflict management, State believed it was crucial to avoid a premature confrontation.   Once Habib had probed Israel's views and those of other central players in the area, it would be appropriate to take a hard look at U.S. options to bring about a halt in the fighting, cessation of PLO rocket attacks on Israel, and a strengthened buffer on the Israel-Lebanon border.   If Habib found Begin determined to pursue a course that could undercut the U.S. ability to lead the peace process, subsequent negative steps could be taken against Israel.   State therefore suggested continued attempts to internationalize the problem of Lebanon, bring about an Israeli pullout, and conduct forward planning on American participation in a peacekeeping force after the cease-fire had been restored.

In contrast, Defense believed that Habib's efforts to restrain Israel would have been bolstered if he were authorized to issue a warning to Begin.   Without an agreement on a cease-fire and the withdrawal of Israeli forces, the United States would be required to take such actions as a curtailment of security assistance to Israel, an acceleration of American arms sales to Jordan, and an elimination of American diplomatic support for Israel in the United Nations.   The most controversial option considered by the Special Situations Group was for Habib and a PLO representative to meet. A classic nonstarter, this alternative was not seriously considered, although it had been offered in earnest.

In mid-June, there was a National Security Planning Group meeting, the first one since the initial team returned from the economic summit.   The emphasis was on how to achieve enough consensus to issue a National Security Decision Directive (NSDD) on Lebanon.   The White House took the lead in trying to avoid arguments over bureaucratic rights and wrongs as it sided with State on the main issue of the discussion: how to achieve a linkage between Israel's invasion of Lebanon and Jerusalem's policies in the stalled Palestinian autonomy negotiations.   As usual on political/military concerns, Defense was isolated and yielded to a White House/State-led coalition as the officials "round-tabled" the issues.

Jerusalem Returns to Washington in Mid-Crisis

From 11:20 A.M. to 1:30 P.M. on June 21, Prime Minister Begin was in a meeting at the White House. The president, the vice president, Secretary Haig, Secretary Weinberger, Assistant to the President Clark, and Ambassador Samuel Lewis attended. The issues at the first Oval Office session were Lebanon and the Arab-Israeli peace process, which received high and low emphasis respectively. At a working luncheon from 12:15 P.M. to 1:30 P.M. in the White House Cabinet Room, participants gave Lebanon high emphasis compared to American-Israeli military links. Assistant Secretary Veliotes and the Autonomy Talks Negotiator Ambassador Richard Fairbanks came to these discussions. Finally, there was a follow-up meeting between Begin and Haig at 4:00 P.M. at the prime minister's hotel. In addition to Veliotes and Fairbanks, Geoffrey Kemp of the NSC staff joined this session.

Begin's visit of June 1982 was the nadir of U.S.-Israeli summitry. According to Israeli sources, rather than summarizing suggested guidance from 3 x 5 note cards prepared by the NSC staff, the president curtly read the guidance to the prime minister. In so doing, Reagan cast a chill on the bilateral relationship. And the threat of sanctions, in the event of Israeli noncompliance with the American agenda of immediate cease-fire and withdrawal, hung in the Oval Office atmosphere. This threat was not in the air during the afternoon session between the prime minister and Secretary Haig. The secretary, however, was operating under the handicap of being down on the power curve and on the way out; therefore, Haig was not as credible a representative of administration thinking as was White House aide and "first friend," Judge Clark.

Despite the more favorable treatment Begin received from Haig, the prime minister rejected even the appeals of the secretary, Israel's only friend-in-court at the time. A weakened and isolated Haig told Begin that the United States expected Israeli settlement activity on the West Bank to cease and said that there should be rapid progress toward an agreement for Palestinian autonomy once the Lebanon problem had been solved.[17]

Begin adamantly rejected the idea of linking Israel's supposed vulnerability regarding Lebanon on the one hand with concessions expected from Jerusalem on the other. Haig proposed what might be termed "positive linkage," that is, Israel's need to extricate itself from Lebanon meant that the United States could achieve other diplomatic goals from Jerusalem, such as concessions on Palestinian autonomy. While the State Department was using a positive approach, the Defense Department devised "negative linkage"-- sanctions against Israel unless it ended the fighting and withdrew. Neither approach could succeed, however, because America has little leverage over its allies, especially those that are on the front line of conflict and in possession of a strong domestic political base in the States. Israel is perhaps the only nation that fits these criteria.

Conclusions

As war began, the administration added another element to its policy of restraining Israel, appeasing Syria, imploring Saudi Arabia, reassuring Jordan, and placating the Palestine Liberation Organization. The new strategy was to threaten an ally--Israel. One goal was to compel Jerusalem to follow Washington's preferences in the conduct of Israel's war in Lebanon against the PLO. Just as American diplomatic efforts were unable to still the guns of June and avert war, White House reorganization plans and subsequent threats of sanctions against Jerusalem were not able to contain the war. The shooting started according to the timing set by the "odd couple" of the Near East, Abu Nidal and Ariel Sharon.

Secretary of State Alexander Haig sought to use the Lebanon crisis as an opportunity to move into a higher diplomatic gear for stimulating the peace process, but the rest of the administration engaged in a downshift diplomacy of punishing Israel. This shift inadvertently backfired by slowing the PLO's exit from Beirut, ultimately prolonging the war. Threats of diplomatic sanctions failed to restrain Israeli force yet encouraged the PLO to hold out for better terms. As a result, Israeli force stalled before the environs of Beirut without a diplomatic boost from Jerusalem's principal ally, the United States of America.

6

Force Sans Diplomacy

The Diplomacy/Force Mix

Accommodation and Coercion

Finding the appropriate combination of diplomacy and force is difficult. If there is too much force in relation to diplomacy, the result may be escalation; too little force in relation to diplomacy may lead to noncompliance. Hence, a central concern of policymaking is how to combine threat with promise, and coercion with accommodation. The optimal mix of negative and positive incentives must depend upon the adversary's behavior and the particular set of circumstances prevailing at the time. Prior to the Israeli invasion of Lebanon, the American approach contained too much diplomacy in relation to potential force. Syrian noncompliance with the U.S. request to remove its missiles from Lebanon may have resulted from the American approach that favored diplomacy over force.

During the Israeli invasion of Lebanon, Washington undercut Jerusalem's threat of force with uncoordinated diplomatic initiatives from competing bureaucracies--a dual-track contest between the White House staff and State, with the president on the sidelines. In the two years following Israel's invasion, the White House staff seized the initiative from State and began to use too much force in relation to diplomacy; escalation between the United States and Syria ensued. Meanwhile, the president remained relatively inactive regarding U.S. decisionmaking on Lebanon and Syria.

Phases of the Lebanon Conflict

A first stage of America's concern over Lebanon began with the missile crisis in May 1981, peaked during July with the cease-fire, and tapered off eighteen months later. A second American phase followed a partial Israeli withdrawal from the mountains around

127

Beirut. In this stage, the United States employed naval and air power on behalf of the minority-rightist government of Lebanon during 1983, there were attacks on Americans during April and October of that year, and American troops began to withdraw under pressure early in 1984. This second American stage differed from the first because it depended more upon force than diplomacy. During the first phase, American diplomacy attempted to manage Syrian-Lebanese rightist clashes, the Syrian-Israeli missile confrontation, and the Israeli-Palestinian "border" conflict.

The Israeli stage began with the June 1982 invasion and reached a zenith as the PLO withdrew during September. It began to level off after massacres in two Palestinian refugee camps some three weeks later. Diplomacy without force characterized Washington's first phase; force not coordinated with diplomacy typified both Washington's second stage and Jerusalem's, as well. Given the acute tension between Israel and the Arab states, it is understandable that threat dominates promise in this conflict zone. In light of the difficulty Jerusalem has in reaching accommodation in a hostile environment, its superior capabilities relative to the Arab adversaries, and the intransigence of all the actors, it is not surprising that force is a normal part of the intercourse among the parties to the Arab-Israeli conflict.

Knowing that force is part of the norm, Washington needs to devise a way to extract the best from a bad situation, that is, one in which the parties use force. Just as Washington took advantage of a war initiated by Cairo and Damascus against Israel in 1973 to further the peace process, the United States should have done the same with a war begun by Jerusalem in 1982. Secretary of State Kissinger had used the 1973 war to launch his step-by-step peace process, and Secretary Haig deserved the opportunity to do the same in 1982. Rather than seeking some diplomatic benefit from Israel's use of force, however, the United States and Israel worked at cross purposes.

Washington Versus Jerusalem

The negative sanctions Washington decided to impose during the course of the Lebanon War illustrate the conflict between American diplomacy and Israeli force. Jerusalem's invasion prompted the administration to delay notifying Congress formally about the scheduled sale of seventy-five F-16 aircraft to Israel. During mid-June 1982, State had informed the'White House that a decision had to be made immediately on whether to proceed with or delay this formal notification. If no action were taken, it might have conveyed the impression that by doing nothing the United States was actually delaying notification. On May 24, the administration had informally notified Congress of the proposed sale, worth $2.7 billion. A twenty-day, informal notification period had ended June 13, three days before State alerted the White House of the need to act.

Whether to proceed or delay presented the administration with a classic policy dilemma. On one hand, going ahead with formal notification would have bolstered critics who could charge that the administration was rewarding Jerusalem for invading Lebanon. Thus, American relations with the Arab states could have been damaged if formal notification had gone forward. Even though deliveries would not have commenced until 1985, Moscow and Damascus could have asserted that the F-16 aircraft transaction represented a major resupply of Israel because Damascus had claimed significant Israeli air losses. Such an argument could have justified a large Soviet resupply of Syria, an action that Washington sought to deflect.

On the other hand, delaying the arms sales until there was clear evidence of Jerusalem's intentions could have complicated Habib's task of designing a framework for a lasting peace with Israel's cooperation. Indeed, delay could have harmed the peace process itself, thereby destroying the opportunity for accord presented by the invasion. Delay also could have decoupled diplomacy and force even further. Punishing Israel by holding up an arms sale would have sent a message that the United States would not permit the destruction of the Palestine Liberation Organization. Thus, that organization could hold out for terms of its own design, in anticipation of even greater support from the United States in the future.

State came down on the side of timely notification, although it lost to the advocates of delay. According to former officials of the department, State reasoned that, on balance, it was better to get the issue out of the way in order to bring Prime Minister Begin in agreement with American diplomatic initiatives. Although State did not mention the effect of notification on reinforcing Israeli military power in Lebanon, advocates of delay took their position precisely to avoid Washington being "tarnished" by Jerusalem's excessive use of force. Delaying an inevitable notification of a military sale to an ally, however, was an insufficient punishment to control Israel and not enough to appease hard-line Arab states, such as Syria.

With respect to Arab moderates, State was willing to trade off the short-term costs of not mollifying them in order to take advantage of the long-term opportunity for diplomatic innovation provided by Israel's use of force. The rest of the administration, however, refused to buy State's strategy of making the best of a bad situation. As a result, Washington had fewer positive inducements to motivate Jerusalem. Also during mid-June, the administration made a pronouncement to the allies that the West should not dwell on the past because much had to be done quickly if Lebanon were to have a future. This statement was intended to take the focus away from Israel's prior misdeeds and shine the light on Lebanon's future instead. The administration, however, retained its backward-looking approach of punishing Israel despite the implication in the statement to the contrary.

Where Will the PLO Fighters Land?

One reason why Washington decided not to tie its diplomacy to Jerusalem's use of force was its assessment on the likely disposition of PLO fighters once they departed from Beirut. During mid-June, the administration inaccurately concluded that the PLO would have to relocate primarily in Syria after its defeat. In this event, the organization would have become more dependent on Syria, more radical, and far less cohesive. The defeat of the PLO's conventional army would help the hard-liners, who had long argued that "Palestine" can be liberated only by a united and radicalized Arab world. Frustrated and desperate, the Palestinians not only would turn to terror against both the United States and Israel but also would use subversion to destabilize moderate Arab governments.

Although there were good reasons for Washington to believe the gloomy scenario about the radicalization of a defeated PLO, it turned out to be untrue. But Arab moderates themselves were spreading this pessimistic line at the United Nations. Tunisia, for instance, held that continuing American support for Israel against the PLO during mid-June weakened Arab moderates. In the context of the "loss" of Egypt after the Camp David peace accord with Israel and the fall of the Shah of Iran, a case could be made that the defeat of the PLO in Lebanon weakened the moderate Arab states. On balance, however, these moderates actually may have been strengthened by the destruction of that organization's conventional army in Lebanon, the departure of most of the remaining combatants to Tunisia, and the dispersal of the rest throughout the Arab world. Even before the PLO withdrawal from Lebanon, the peace process received a shot in the arm in the form of the Reagan initiative and increased Jordanian risk-taking for peace. Later in 1985, King Hussein threw down a gauntlet by daring Arafat to join Jordan in a mutual approach to Israel. The king ventured to make this bold challenge because Israel's invasion had weakened the Palestine Liberation Organization relative to the moderate Arab states.

The Incredibility of Israel's Threat to Take West Beirut

Another factor mitigating against Washington coordinating its diplomacy with Jerusalem's use of force was the belief among policy analysts in the administration that Israel would not invade West Beirut. Certainly, there was no need to reinforce the credibility of Jerusalem's warning to take all of Beirut if one did not believe in the threat. American analysts thought that Israel had three options regarding West Beirut: (1) psychological warfare, (2) commando raids in cooperation with Lebanese rightists, and (3) invasion. The consensus was that Israel was unlikely to use psychological warfare exclusively but would continue with raids. Also, Jerusalem was likely to be deterred from invading by two concerns--Israeli casualties and Begin's forthcoming June 21, 1982, meeting with Reagan.

A further deterrent to an Israeli invasion was Habib's presence in Beirut. Once he had departed, the prospects for a showdown between Israel and the PLO would have risen. Critics in Jerusalem had soured on Habib and incorrectly alleged that he purposefully had interposed himself between Israeli forces and PLO fighters in Beirut. There was overwhelming support in Washington publicly praising Habib's efforts in order to show Jerusalem that he had the full support of a unified administration. Because Habib's interlocutor role compelled him to visit Beirut, some Israelis believed that he used the trips to thwart an invasion by the Israel Defense Forces. In fact, Habib's very presence did interfere with an Israeli attack on West Beirut, thereby reducing the credibility of the threat to invade.

Unknown to Habib's Israeli detractors, he (and Haig) stood virtually alone in recognizing the need to use the threat of Israel's prospective invasion of West Beirut as a motivating factor to induce a PLO withdrawal. Jerusalem was engaged in the traditional game of coercion, and it needed all the diplomatic backup it could find. By

picking unnecessary fights with one of its strongest supporters--
Habib--Jerusalem undermined its own goal of encouraging a PLO
pullback without the need to expend more blood and treasure.
Rather than lining up their vectors with those of Habib, some in
Jerusalem unsuccessfully attempted to discredit him.

The American Diplomatic Approach

The fact that Israeli force was not coordinated with American
diplomacy does not mean that diplomatic activity or objectives were
absent. Indeed, the United States had an extensive set of goals that
guided the Habib mission: (1) strengthening the authority of the
government of Lebanon, (2) effecting a dramatic reduction of the
Syrian presence, (3) ending the Palestinian use of Lebanon as a
state-within-a-state, (4) terminating Israel's security enclave
patrolled by Lebanese renegade rightists in southern Lebanon, and
(5) strengthening the capabilities of the peacekeeping forces.

To reinforce the government of Lebanon, Habib would use a
diplomatic contact group that included France, Saudi Arabia, and
the United States. This group was supposed to gain support for the
national unity government. In addition, Habib was to ask
Jerusalem to pull its forces away from the presidential palace.
Then, if the Israelis cooperated, the government of Lebanon would
not appear to be acting under duress. The Lebanese Armed Forces
were to be deployed throughout West Beirut in conjunction with the
resumption of such city services as electricity and water. Habib
also was going to urge other governments to reestablish a
diplomatic presence in Beirut and give visible and active support to
the government of Lebanon. With an enhanced capability for the
central government, a reduction in the Syrian military presence was
possible. In addition, Habib was to encourage Begin to stop linking
Israeli and Syrian withdrawal publicly. And the envoy was to ask
Damascus to be flexible, especially in allowing Syrian forces to be
replaced by Lebanese Armed Forces units at critical geographical
points.

In connection with Habib's aim to end the PLO's use of
Lebanon as if it were a Palestinian state, he hoped to capitalize on
the inter-Arab consensus for controlling the Palestinians by having
Lebanese authorities begin early discussions with the PLO on its
disarmament. He also wanted to urge flexibility on Begin if a trade
of PLO disarmament for the continued presence of its leadership in
Beirut became necessary. Habib could work with the diplomatic

contact group to make sure that once disarmed, the PLO would remain so. At the same time, he would seek to have Lebanese rightist militias mainly in East Beirut and in its nearby mountains (as opposed to the renegades under Israeli control in southern Lebanon) place their forces under the central government's authority. The outlaw rightists had so little legitimacy that the administration simply hoped they would fade away.

Further, Habib's instructions were to negotiate an end to Israel's security zone in southern Lebanon. He hoped to obtain Begin's acceptance of the idea that Lebanese outlaw Major Sa'ad Haddad must go, especially because his enclave would have made little sense under the proposed security arrangements patrolled by a multinational force for the south. The idea that Haddad's units would be integrated into the government of Lebanon's armed forces, however, was a nonstarter because Jerusalem trusted the Lebanese under Israel's command more than any international force.

On the related goal of strengthening peacekeeping operations, Habib would try to nail down Lebanese acceptance of a forty-kilometer zone patrolled by an outside force in exchange for Jerusalem's termination of its security zone in southern Lebanon. He also intended to initiate discussions with the Lebanese Armed Forces to determine their needs in relation to sharing responsibilities with a multinational peacekeeping force. Washington itself would decide how to structure the force (for example, whether to seek an expansion of the United Nations Interim Force in Lebanon [UNIFIL] or to pursue a non-UNIFIL force) and determine its degree of participation in a non-UN peacekeeping force.

The Incredibility of the U.S. Approach

The goals and initiatives of the Department of State were a combination of prayerful hope and wishful thinking. Underlying its vision of the future were two assumptions: first, that the combatants and factions would voluntarily yield authority to the central government and, second, that the government could perform as a unitary actor despite the centrifugal pull of the contending factions in the Lebanese social order. It is one thing to work toward the goal of strengthening the authority of the government of Lebanon; it is quite another to imagine that such efforts actually would have the intended effect. Why would Syria allow the central government to expand its authority and possibly become a threat to the long-held Damascus goal of exercising suzerainty over Lebanon? It is difficult to imagine a set of incentives that would motivate Syria to strengthen the central government's authority in order to permit a decrease in the Syrian military presence in Lebanon.

Why should armed Palestinians contemplate a disarmament regime while they hoped for additional American military sanctions against Israel? The PLO had little incentive to disarm while Washington was deflating Jerusalem's threat to invade West Beirut. Moreover, American policy assumed that Israel would consider relinquishing the security zone it had just fought to strengthen in favor of an untested multinational force of countries, all of which opposed Israel's invasion. Thus, American diplomacy was detached from the harsh realities in Lebanon. Meanwhile, Israeli force hammered away at the political will of the armed Palestinians to coerce them to flee.

Multiple Voices and Dual-Track Diplomacy

Too Many Speakers for the U.S.

Among the factors that prevented the proper union of American diplomacy with Israeli force were the negative sanctions against Israel, an incorrect estimate that the PLO would have to end up in Damascus, and the administration's belief that Israel was unwilling to attack West Beirut. Another reason was that American intentions were transmitted via multiple speakers. However, although several voices spoke for the United States, they did not misuse diplomatic channels to convey conflicting messages about American policy toward the PLO in Lebanon. Incoherence, rather than deceit, was the order of the day.

Frustrated by the bureaucratic disarray, Haig complained that mixed signals continued to bedevil United States diplomacy.[1] He had a point, as the following facts demonstrate. On June 13, 1982, Israel tightened its noose around Beirut, leaving the PLO with no exit. The siege of Beirut had begun. Israel's objective was to create the appearance of a credible threat to take West Beirut by force so that the PLO would have to choose between surrender and annihilation. On the same day, King Khalid of Saudi Arabia passed away and was succeeded by Crown Prince Fahd. The U.S. delegation to the funeral included the vice president, Secretary of Defense Weinberger, Senator Charles Percy, and Deputy Assistant to the President McFarlane. This delegation met with Fahd on

June 16. Upon examining the cable reports of these meetings, Haig feared that what Bush and Weinberger had said to the Saudi leaders would have the effect of undercutting the pressure the United States and Israel were bringing to bear on the PLO.[2] That is, after hearing reassuring American statements from the Saudis, the PLO may have decided to play for time to obtain better conditions for withdrawal than those offered.

The discussions of the American delegation in Riyadh did, in fact, undermine Israeli military pressure. In addition, they coincided with American efforts to compel Israel to accept a cease-fire. According to the Israeli press, the United States had requested that Israel agree to a forty-eight-hour period in which all fighting would be stopped in the Beirut area.[3] The Israeli cabinet met in Jerusalem on June 17 and decided that Israel would continue to maintain the cease-fire and react only if attacked.[4] The fighting, however, continued as both sides blamed the other for cease-fire violations.

On June 23-24, events converged to reduce pressure on the PLO. There were published reports in Israel suggesting that the United States would join in the demand that the Israel Defense Forces withdraw about ten kilometers from Beirut.[5] Other accounts reported that Habib had suggested an Israeli withdrawal five kilometers from Beirut.[6] Such reports undercut Jerusalem's coercive diplomacy. Also, there were public statements from Washington that undermined Israel's military pressure on the Palestinian leadership. White House Deputy Press Secretary Larry Speakes said Begin had promised President Reagan that Israel would not go further into Beirut.[7] Begin, however, had said only that Israel had no intention of attacking West Beirut.

While the White House was publicly undermining Israeli coercion, Habib was privately reinforcing Jerusalem's military pressure. According to former officials, Habib had met with the Lebanese National Salvation Council the previous day to articulate precise demands for the council to pass on to the Palestine Liberation Organization. He stressed that the Israel Defense Forces had the PLO by the throat and could tighten the grip at any moment. This ominous warning to the PLO was strengthened by the beginning of an evacuation of some American citizens from Beirut. Thus, although pressure on the PLO had been relaxed by Washington's actions, the hope remained that the Palestinian leadership would accept Jerusalem's withdrawal terms as reinforced by Habib's diplomacy.

No Dual-Track Diplomacy

Without doubt, the fact that several officials spoke for the United States added to the confusion about America's policies. But a less compelling case can be made that dual-track diplomacy marred the effective transmission of U.S. initiatives. There are two schools of thought on this issue. One school, championed by Haig when he was secretary, lambasted the administration for speaking through multiple diplomatic channels on the subject of Lebanon. The other school, led by Clark when he was national security adviser, denied that multiple diplomatic channels existed. Indeed, this clash with Clark was one of the reasons Haig was ultimately sacked.

A confused structure of authority resulted in several individuals speaking with minimal coordination. This lack of coherence helps explain Haig's mistaken belief that the Reagan administration spoke privately on Lebanon. Consider the structure of authority. The president downgraded the position of national security adviser upon assuming office in 1981. Richard Allen, the first incumbent, was qualified for the position, but he reported to the president through Counselor to the President Edwin Meese, a man of limited experience in foreign affairs. Subsequent appointees--William Clark, Robert McFarlane, John Poindexter, Frank Carlucci, Colin Powell, and Brent Scowcroft--reported directly to the President.

The national security system in 1981-1982 was prone to produce a cacophony of speakers. Allen did not have the clout to settle turf battles between Haig and Weinberger; thus, they often sent contradictory messages. Meese had neither the time nor the background to supervise the NSC system, and the president had neither the inclination nor the experience to do so. Consequently, Haig and Weinberger fought without referee, and though Meese had the authority, Allen had the responsibility. This gap produced an uncoordinated system of private pleadings taken directly to the president, who was a relative bystander in the bureaucratic warfare of his subordinates. Weinberger had a political key to unlock the south entrance to 1600 Pennsylvania Avenue; that is, he was a master of the "back-door" approach to the president. He also knew that those who opened it first could make a particular decision go their way. "Going back door" meant circumventing both the NSC staff at the White House and the interagency process dominated by the State Department.

Consider the NSC staff as a corporate marketing department that derives and synthesizes options from the interagency process and presents coherent policy packages to the president. In an era of multiple policy sources, State alone cannot reign unchallenged over the interagency process. And in this regard, the coordinating role that the NSC staff plays leads to collisions with State and other departments. The Haig-Clark matchup stemmed from the NSC staff attempt to coordinate and select among the options that flowed in for presidential decision. Not unexpectedly, the Haig-Clark battles lent credence to false rumors of a dual-track diplomacy for Lebanon.

After Haig's dismissal on June 25, 1982, White House aides, such as Chief of Staff James Baker and his deputy Michael Deaver, were eager to dispel speculation that Haig's departure was a result of policy differences over Lebanon. Secretary Haig's confidants, however, criticized what they alleged were policy signals being sent to the Arab world from the White House that contrasted with messages from State. For example, Haig learned from Habib that the Saudis may have been saying things to the Lebanese leadership that did not reflect Jerusalem's position, as State knew it, about a possible disengagement of Israeli forces from the area around Beirut. National Security Adviser Clark supposedly had assured the Saudi ambassador in Washington that the United States had obtained Israel's agreement to withdraw its forces five kilometers, or about three miles, from Beirut. On June 18, the wife of this Saudi ambassador paid a visit to First Lady Nancy Reagan and brought a letter signed by the wives of six Arab ambassadors in Washington. The message called for an end to the bloodshed in Lebanon. She asked Judge Clark to attend the meeting, and State offered no objections when he notified the department of his plan to be present.

The standard operating procedure is for a State Department representative to take part in any meetings that White House officials at Clark's level hold with foreign envoys. Four days after the first lady's session, the Saudi ambassador met with Clark. The White House again checked with State; the department did not object but failed to send a representative to the meeting. Two days later, Ambassador Habib informed Washington of reports from the PLO, via the Lebanese, that Judge Clark had given assurances of an Israeli withdrawal. He has denied this, and the Saudis claimed that they had never passed such information to the PLO or the Lebanese. Haig himself met with the Saudi ambassador the day after Clark's meeting to say that the United States saw no way out of the situation except for the PLO to withdraw. Thus, Haig attempted to link Israel's threat to use additional force with the American diplomatic objective of effecting a PLO withdrawal with minimal bloodshed.

On the evening of Tuesday, June 22, Special Envoy Habib met with Israeli Defense Minister Sharon at the Beirut-area headquarters of the Lebanese rightist militia leader Bashir Gemayel. Because Habib had hoped to avoid meeting an Israeli under the auspices of Lebanese rightists, neither Bashir nor any of his men were present. Sharon's opening position was that he would not agree to any disengagement or pullback of the Israel Defense Forces. On the one hand, Habib acknowledged that the disposition of the Israeli forces made a five-kilometer pullback a virtual impossibility. On the other hand, he needed to secure some type of symbolic withdrawal that might be achieved near the airport and/or the palace. Sharon showed surprising flexibility by agreeing to remove Israeli military posts around the Lebanese presidential palace. Given the fact that these positions had been an irritant to the Lebanese leadership, their removal would have created a better atmosphere for Habib's planned meeting with the National Salvation Council of Lebanon.

After the June 22 meeting, Habib helicoptered to Israel to meet with its leaders, not expecting that the cabinet would agree to the controversial five-kilometer withdrawal. But though the government failed to approve a general pullback, it did agree to minor adjustments in the disposition of Israeli deployments around the airport and the palace. Armed with the relatively positive outcome from Jerusalem, Habib returned by helicopter to the American ambassador's residence in Beirut on the evening of June 23.

Meanwhile, in Washington, Haig asked Begin when they met on June 22 to consider a pullback as part of a package in which the PLO would agree to leave Beirut. But before Begin could discuss the matter at the June 24 cabinet session in Jerusalem, the PLO received the incorrect impression that Israel had agreed to unilateral disengagement. Haig claims that such misinformation came from the Saudi ambassador in Washington, who had just met with Clark.[8] Haig was concerned with Clark's purported intervention because, at the same time, the secretary was telling the Saudis that Washington could not guarantee that Jerusalem would refrain from invading West Beirut. In this respect, the only way to prevent an attack was to end the PLO presence there. If Clark, in fact, had informed the Saudi ambassador that the Israeli forces would pull back, it would have encouraged the PLO to resist Jerusalem's pressure.

Although Haig had good reason to believe a dual track operated, Bernard Gwertzman of the *New York Times* wrote that his interviews did not substantiate the two-channel idea.[9] Given the positive outcome from Jerusalem on the cosmetic changes and the simple fact that the Saudi ambassador had a meeting at the White House, one can understand how rumors of an Israeli pullback may have begun. In light of the history of White House-State disputes, it is reasonable that a dual-track idea would be put forth to explain the stalemate in negotiations over the PLO withdrawal from Beirut. Advocates of the multiple diplomatic channel hypothesis had a persuasive argument based upon circumstantial evidence. However, the overwhelming weight of direct evidence suggests that the dual-track idea should be rejected. Nevertheless, the many voices speaking out from Washington made it difficult to synchronize American diplomacy with Israeli force.

Haig Is Fired

Regarding people and politics, Haig's departure stemmed partly from his power struggles with White House staffers. In addition to such bureaucratic rivalry, there were serious policy disputes. Despite denials from the White House, Haig and Clark differed over Lebanon and on such issues as the Argentine-British clash over the Falklands and whether to permit U.S. technology to be used by companies in Western Europe for the construction of a natural gas pipeline from Europe to the Soviet Union. Clark tilted towards Argentina, took a hard-line position in favor of restricting the use of American technology for the pipeline, and wanted to disassociate the United States from Israel's use of force in Lebanon. Haig held the opposite view on all three issues.

On the day that Haig was fired, June 25, 1982, the Special Situations Group convened in the White House Situation Room. The formal agenda included a variety of topics on Lebanon, such as the president's correspondence with Prime Minister Begin and instructions to Ambassador Habib. According to former officials, however, a discussion of Secretary Haig's resignation and how to play it to the public actually dominated the meeting. The chosen line was that the departure was not motivated by policy difference. Rather, Haig was allegedly involved in a trivial pursuit game over turf and perks, such as where he would be seated in relation to the president and whether the plane he used in the Falklands war shuttle diplomacy had windows.

The point of this public relations offensive was to shift the blame from the White House to Haig--a damage control ploy. His adversaries tried to paint him as a power-hungry, overly sensitive, and politically isolated person whose departure was the result of his own peculiarities. White House "spin doctors" held a series of backgrounders for the press to insure that the party line became the "spin" given to news accounts of the resignation. However, although Haig did not document policy differences in his resignation statement, the White House tack failed. John Goshko, a reporter for the *Washington Post*, wrote that the White House had become increasingly unhappy with Haig's advocacy of an accommodative line toward Israel's attempts to crush the Palestine Liberation Organization in Lebanon.[10] Ultimately, however, though differences on issues were significant in the firing of Haig, the fact that he was not considered to be a team player by the White House staff was a very important factor, as well.

Shultz Joins the Team

The White House quickly announced the appointment of George Shultz, who the staff believed would be more of a team player than the fallen Haig. They sought to deflect speculation about why Haig had left by putting the spotlight on his replacement, a tactic that failed because the Haig dismissal was such good press copy. Like Weinberger, Shultz had been an executive of the Bechtel Corporation, a company with extensive contracts in Arab countries. Hence, there was concern in pro-Israel circles that State, under Shultz, would join the White House/Defense coalition and take a tougher line than Haig had toward Israel's use of force.

A comparison of the congressional testimony of Haig and Shultz reveals their differences in approach toward the Middle East.[11] On November 12, 1981, Haig reviewed American policy for the area in a congressional hearing. Being the globalist that he is, Haig emphasized the Soviet threat, rather than the Arab-Israeli conflict. He discussed a regional consensus of strategic concern about threats posed by the Soviet Union and its proxies and stated that American efforts to resolve local conflicts could benefit from this consensus among its friends. Haig asserted that U.S. policy was integrated into a balanced strategy--an approach which recognized that the Arab-Israeli peace process and security cooperation against the

Soviet threat must reinforce one another. Although he mentioned the peace process in terms of the autonomy talks then taking place between Egypt and Israel, with the United States on the margin, he did not refer to the Palestinians by name.

George Shultz's confirmation hearings on July 13 and 14, 1982, stand in contrast to Haig's. Almost as if Shultz had been captured by regionalists at State on the way to the hearings, the secretary-designate focused squarely on the Palestinian issue and scarcely mentioned the Soviet Union. Shultz said that the Lebanon crisis highlighted his concern that the legitimate needs and problems of the Palestinian people had to be both addressed and resolved.[12] Shultz introduced the Soviet Union only in the context of American ties to oil-rich Arab states, emphasizing the importance of strengthening relations between these nations and the United States to thwart Soviet designs on them. Had Shultz spoken in the aftermath of the American decision to sell an air defense system to Saudi Arabia (which had to be justified in terms of the Soviet threat) rather than in the middle of the Lebanon War, he, like Haig, may have been less concerned with the Palestinian issue and more worried about the Soviet Union. In spite of such differences in historical context, however, the statements of the two secretaries reveal major differences in approach toward the Middle East in general and to the Palestinian issue in particular.

Bureaucratic Dynamics and Ideas

Washington is a town where politics and personalities are intertwined, where pundits keep standings on who is up and down and who is in or out, and where bureaucrats take advantage of changes at the top to promote their own agendas. As Haig faded and Shultz rose, globalists appeared to be going down and out, and regionalists seemed to be on their way up and in. It appeared that Soviet-bashing, which was chic under Haig, would become out of fashion under Shultz. But the rise of regionalists was due more to the fact that they used the temporary state of flux to push their platform than to any convergence between their ideas and those of Secretary Shultz. In the key issue of the relationship between bureaucratic dynamics and ideas, it seems that policy changes result when people in organizations can assert themselves, rather than when there is a change in the views of elites.

In terms of the relationship of diplomacy to force, the shift from Haig to Shultz signaled an even wider gap between Washington and

Jerusalem. Haig had acknowledged the need to coordinate Washington's diplomacy with Jerusalem's use of force, but the smart money anticipated that State under Shultz would side with the White House and Defense against Israel. A unified Washington then would be able to compel Jerusalem to forgo an invasion of West Beirut, accept a cease-fire, soften its demands for unconditional PLO surrender and departure from West Beirut, and withdraw from Lebanon without attaining guarantees for the security of Israel's borders. For the most part, however, the smart money was wrong; Haig's ideas persisted, even in the absence of the man himself. And the White House, State, and Defense were unable to present a unified front to coerce Israel. In the end, it was Jerusalem's force that coerced the PLO to sue for peace.

The Diplomacy of the PLO and Israel's Force

Why Would the PLO Leave Lebanon?

In addition to the Jerusalem-Washington nexus, Secretary Shultz implied another facet of the relationship between diplomacy and force when he granted the effectiveness of Israel's use of force to achieve a PLO withdrawal from Beirut. However, he suggested that force and diplomacy must be balanced and that Israel had gone too far.[13] His acknowledgement suggests a major theme of this book--force and diplomacy must be used in harmony. One aspect of the force/diplomacy relationship in the Middle East is the way in which the diplomatic efforts and the situation of the PLO interacted with Israel's use of force to compel that organization to flee from Lebanon. In other words, how great a role was played by force and by diplomacy in the PLO's decision to accept American-Israeli terms for withdrawal from Beirut?

The Reagan administration offered two conflicting answers to this question. One held that it was explicit PLO policy to withhold concessions when it was under armed attack by Israel and to moderate its demands in periods of relative calm. Those who maintained this view believed that the PLO decided to withdraw and accept harsh American-Israeli conditions because it lacked diplomatic support in the Arab world in general and within Beirut in particular. Even academic advocates of this approach, however, have acknowledged that Israel's use of force played a crucial part in the PLO withdrawal decision. An historian of the Palestinians, Rashid Khalidi, grants that, as Israeli attacks peaked in intensity during the first twelve days of August, it became clear that the Palestinian combatants had no alternative to evacuation.[14]

The second interpretation among Reagan administration officials gave more weight to military facts on the ground, rather than to the diplomatic isolation of the Palestine Liberation Organization. They believed that Israeli military actions reinforced the diplomatic isolation of the PLO and thereby prompted a withdrawal decision. Thus, the PLO fled from Beirut not just because they lacked diplomatic support within the Arab world but primarily because of battlefield defeats and the expectation that more military force would follow.

Khalidi, who is close to the PLO, agrees with the first interpretation that diplomatic isolation, more than Israeli force, caused the PLO to pull out from West Beirut.[15] In accordance with China's former chairman, Mao Zedong, Khalidi suggests that the relationship between a successful guerrilla army and the society in which it operates is like that of a fish in water. Because the PLO was isolated from the local population and lacked strong Arab support outside of Lebanon, it was like a fish thrashing about on dry land and thereby vulnerable. Even if the PLO had backing in the local population and from Saudi Arabia and Syria, Israel's use of force still would have been decisive in the pullout decision. A fish swimming in the relative safety of a pond still faces threats from those who troll its waters.

It was true that the PLO was strongly opposed by the rightist militias of the Lebanese Forces and lacked support from central players in the leftist Muslim parties of the Lebanese National Movement. Israel's military attacks on Lebanese civilian areas were designed to root out PLO forces hiding among civilians. These assaults widened the gap between the Lebanese and the PLO, and that organization increasingly came to be blamed by the Lebanese for Jerusalem's retaliatory blows. When the PLO began to build up its armaments against the possibility of being expelled by the rightists, it created additional enmity among the Lebanese. Thus, the core of the PLO problem in Lebanon, according to Khalidi, was that any growth in its local military strength only multiplied its enemies.[16] In short, Israeli force and PLO diplomatic isolation interacted to compel that organization to withdraw from Beirut. The threat of military action enhanced the effect of political alienation and left the PLO with little choice but to flee.

War as Politics and Policy by Other Means

Khalidi cites two schools of thought within the Palestinian leadership on the conditions under which the PLO should depart from Beirut.[17] The first held that there was no alternative to a pullout in light of the bleak military situation on the ground. This group wanted a minimum political quid pro quo but would not have haggled too long over the details because the pullout was inevitable. What this faction desired was some type of American recognition to aid the PLO's transition from a primarily military body to a political one. This school of thought was at its height of influence in mid-June but was discredited by early July. Thereafter, critics satirized its advocates by calling it the "withdrawal now" movement, a take-off on the name of Israel's "peace now" group.[18]

The longer Israel delayed its attack on West Beirut, the stronger the Palestinians in the second school of thought became. This faction viewed the war in political, rather than military, terms. Because the war was far from over as a political event, this group believed it was advisable to hold out for better terms, using negotiations as an open-ended, strategic tool with which to extract the maximum from a grim situation. To paraphrase Von Clausewitz, the second group viewed war as an extension of policy and politics by other means.

During the third week of June, the PLO position began to harden around a commitment to withdraw in principle while refusing to accept the original American-Israeli conditions. The PLO attempted to play the delay game in order to discover novel elements that would improve its situation. A French offer to mediate on June 15 was just such a factor. With an irresponsibility that was unbecoming in a great power, France had called on the PLO to hold out for: an unequivocal condemnation of Israel, unconditional Israeli withdrawal, noninterference by Jerusalem in Lebanese affairs, Lebanese-Palestinian negotiations to regulate the PLO's status in Lebanon, and self-determination for the Palestinian people with their own state on the West Bank and Gaza. Without American knowledge, France put forth this maximalist program, even though it had little diplomatic clout among the parties and scant military force in the immediate area.

Misusing its position as a transmitter of American messages, France prolonged the agony of withdrawal by the armed Palestinians and added to the mounting casualties during the siege of Beirut. Furthermore, the French diplomatic initiative helped to discredit Israel's threat to use additional force in the seizure of West

Beirut. Thus, France ingratiated itself with the PLO at the same time that it presented itself to the United States as an aid to American policy. Secretary Haig was keen on the prospects of involving the French. Unaware of Paris's duplicity, he wrote that the French had offered valuable support for the U.S. position on a PLO withdrawal.[19] So, France prolonged the war by saying one thing to the United States and another to the Palestine Liberation Organization.

The Re-Partition of "Palestine"

Bolstered by French diplomacy, the PLO pursued two approaches to enhance its bargaining position during July. The first was the Franco-Egyptian United Nations draft resolution of July 28, 1982; the second was the July 20 visit to Washington by an Arab League delegation. The draft resolution built upon the French position that led the PLO to hold out for improved political terms in mid-June. The core of the draft involved linking Lebanon with the question of "Palestine"--the use of the PLO withdrawal crisis as an occasion for another partition of Great Britain's former Mandate of Palestine. This partition would create a Palestinian state in the West Bank and Gaza.

The central benefit for the PLO of the Arab League's visit to Washington was to open a dialogue in exchange for some move by the organization toward recognition of Israel. One idea that the PLO proposed was mutual and simultaneous recognition between itself and Israel. This proposal would sidestep the U.S. demand that this organization accept UN Resolutions 242 and 338, along with explicit recognition of Israel, as condition for a dialogue with the United States. The United Nations Security Council had passed Resolution 242 in the aftermath of the 1967 war. Given the fact that Israel had seized land from Egypt, Jordan, and Syria during the fighting, this resolution called for a trade of land for peace. Resolution 242, however, did not mention the Palestinians by name and thus was not acceptable to them. After the 1973 war, the Security Council passed Resolution 338, which called for acceptance of Resolution 242 and direct talks among the belligerents, but it also failed to mention the Palestinians.

Both the mutual and simultaneous recognition, as well as the draft resolution proposal, were nonstarters. Even in a Gulf state--Kuwait--there was little sympathy for the PLO position. A Kuwaiti newspaper editorial expressed more support for the American than for the PLO's view: "The U.S. refusal to meet with the Palestinian member in the Arab ministerial delegation to Washington was expected in view of that administration's rejection to meet [sic] with PLO officials as long as the organization does not recognize Israel and the Security Council Resolution 242."[20] So it is not surprising that two Arab League delegation members, Saudi Arabia and Syria, declined to back the strong political demands of the PLO in discussions with the United States. In reporting on the delegation's meeting with President Reagan, one member of the committee--the Saudi foreign minister--even mentioned a desire to bring about the integration of Lebanon.[21] This was a euphemism for expelling all foreign forces from Lebanon, including the PLO combatants.

Partly as a result of its failure to obtain the strong backing of the Arab delegation to Washington, the PLO ultimately decoupled withdrawal from an overall political settlement. Unlinking pullout from settlement opened the way for the PLO to accept the terms proposed by Habib in mid-June. Khalidi posits that the failure of Saudi Arabia and Syria to reinforce French diplomatic backing of the PLO and the organization's isolation from political allies within Lebanon proved decisive in the PLO's choice to accept the Habib withdrawal conditions.[22]

In contrast to Saudi Arabia and Syria, France provided solid diplomatic support for the Palestine Liberation Organization. Paris preferred the formula of a "political plus" to balance any "military minus." Specific steps towards Palestinian aspirations for statehood were seen as a political bonus to compensate for any Israeli-inflicted decline in the PLO's military capacity in Lebanon. So, the diplomatic isolation of the PLO was important in its decision to withdraw from West Beirut; more important, however, was Israel's actual and potential use of force. Thus, military factors enhanced the effect of the organization's political isolation. Diplomatic initiatives and force employment marched side by side, but not hand in hand, throughout the war.

Conclusions

Washington's negative sanctions against Jerusalem undercut the credibility of Israel's threat to invade West Beirut and thereby strengthened the willingness of the PLO to hold out for better conditions than those being offered by Jerusalem. The administration's inadequate assessment of where the PLO would land after its flight from West Beirut discouraged policymakers from linking U.S. diplomacy to Israel's threat to enter West Beirut. And Washington's perception that Jerusalem was unlikely to order its forces into West Beirut, for fear of additional casualties and a negative American reaction, also worked against synchronizing diplomacy and force.

Although American diplomatic initiatives abounded after Israel's invasion, they were not coupled with Jerusalem's military policies. As a result, the credibility of Israel's threat to use additional force in Beirut was lowered. There also was a lack of coordination within the administration, a failure that derived from presidential uninvolvement. But though there were several voices speaking for the United States, there does not appear to have been a purposeful use of diplomatic channels to convey conflicting messages about the PLO to the Saudis or Lebanese. Rather, personality differences and role conflicts interacted to produce policy clashes, which, in turn, contributed to a foreign policy in disarray.

Despite an incoherent American policy, the diplomatic isolation of the PLO reinforced by Israeli military pressure, caused the Palestinian leadership to abandon West Beirut. Lebanese civilians, caught in the midst of the fighting, increasingly began to blame the PLO for Israeli military retaliations, thereby compounding the organization's political alienation. Finally, American diplomatic initiatives failed to reinforce Israeli military activities and hence unintentionally delayed the PLO's withdrawal from Lebanon.

7

The Siege-Squeeze War

Jerusalem's Siege of Beirut: An Overview

June and July

Israel's military siege was designed to induce the PLO to depart from Beirut before the U.S. diplomatic squeeze on Jerusalem compelled it to lift its blockade. On the day Secretary Haig resigned, June 25, 1982, Israel bombed Palestinian positions in West Beirut, prompting his sharp statement against the assault to Jerusalem's ambassador to Washington, Moshe Arens. Despite the criticism of Israel by Haig, on the day after his resignation, the United States sided with Jerusalem in vetoing a French draft resolution at the United Nation Security Council, in a 14-to-1 vote. This draft called for an immediate cease-fire, an Israeli pullback to ten kilometers from Beirut prior to a total withdrawal, a simultaneous removal of PLO forces to existing camps, and the introduction of UN observers to supervise the truce and disengagement. The United States vetoed the draft because it failed to call for the elimination of armed Palestinian elements from Beirut and elsewhere in Lebanon. During an emergency special session, the UN General Assembly voted 127 to 2 to call for an unconditional Israeli pullout and cease-fire by June 27, as well as Security Council consideration of practical ways and means to ensure Israeli compliance in accordance with the UN Charter if it failed to comply; the United States and Israel cast the dissenting votes. On that very day, Israel destroyed additional Syrian missiles in the Bekaa Valley of Lebanon.

Attempting to mix diplomacy with force, Jerusalem also proposed a plan by which the Lebanese army would enter Beirut and the PLO would lay down its arms en route to Syria. Furthermore, Israeli aircraft dropped propaganda leaflets in a psychological warfare campaign to frighten the residents of West Beirut into leaving. Two days later, Prime Minister Begin offered to allow PLO fighters to leave Beirut with their personal weapons and stated that Israel had no desire to humiliate them. On July 4, the Israeli cabinet issued a statement declaring that it would reject any peace proposal that would leave the PLO with a political or organizational presence in Lebanon. Jerusalem tightened the noose that encircled West Beirut, preventing food, water, and fuel from entering. The reinforced blockade prompted passage of a Security Council resolution that called for Israel to respect civilians' rights and to restore vital facilities in Beirut. Israel responded by bombing additional Palestinian neighborhoods in West Beirut, yet it consented to a temporary cease-fire on the afternoon of July 5.

On the next day, President Reagan announced an agreement in principle to send a small contingent of U.S. troops to join a multinational force for temporary peacekeeping in Beirut if a settlement were reached. The proposed force was to separate Palestinian and Israeli troops, help in the evacuation of PLO fighters, and arrange for the Lebanese army to assume control of the city. According to former officials, the White House stepped up its pressure on Jerusalem with a message stating that Israel Defense Forces actions at crossing points over the past seventy-two hours had made negotiations impossible. Although some pressure on the PLO was necessary, Jerusalem's twenty-four-hour deadline for that organization's withdrawal was unacceptable to Washington. If Jerusalem failed to cooperate, Washington stated that it would have to consider other ways to talk with the relevant parties--a diplomatic euphemism for Habib's opening of direct contacts between the PLO and the United States.

Jerusalem may have caved in to Washington's pressure the next day. Israel stated that it had not issued an ultimatum and that Habib could have additional time to negotiate a PLO departure; nevertheless, Israel reemphasized, there could be no PLO presence in Beirut. Jerusalem also said it would react only if attacked, and would open one crossing point. On July 11, however, following an exchange of artillery and rocket fire between Israeli forces and Palestinian fighters that lasted for fifteen hours before another cease-fire was called, the negotiations reached an impasse. Three days later, Washington sent a message to Damascus asking Syria to accept PLO combatants, despite the fact that it had earlier rejected a similar request. On July 16, State sent a letter to Congress on possible Israeli violations of arms agreements. Shultz, sworn in as secretary of state, promptly convened a panel of experts to discuss the Middle East. On July 19, the vice president met with the French ambassador to Washington regarding Lebanon, and the president met with the Saudi and Syrian foreign ministers the following day and suspended the sale of cluster bomb munitions to Israel.

On July 22, Special Envoy Habib began a journey to the Middle East. His goal was to enlist the support of Arab regimes in accepting PLO fighters evacuated from Beirut. As yet one more cease-fire collapsed during the third week of July, Habib left for Damascus. Thereafter, Israel launched air strikes on PLO targets south of Beirut and additional attacks on Syrian missiles in the Bekaa Valley. From July 25 to 27, Israel continued bombing West Beirut, and there was heavy ground fighting around the airport. And for the first time since the invasion, Israeli planes bombed a heavily populated residential area near the heart of West Beirut, causing many civilian casualties. Habib returned to Beirut on July 28 amidst heavy air strikes. One day later, the United Nations adopted a Spanish resolution calling for Israel to lift its blockade. The United States abstained, ostensibly because of lack of time to consider the draft.

Soon after, an Arab League ministerial group called for withdrawal of all Israeli and PLO forces, a remarkable declaration considering the source. The following day, however, the intensive land, air, and sea bombardment of Beirut was resumed, as Washington and Jerusalem argued over the possibility of "proximity talks" between Habib and the PLO in Beirut. President Reagan met with Egyptian Deputy Prime Minister and Minister of Foreign Affairs Kamal Hassan Ali, and Vice President Bush met with Israeli Ambassador Moshe Arens. As July closed, Secretary Shultz got into the act by suggesting to Israel that the Arab ministerial declaration was constructive, that a firm cease-fire was necessary, and that Jerusalem must respond to violations proportionately. (The proportionality criterion was a standard that Haig also had advocated.) Meanwhile, the Lebanese prime minister gave Ambassador Habib a detailed plan from the PLO for the pullout of its approximately 6,000 fighters in Beirut.

August

As August opened, another cease-fire collapsed. Once again, Israel took complete control of Beirut International Airport and bombarded PLO positions, as well as residential areas of West Beirut, for fourteen hours before yet another cease-fire was arranged. On August 2, Israeli Foreign Minister Shamir met with the president, along with the secretaries of state and defense. Shamir was told that it was crucial both to end the violence and to allow food and medical supplies to enter West Beirut. Washington also gave renewed assurance through Envoy Habib that the PLO had agreed in principle to evacuate. Nevertheless, Israeli forces advanced into West Beirut and strengthened their siege of PLO strongholds. With the United States abstaining because the PLO was not criticized, the UN Security Council adopted a resolution that demanded an immediate cease-fire, withdrawal of Israeli forces, censure of Israel for failure to comply with six prior resolutions, and return of Israeli troops to positions held on the first day of August. As if in reply, Israeli aircraft, gunboats, and artillery rained shellfire across West Beirut, and Israeli armored units made a rapid advance toward Palestinian camps and neighborhoods on the outskirts of the capital.

The president publicly called for a cease-fire on August 4, and Washington sent yet another sternly worded statement telling Jerusalem to observe the cease-fire in place, that is, one in which both sides not only held their fire but also held their positions. In a succinct statement on the proper union of diplomacy and force, however, Israel advocated a combined political/military approach: If a military option were foreclosed, a political solution would be impossible. Thus, Jerusalem, with good reason, believed that UN and U.S. entreaties for Israel not to invade West Beirut merely encouraged PLO procrastination. Israel, in effect, attempted to synchronize diplomacy with force but was hindered by pious pleas from New York, Washington, and even the Vatican. Although the United States vetoed a Soviet draft resolution on August 5 that called for the suspension of military aid to Israel (the vote was 11 to 1, with 3 abstentions), Washington's diplomacy remained out of sync with Jerusalem's use of force.

Over the next two days, Israel not only maintained its military pressure but also intensified its diplomatic campaign. Jerusalem opposed the introduction of a multinational force prior to evacuation: The PLO would stay under the protection of the outside force because the Palestinian fighters had no place to go. Israel even wanted a list of both destination countries and Palestinian combatants. It also proposed that the multinational force should enter at a geographical halfway point and be prepared to depart if the remaining Palestinian fighters refused to leave. The following day, Israel complemented its diplomatic offensive with intensified military pressure. Although the cabinet, in a well-timed diplomatic gesture, authorized the restoration of West Beirut's water supply, it also continued to exercise military force both within Beirut proper and outside the city, against PLO targets behind Syrian lines.

On August 11, Syria announced that it would accept both PLO fighters and leaders. Although Jerusalem partly fulfilled its intentions toward Damascus by putting military pressure on the PLO, these military activities boomeranged because they caused Washington to buckle. The United States believed these attacks hindered, rather than facilitated, such talks. Jerusalem seemed to respond to Washington's demands and threats of negative sanctions with continued strikes and naval landings north of Beirut. At the August 12 Israeli cabinet meeting, however, Defense Minister Sharon was disciplined for conducting an unauthorized massive bombardment of Beirut. Schiff and Ya'ari state that the cabinet divested him of his authority to activate the air force.[1] In addition, the cabinet voted 15 to 2 against continuing the siege and accepted a cease-fire that began the next day.

Negotiations resumed on August 14 and continued for three days, with the PLO insisting that French forces should enter West Beirut on the first day of the withdrawal. The Israeli cabinet agreed to end the siege of Beirut and allow the introduction of the multinational force on day one of the PLO evacuation. It insisted, however, that, as part of the settlement, Syria should leave Lebanon entirely. To avoid the impression that the cabinet lifted the siege in response to the U.S. squeeze, Israel leaked reports that Begin had decided to end the blockade before Reagan's intervention. On August 18, the government of Lebanon decided to ask the United States, France, and Italy to contribute troops for a multinational force that would oversee the evacuation of PLO fighters. And on the following day, the Israeli cabinet decided to put forward a proposal for the evacuation of Palestinian and Syrian forces from West Beirut, formally ending the ten-week encirclement of the city.

Between August 21 and September 1, the PLO leaders and fighters withdrew from West Beirut, Bashir Gemayel was elected president of Lebanon two days after the evacuation began, and American marines arrived in Beirut as a part of the multinational force, on August 25. The Israeli blockade had succeeded. Jerusalem's encirclement of Beirut and Washington's attempt to end the blockade were reminiscent of the previous SAM-site game that asked whether a Syrian surface-to-air missile could take out an

Israeli aircraft before that plane could kill the missile. In fact, the answer was no. Similarly, the siege-squeeze game asked if Jerusalem's siege of Beirut could compel the PLO to exit before Washington's squeeze on Jerusalem induced it to lift the siege. The answer was yes.

Washington's Squeeze on Jerusalem

Reports to the Congress

The Reagan administration's pressure on Israel during its siege of Beirut included presidential telephone calls and letters, entreaties from Secretary Haig, warnings from Secretaries Shultz and Weinberger, delays in notifying Congress about the shipment of aircraft destined for Israel, reports to Congress on the possible misuse of American-origin armaments, and a suspension of the sale of certain types of weapons used by Israel in Lebanon. Some officials within the administration were opposed to punishing and pressuring Israel via reports to Congress on possible violations of U.S. legislation restricting the use of American-origin arms.

Bob Woodward describes Director of Central Intelligence William Casey's reaction to the issue of whether the United States would be seen as an accomplice in Israel's invasion of Lebanon because Jerusalem used American-supplied equipment. Casey expressed his intensity in profane language, asking how the United States could use Israel's invasion of Lebanon for the American "national interest."[2] In other words, Casey was opposed to punishing Israel through reports to the Hill. Rather, the director wanted to use Israel's invasion to further America's aims in the region; he saw crisis as an opportunity for change--a central theme of the current inquiry.

Despite Casey's opposition, a report appeared on the possibility of sanctions. It stated that the administration had determined that Israel might have violated its arms agreements with the United States by using American-made military equipment during the invasion of Lebanon, and that the executive branch planned to inform Congress about the finding.[3] Under the terms of the Arms Export Control Act, the executive branch has the authority to suspend military aid if a recipient is in substantial violation of a military assistance agreement with the United States. Accordingly, Acting Secretary of State Stoessel wrote to Senator Charles Percy, chairman of the Senate Foreign Relations Committee, and to

Speaker of the House Thomas O'Neill, on July 15, 1982, pursuant to the requirements of the Arms Export Control Act. Arms shipments to Israel under the U.S. Foreign Military Sales program are governed by the U.S.-Israel Mutual Defense Assistance Agreement of July 23, 1952, which provides that:

> The Government of Israel assures the United States Government that such equipment, materials, or services as may be acquired from the United States under the provisions of...the Mutual Defense Assistance Act of 1949...are required for and will be used solely to maintain its internal security, its legitimate self-defense, or to permit it to participate in the defense of the area of which it is a part, or in United Nations collective security arrangements and measures, and that it will not undertake any act of aggression against any other state.[4]

The bottom line is that Israel promised the United States to use American-origin equipment only for self-defense and not for "aggression" against any other state. Hence, according to this agreement and the terms of the military sales program, Acting Secretary Stoessel filed the report to Congress.

The Stoessel report held that Israeli forces entered Lebanon on June 6, 1982, and used a large quantity and variety of American-origin equipment. As a result, the report concluded that Israel may have committed a "substantial violation."[5] State routinely prepared the report after Israel's June 6 invasion but held it up because of Prime Minister Begin's visit of June 18-21. The department released the report on July 15 only after being pressured to do so by Defense at a White House meeting.

According to former officials, Defense noted that such documents had been submitted in connection with several previous Israeli incursions into Lebanon, as well as its raid on the Iraqi nuclear reactor in June 1981. Defense criticized State's delay in submitting the document, noting that such documents typically were released within a week or two of a reportable incident. On June 30, Defense forwarded to State a listing of Foreign Military Sales equipment believed to have been used by the Israel Defense Forces in Lebanon. Although such a listing had not been required in the past, Defense sent it to State to expedite the submission of a report to Capitol Hill. Thus, Defense was trying to push State to take a step that would demonstrate American displeasure with Israel.

Secretary Haig, however, delayed submission so as to avoid losing the diplomatic benefits that the invasion held for the peace process.

The operative portion of the Stoessel document--that a substantial violation may have occurred--is standard wording that meets the minimal reporting requirements while avoiding unnecessary complications in American-Israeli bilateral relations. A comparison with the wording used in reports during the Lebanon War and the Iraqi nuclear reactor bombing demonstrates a similarity in approach and, thus, a continuity in policy. After the Israeli attack on June 7, 1981, that used American-origin F-15 and F-16 aircraft, Secretary Haig reported to Speaker O'Neill that Jerusalem may have substantially violated the 1952 agreement. He wrote that State was conducting an extensive review to consider Israel's contention that the attack was necessary for its defense because the reactor was intended to produce atomic bombs and shortly would have become operational. The Israelis also claimed that, once functional, an attack could not have been carried out without exposing the inhabitants of Baghdad and elsewhere to massive radioactive fallout. Although State promised to inform Congress of the outcome of its thorough review, the department did not issue a follow-up report; indeed, it is doubtful if there was any review whatsoever. In effect, then, State's approach was to avoid allowing Jerusalem's misdeeds to affect ongoing bilateral relations. By contrast, Defense would have punished Jerusalem for each act of noncompliance with American legislation, regardless of Israel's motivation or the ramifications of the action.

The Cluster Bomb Unit Flap

A specific case of the use of American-origin equipment in Lebanon by the Israel Defense Forces was its employment of cluster bomb units--CBUs. (These weapons spread pellet-sized explosives over a wide area and are particularly damaging to people as opposed to property.) Journalist Judith Miller reported that the United States decided to ban cluster shells for Israel, a policy supposedly based on a government review of Israel's statements about its use of CBUs.[6] This policy decision began with an initiative from the Pentagon.

The following describes the position of the Department of Defense in mid-July 1982 regarding the cluster munitions issue, according to former officials. On December 16, 1976, the government of Israel provided assurances to the United States on

its use of CBUs, commitments that were reaffirmed in an exchange
of letters on April 10 and 11, 1978. The assurances covered only
air-delivered munitions, but the Pentagon also had artillery
ammunition for 155-millimeter howitzers, a weapon that employed
a similar cluster bomb concept. Defense also noted that 4,000
rounds of artillery ammunition were scheduled to be transferred to
Israel, but, in view of the uncertainties in Lebanon, the department
planned to withhold shipment until the situation was clarified.

NSC staffers entered the fray on the side of State, which
opposed delay. They held that, at a time in which Washington was
trying to prevent Jerusalem from invading West Beirut, Defense's
proposal for delaying delivery could harm American efforts. These
officials believed that the threat of sanctions would be more
effective in obtaining Israeli compliance to forgo invasion than the
actual implementation of sanctions. The staffers correctly held that
Israel was likely to adopt a legalistic approach and claim that
American actions were unwarranted because artillery shells, as
such, were not included under the assurances. In the end, however,
Defense prevailed. The White House announced that the transfer of
a shipment of cluster-type artillery shells had been suspended until
completion of an interagency study on whether or not Israel's use of
the weapon in Lebanon violated an agreement with the United
States.[7] Jerusalem acknowledged that it had used the cluster
weapons but contended that it had not contravened any U.S.-Israeli
accord.

The cluster munitions story did not end with the White House
decision to delay the July 19 shipment of 4,000 units. The fact that
the administration scheduled an additional 22,000 units for delivery
through December 1982 underscored the need to decide whether to
discontinue both shipments and future sales or maintain the
suspension then in effect for another six months. On July 23, State
drafted a memorandum, with NSC staff concurrence, favoring
maintenance of the suspension. In a counter-memo of July 24, the
Office of the Secretary of Defense advocated canceling delivery and
prohibiting future sales. Washington did not even consider the
option of resuming deliveries without implying an Israeli violation of
the Arms Export Control Act.

One rationale for continuing the suspension of cluster bomb
munitions was that State and the NSC staff believed that to cancel
shipments and prohibit future sales would provoke Prime Minister
Begin to attack West Beirut just when the administration was
encouraging him not to do so. Israeli sources confirmed that the

hawks in the cabinet would have been strengthened by any American decision other than the resumption of sales or continuation of the suspension. Continuing the suspension also had the benefit of minimizing public fanfare, and the practical effect of the suspension would be the same as cancellation. Thus, the deliveries could be halted with less political risk.

However, the Office of the Secretary of Defense strongly opposed State and the NSC staff. Defense contended that State had "fuzzed over" the legal issue, for example, with the circumlocution that Israel might have been in violation of the 1978 agreement with the United States. The evidence supposedly was overwhelming that Israel consistently had violated U.S. terms for the use of American-origin weapons. After employing cluster bombs in Lebanon during 1976, Jerusalem had formally agreed not to use them in close proximity to population centers and then only against military targets, such as regular armed forces in wars of the scale of 1967 and 1973. During 1978, when Israel may have been in violation of the 1976 agreement, Washington and Jerusalem signed yet another formal accord. And in June 1982, Israel used cluster bomb units against irregular forces in Palestinian civilian population centers. One month after State had sent a demarche to Israel, Jerusalem acknowledged that it had continued to use such munitions. It implied that any civilian population center that encompassed PLO military forces ceased to be civilian, and, thus, there were no applicable restrictions on the use of American-origin equipment.

The Department of Defense's main critique of the government of Israel was based on a strategic-political argument. According to former civilians in the Office of the Secretary of Defense, the Southwest Asian security strategy required Arab friends to prevent an eventual Soviet suzerainty over the Gulf area and a consequent tilt in the global balance of power. Radical Arab propaganda portrayed the United States as acquiescing in the systematic destruction of West Beirut and in the killing of Palestinian and Lebanese civilians. Consequently, a public American decision to discontinue cluster bomb deliveries would help disabuse this perception.

Defense's rationale for cracking down on Israel by cutting off the sale of cluster munitions was strengthened by Cairo. The Egyptians held that any American request for facilities in Arab states, for example, in the Gulf, would be inconsistent with U.S. sales of equipment that enabled Israel to invade Lebanon. Furthermore, Egypt believed that Arab Gulf states should provide defense facilities to the United States only if it moved expeditiously to resolve the Palestinian problem. Egyptian rhetoric, however, was discredited by the actions of these Gulf states.

Meanwhile, as Cairo was linking Arab facilities in the Gulf with an American solution to the Palestinian problem, Riyadh was stepping up joint contingency planning with Washington to meet the Iranian threat, in light of the serious losses Iraq had begun to sustain in its two-year-old war with Iran. The moderate Arab states were split regarding the relative importance of the Israeli threat to the PLO in Lebanon and the Iranian threat to the Gulf states. Arab moderates could not make a concerted effort to reinforce the arguments of their allies at Defense. Thus, the effort to build an interagency coalition and impose meaningful sanctions on Israel, and, in particular, to cut off the sale of cluster munitions ultimately failed.

Jerusalem Comes to Washington

Another opportunity for Washington to squeeze Jerusalem came with Shamir's planned visit to the White House. Based upon reports of former officials, the NSC staff held that Israel itself needed to be flexible in its siege, at least for humanitarian purposes. The staff warned that the government of Israel might decide that it could no longer afford a no-win war of attrition or a political outcome that its adversaries would count as a PLO victory. Therefore, Jerusalem might opt for a military solution on West Beirut and would be interested in assessing how Washington might react to such a contingency. The staff advocated that an American response to such a query should highlight the grievous consequences for U.S.-Israeli relations if Jerusalem ordered an invasion of West Beirut. Because Washington was convinced that the PLO could be extracted by diplomatic means, Jerusalem needed to be flexible in its use of military pressure. Furthermore, the NSC staff stressed that American willingness to assist Israel in Lebanon should be linked to Israeli commitments to greater flexibility on the Palestinian autonomy negotiations and easing restrictions on the inhabitants of the West Bank and Gaza.

The State Department's position on the Shamir visit generally was similar to that of the NSC staff. Former officials report that State focused on Israel's broad choice between diplomacy and military force to induce a PLO withdrawal from West Beirut. The department also asserted that the United States could not afford to paper over its differences with Israel on Lebanon, but it was more circumspect than the NSC staff regarding the need to avoid a confrontation with Jerusalem. In contrast to the NSC staff, State stressed the similarity of goals between Washington and Jerusalem: the removal of all armed PLO personnel and the assertion of the government of Lebanon's authority throughout the city. State also called for a clear declaration of America's opposition to an Israeli invasion of West Beirut, stressing that an effort to impose a military solution would have the gravest impact on U.S.-Israeli bilateral relations. The department expressed serious doubts concerning the utility of Israeli pressure tactics, particularly the curtailment of electricity and food.

State declared that the needs of all parties had to be met in devising a compromise on the timing of the multinational force's entry into West Beirut. The United States believed the multinational deployment should not occur until the PLO evacuation was well under way. That organization, however, wanted the outside forces to be in place prior to its withdrawal. After resolving the West Beirut crisis, the United States hoped to turn immediately to the broad problems of Lebanon. These issues included the establishment of a strong central government able to exert its authority throughout the country and the withdrawal of all foreign military forces in a manner consistent with Israel's security.

To this end, Washington needed a clarification of Jerusalem's security requirements after a PLO evacuation. For example, what was the future status of Israel's renegade Lebanese Major Haddad and his security enclave in southern Lebanon (on Israel's northern border)? According to the department, the continuation of such a force, independent of the government of Lebanon, could be counterproductive to U.S. goals. Finally, State expressed concern about Israel's use of American-controlled equipment.

As a military backdrop to the political drama being played out in Washington, the fighting in Beirut escalated. Israel bombarded PLO positions and residential areas of West Beirut by land, sea, and air for fourteen hours on August 1 in the most intense shelling of the besieged capital since the invasion commenced on June 6. The bloody onslaught lasted from 3:00 A.M. to 5:00 A.M., when a cease-fire arranged by Special Envoy Habib took effect. Meanwhile, a three-way meeting had been scheduled for the day of the intensified bombing. The armed Palestinians and the Lebanese, and thus indirectly the Americans, had planned to discuss a timetable for the withdrawal of PLO fighters from West Beirut. But the meeting was canceled because of the bombing, prompting Lebanon's President Elias Sarkis to remark that the large-scale Israeli raid had come just as the parties were making progress in the negotiations.[8]

Back in Washington, the White House leaked to the press that the president would be firm in his meeting with Shamir.[9] Although Reagan did not explicitly criticize Israel for its massive bombardment of Beirut on August 1, he seemed visibly perturbed by the breakdown of the cease-fire. As promised, he was steadfast in his meeting with the Israeli foreign minister. Consistent with White House expectations, Shamir stated that President Reagan sent Prime Minister Begin a firm, but nonthreatening, message.[10] Not only did the Israeli Minister fail to detect a threatening tone in the president's remarks, Shamir came away assured that U.S. policy had not shifted after Shultz replaced Haig.[11]

Meanwhile, the State Department declared that the United States was extremely concerned about the interruption of the truce. This statement clearly demonstrated the gap between diplomacy and force in the relations between the two allies. In asserting that Jerusalem's continued use of force served no useful purpose and made it almost impossible to conduct negotiations, the State Department again devalued the currency of Israel's coercive diplomacy and, paradoxically, may have thereby prolonged the fighting Washington wished to end.

Following guidance from State and the NSC staff, the White House warned of grievous consequences for American-Israeli relations if Jerusalem ordered an invasion of Beirut. Israel asserted that it wanted to assist Habib in ending the bloodshed and argued that PLO fighters would not depart unless its leadership was convinced that it had no choice but to organize a general evacuation. Jerusalem believed the PLO was using negotiations as a tool to delay its departure--the organization had even acknowledged that it needed Habib only to ensure a supply of water and electricity. As Israel saw it, then, there was no way to induce the PLO to evacuate except via intense military pressure and a threat of further escalation until it complied. And the breakdown in the cease-fire had not ended the negotiations; on the contrary, renewed fighting actually had enhanced the prospects for a rapid resolution of the conflict.

Jerusalem claimed that by accomplishing its military goals in West Beirut, a new political situation would evolve that, in turn, would create novel horizons and opportunities for peace: Lebanon would become a part of the free world without Syrian or PLO domination. However, the White House leadership believed that the Soviet Union profited whenever Israel over-reacted. One high-level official suggested that police officers chasing a group of suspects should not fire wildly into a crowd to apprehend them but ought to use other means of capture that would not harm innocent civilians; otherwise, the suspects might win the sympathy of the crowd. Similarly, he said, Israel should not use military force against Lebanese civilian areas simply because PLO forces were hiding there. Ultimately, the White House's empathy for the plight of the Palestinians paved the way for a drive by that organization to win concessions. The race had begun in the war for Washington.

The PLO's War for Washington

Diplomatic Shock Troops for the PLO

As the conflict intensified, Israel increased the military force it applied to Palestinian targets in and around Beirut. The PLO's response was to exert diplomatic pressure on Jerusalem at the global level. The Israel Defense Forces battled in Lebanon with military might, and the PLO fought a war in world capitals with diplomatic briefs urging international political support. Jerusalem battled for Beirut, but the PLO fought for Washington via Riyadh, Cairo, and Paris. As American intelligence had anticipated, the PLO's primary goal was to transform the fighting from military battles it could not win to international political warfare where victory was conceivable.

The shock troops in the PLO strategy to storm Washington were Saudi, Egyptian, and French diplomats. Fresh from a November 1981 air defense package victory over the pro-Israel lobby on Capitol Hill, Riyadh was in a strong position to carry the Palestinian banner through the diplomatic corridors of Washington. The main Saudi goal was to induce the United States to squeeze Israel so that Jerusalem would: (1) not launch an attack on West Beirut, (2) lift the siege of the city, (3) consent to a cease-fire, (4) withdraw its forces, and (5) leave a PLO-armed presence in Lebanon.

According to former officials, Riyadh specified the conditions under which the PLO would withdraw as of mid-July. First, the multinational force should arrive before the PLO would depart so that Palestinian fighters could leave under the cover of the outsiders. Second, the United States should commit itself publicly to guaranteeing the safety of the existing Palestinian fighters, as well as the remaining families. Third, the combatants should exit only via routes agreed upon by the PLO, and its units should be accompanied by the multinational force to places designated by the Palestinian leadership. The heavy emphasis on the international force, with special reference to French units, was a PLO tactic either to avert an Israeli attack while departing or even to avoid the need to withdraw at all.

A related approach in the war for Washington was for the PLO to seek a direct dialogue with the United States. As early as the first week of July, State had hinted to Israel about the possibility of U.S.-PLO contacts. If Israel failed to cooperate with Habib, the United States would consider other ways to preserve its credibility. This warning could be interpreted to imply that the administration would open up a more direct communication line to the PLO than the UN, Saudi, and French connections. To reinforce this message to Jerusalem, State leaked Deputy Secretary Stoessel's talking points for his meeting with Israeli Ambassador Moshe Arens, when Stoessel had implied that direct contacts between the United States and the PLO were, indeed, possible.[12]

During the third week of July, additional talks occurred, via the Saudis, aimed at exploring the possibility of contact between the PLO and the United States. These talks were sensitive because Washington had pledged to Jerusalem, as a part of the September 1975 Sinai II withdrawal negotiations, not to deal directly with the PLO until that group both recognized Israel's right to exist and accepted UN Resolutions 242 and 338. (These resolutions recognize that right and explicitly commit the parties to a negotiated settlement.)

A PLO emissary, Khaled al-Hassan, traveling on a Kuwaiti passport, was in Washington during the third week of July as a member of an Arab League delegation. Except for Hassan, the other members had meetings with American officials, including a session with the president on July 20. Hassan wanted to hammer out the wording of a statement acceptable to the administration via the Saudis and Syrian foreign ministers. As a founding member of the PLO centrist group--Fatah--he was regarded as a pro-Saudi voice who also reflected the views of Arafat. In an interview, Hassan declared that the PLO would leave Beirut and urged that, after this withdrawal, the United States and the PLO should begin discussions as a first step on the road to peace.[13] Hassan praised

President Reagan's demands to Israel that the fighting in Beirut must end, expressed satisfaction about the beginning of a change in American policy toward the PLO, and acknowledged that group's support for Franco-Egyptian efforts to add specific language about Palestinian self-determination to UN Resolution 242.

The Talk About the Talks in Washington

On July 23, 1982, the same day that Hassan was in Washington hoping to cut a deal on the "recognition" of Israel and receive a political bonus in the form of direct talks with the United States, additional evidence of an American overture to the Palestinians surfaced. Unnamed administration officials leaked word to the press that the United States probably would authorize direct contacts with the PLO if American peacekeeping forces were sent to Beirut and an emergency arose affecting the troops' security.[14] The officials claimed that such a hypothetical situation would be consistent with precedent established during the 1975-1976 Lebanon civil war. At that time, an American security officer in Beirut received authority from Washington to make contact with the PLO to help insure the protection of Americans during the civil strife. Therefore, as part of its bargaining position for agreeing to leave Beirut, the PLO was eager to establish links with the United States as a political bonus to offset its military defeat by Israel.

On July 22, 1982, in response to news reports of backstage moves involving the PLO, both the White House and State issued strong but not believable denials. The *Washington Post* reported that a PLO emissary was in Washington, where he had been dealing indirectly with the administration.[15] Here is a case where Washington adroitly but ultimately without effect used the threat of direct contacts with the PLO as a tool to influence Jerusalem and curry the favor of moderate Arab states. Hints related to private diplomacy between Washington and Jerusalem were more likely to be effective as levers than public warnings because public exposure could have produced a pro-Israel, anti-PLO backlash among the American people. Once the talks appeared on centerstage due to ill-advised leaks from unnamed American officials, therefore, State concluded that U.S. diplomatic energies should be concentrated on getting the PLO out of West Beirut. Thus, the "talk about talks" phase of negotiations ended with little fanfare.

In the final analysis, the threat of direct American contacts with the PLO neither compelled Jerusalem to cease its military action in

Beirut nor gained the favor of moderate Arab states. Moreover, by raising the specter of direct talks and then abruptly backtracking, the administration appeared to be vacillating to both Israel and the Arab parties. The bottom line is that the United States could effectively use the threat of talks with the PLO to pressure Israel only if such threats had been confined to those two governments.

Proximity Talks in Beirut

Although the indirect talks approach ended in Washington, the administration continued to toy with a variant of this idea in Beirut. Former officials confirmed that, at the end of July, the White House authorized Habib to hold proximity talks on a contingency basis and only when needed: PLO representatives could be on one floor of an apartment building, Lebanese negotiators on another, and Habib on yet a third. The administration explicitly proscribed contact between Habib and the PLO representatives. Israeli reaction to this approach--quickly dubbed the "flooral" proposal--was unequivocal rejection. Jerusalem reminded Washington that Israel had opposed proximity talks for fifteen years and hinted that if the United States adopted this idea, it could spell the end of the Habib mission. Jerusalem noted the paradox that as the Israel Defense Forces broke the backbone of the PLO, the United States took steps to break its 1975 commitment to Israel.

Some Washington officials flirted with the proximity idea as a way of pressuring Israel, but Habib did not. He simply wanted the relevant parties nearby to encourage rapid progress. Especially in light of the breakdowns in telephone service and other communication lines during the siege, it was important for the parties to be close together. Once the bargaining process entered what diplomats called the "endgame," Habib wanted a structure that would facilitate fast action. He requested and received authority from Washington to negotiate PLO withdrawal from West Beirut via the government of Lebanon, and, if he believed circumstances warranted doing so, Habib was authorized to conduct the negotiations in proximity to that organization. The idea may have come originally from the Lebanese, who apparently suggested proximity talks at the end of July. These Lebanese leaders simply believed that there was an opportunity to speed up the negotiating process if the parties were in the vicinity. As with many diplomatic disputes, the proximity talks episode ended with a compromise. Rather than negotiating with the PLO via the Lebanese in the same house, an adjacent building would be used. Israelis, of course, defined "adjacency" to mean hundreds of meters away.

Where the Habib mission may have erred was in failing to sound out Jerusalem informally while it sought formal authority from Washington to bring the parties together in one building. Given Israel's sensitivity to the idea of proximity talks in prior situations regarding the PLO, it should have been apparent to State that such negotiations would further alarm Jerusalem at a time in which it was already apprehensive over Washington's backstage moves toward the PLO. State simply failed to synchronize two major initiatives: (1) its strategic warnings to Jerusalem concerning the possibility of enhanced status for the PLO if Israel failed to cooperate and (2) Habib's request to have the relevant parties nearby. Rather than merely granting Habib the authority he requested, State should have raised with Israel the delicate problem Habib faced. How was it possible to bring the parties near enough to make rapid progress possible but not so close as to raise the status of the PLO as a negotiating partner to a level equal to Israel? If Jerusalem had the opportunity to answer such a query, the outcome may have been more favorable.

Prior to the flap about proximity talks, Habib had been given broad guidelines that were worked out with Haig and approved by the White House. Leslie Gelb, former director of Politico-Military Affairs at State in the Carter administration and also a national security correspondent, stated that Habib's instructions included avoiding anything that could be interpreted as a signal of an American willingness to establish direct contact with the Palestine Liberation Organization.[16] The broader authority Shultz granted Habib contrasted sharply with the narrower guidelines under which he had operated during Haig's tenure. But irrespective of Shultz's preference to grant a wider mandate for Habib to decide whom to use as an intermediary and how, Washington policy gravitated back to the standards set by Haig and Habib when Jerusalem shot down the "flooral" idea. Like the abortive notion of indirect discussions in Washington, the Beirut proximity talks faded away.

A Political Plus for a Military Minus

In addition to opposing proximity talks because they represented an incremental buildup in the status of the PLO, Jerusalem was concerned about the juxtaposition of discussions on direct contacts with possible changes in the U.S. approach to the Palestinian issue in general. The idea for a shift in the American position may be traced to several sources. One was a Jordanian proposal made during the first week of July 1982, seeking a political bonus for the PLO in exchange for its agreement to withdraw from West Beirut. Amman had called for a new initiative based upon a revision of UN Resolution 242. Because this basic document failed to mention the Palestinians by name, referring to them only as refugees, the PLO had long sought this revision. Although not unexpected, it was ironic that the organization would use the occasion of its military defeat to press for a diplomatic payment from Washington in return for the PLO exit from Beirut.

As a light-hearted aside regarding possible PLO destinations after departing from West Beirut, a Lebanese official was quoted as saying if Palestinian fighters go to Syria, it is like going to jail; to Algeria, it is a type of oblivion; Egypt, it is disarming and a government in exile; to Jordan, King Hussein's united kingdom plan that would subordinate the PLO; and to South Yemen in the Gulf, it requires swimming.[17] Amman was one advocate of the idea of extracting a bonus for the PLO in exchange for its withdrawal from Beirut; so, too, were Cairo and Paris, both of which called for a political plus to compensate for any military minus the PLO might suffer.

Egyptian Linkage Diplomacy

In Cairo, press sources reported on Egyptian President Mubarak's message to President Reagan, which said that before or during the departure of armed Palestinian combatants from Lebanon, a solution to the Palestinian problem must be found.[18] Cairo believed that the PLO would not leave Beirut without a political bonus, such as a U.S.-PLO dialogue or a revision of UN Resolution 242 as represented by the Franco-Egyptian draft. Former officials report that Habib, however, opposed any linkage of a PLO departure with steps toward an overall settlement of the Palestinian issue. He held that if the PLO failed to leave in the absence of a political quid pro quo, Israel would move militarily against West Beirut. The special envoy supposedly reasoned that any American initiative to provide a political plus for the departure could prompt Jerusalem to launch an attack. The idea that a PLO bonus could cause Israel to strike probably startled Cairo for it had doubted the credibility of Israel's threat to move on West Beirut in the first place. The Egyptian position was divided into two areas of concern--the PLO in Lebanon and the link between the Palestinian plight in Lebanon and the Arab-Israeli conflict.

Regarding Lebanon, Egypt called for a prompt end to the Israeli encirclement of West Beirut; an immediate pullback of Israeli forces by ten kilometers as a first step toward complete withdrawal; a rearrangement of the Palestinian armed presence, according to principles to be endorsed by a committee comprised of Lebanese and Palestinians; an implementation of a Lebanese cabinet decision of July 14 on the withdrawal of Israeli, Syrian, and Palestinian forces; and the deployment of an international peacekeeping force.[19]

And in connection with the linkage between Lebanon and the Arab-Israeli conflict in general, Egypt advocated a mutual recognition between Israel and the Palestinian people; an affirmation of their right of self-determination; the establishment of U.S.-PLO dialogue; and the cessation of Israeli practices that diminished the rights of inhabitants of the West Bank and Gaza Strip.

At the end of July, Cairo weighed in on behalf of the PLO in the war for Washington, according to former officials. It highlighted the need to resolve the Lebanese conflict in relation to the general Palestinian problem and stressed the twin dangers of growing Islamic fundamentalism and Arab leftist radicalism. To avert these parallel threats, Egypt believed it needed to reposition itself as leader of the Arab world, and showing centrists within the PLO that Cairo could persuade Washington to give them a political bonus would facilitate Egypt's reentry. The return of Egypt into the Arab mainstream would also vindicate President Sadat's opening to Israel and encourage other moderate Arab states to follow Egypt's path toward peace. In other words, to motivate the PLO to join the peace process, Cairo emphasized the need to couple that organization's plight in West Beirut and American gestures to Palestinians in general. Indeed, Egypt explicitly connected its own willingness to accept PLO combatants with a U.S. initiative toward solution of the Palestinian problem.

Cairo preferred a simultaneous linkage of West Beirut, Lebanon as a whole, and the Palestinian issue. Washington preferred sequential coupling, if any at all. Once the immediate West Beirut issue was resolved and Lebanon achieved some stability, then U.S. diplomacy could tackle general issues underlying the Arab-Israeli conflict. In July 1982, Egypt's position was that it would not accept any Palestinian evacuees from West Beirut unless this was part of a comprehensive approach to a peace settlement. In this respect, one source reports that President Mubarak's message to President Reagan stressed that before or during the armed Palestinians' departure from Lebanon, a solution to the Palestinian problem, as a whole, had to be found.[20] As a beginning, Cairo required a clear commitment from all parties, especially Washington, that there would be a dialogue with the Palestinians. In short, Cairo followed a consistent policy of linkage and forcefully stated its views to all the relevant parties.[21]

Hassan Bin Talal, crown prince of Jordan, wrote a statement that, in effect, characterized Egypt's predicament.[22] He criticized the American-encouraged Egypt-Israel peace treaty of 1979 for creating an imbalance in strategic power that had enabled Israel to inflict death and destruction on Lebanon without any deterrent threat by Egypt.   In other words, he believed that Cairo's participation in the Camp David peace process had neutralized Egyptian military power and allowed Jerusalem to launch the invasion of Lebanon.

As a result of criticism from the crown prince and other Arab leaders, Egypt felt a great need to combine any solution to the Lebanese problem with a political reward for the Palestinians. Even if other Arab states had not pressed hard for such a coupling, Egypt felt compelled to be an advocate of the Palestinian cause. Ironically, Cairo's persistent advocacy of linkage diplomacy was undercut by the adoption of an Arab League plan on July 29, 1982, which did not include such a connection. The plan was endorsed by the other moderate Arabs, as well as by the PLO, and it left Cairo in the rather odd position of being more pro-Palestinian than the Palestine Liberation Organization itself. Although Egypt's demands were overtaken by events within the Arab world, Cairo and Paris were undeterred in their efforts to find a political gain for Palestinian military losses.

The Franco-Egyptian Draft Resolution

Like Egypt, France's primary goal at the end of July was to establish a place for the PLO in any subsequent negotiations for a political settlement. France had little faith in American diplomacy because it was focused so heavily on the technical problem of force disengagement, rather than on the Palestinian dimension of the Arab-Israeli conflict.   Indeed, according to the *Middle East Policy Survey* of July 30, 1982 (no. 61), some administration officials described France as undermining Habib's efforts in order to portray themselves as the PLO's "saviors." A first step in persuading Washington to address the broader question of Palestinian rights was for Paris to help the PLO obtain a political "quid" for agreeing to exit peacefully from West Beirut.

Concerning the Palestinian bonus, Cairo and Paris combined their efforts in a draft resolution of July 28, 1982. In the preamble, the draft balanced a reaffirmation to respect the sovereignty of all countries (implicit recognition of Israel's right to exist) with an obligation to respect the national legitimate rights of all the peoples in the Middle East (Palestinian rights of self-determination, that is, to have a state). In the operative section, Part A of the draft demanded a partial pullback of Israeli forces around Beirut as a first step toward their complete withdrawal from Lebanon. Interestingly, the July 28 Franco-Egyptian draft was less balanced in terms of force withdrawals than the Egyptian position of mid-July had been. At that time, Egypt had called for withdrawal of all foreign forces from Lebanon, but the draft resolution demanded a pullout of Israeli forces alone.

Part B of the draft discussed the installation of a new UN peacekeeping force to supervise the disengagement in and around Beirut. Part C supposedly reaffirmed Resolution 242; going well beyond 242, however, this section balanced a call for the security of all states with the need to provide justice for all peoples. The key part of the entire draft was Paragraph 1(b) of Section C that affirmed

> the legitimate national rights of the Palestinian people, including the right to self-determination....[To] this end the Palestinian people shall be represented in the negotiations and, consequently, the Palestine Liberation Organization shall be associated [with the negotiations].[23]

The American Non-Paper

To kill the Franco-Egyptian draft by delaying its submission to the Security Council, the United States prepared a "non-paper" draft resolution for discussions with France and Egypt. Such a document in diplomatic parlance is one that can be used to launch trial balloons or even to express the views of a nation without that state being held accountable for them. In negotiations, diplomats often provide and request the talking points or informal notes their counterparts use in verbal demarches, to ensure that the reporting back to capitals is accurate. Among diplomatic communications, there is the *aide-memoire*, an informal summary of a diplomatic interview or conversation that serves as an aid to memory and is less formal than a *note verbale*, an unsigned letter or record of a conversation. The American non-paper in question can be considered a *bout de papier*--an unaddressed and unsigned sheet of paper carrying brief notes which can be either read from or referred to and left with one's counterparts as an aid to memory.[24]

According to former officials, the preamble of the American non-paper retained the Franco-Egyptian draft's balancing features on respect for the sovereignty of states (for example, Israel) and the legitimate rights of peoples. Both documents explicitly affirmed the phrase "legitimate rights of the Palestinian peoples." But like the Egyptian proposal of mid-July, the U.S. draft demanded the withdrawal of Israeli, Palestinian, and Syrian forces, not just those of Israel.

Although the American goal was to string out the Security Council process with the non-paper, the administration technically may have violated a 1975 accord between Washington and Jerusalem. The United States had agreed that it would not undertake to change UN Resolution 242 without prior consultation with Jerusalem. This resolution, which sought to resolve conflicts between states, did not mention the Palestinians by name. Arafat, in fact, had opposed 242 precisely because it had not dealt with Palestinians as a people. But the United States had introduced the concept of "peoples" as a code word for the Palestinians. When the U.S. non-paper referred to the "legitimate rights of the Palestinian people," this language paraphrased and lifted out of context phrases from the Camp David agreements of 1978, which stated that:

> The solution from the negotiations must also recognize the legitimate rights of the Palestinian people and their just requirements. In this way, the Palestinians will participate in the determination of their own future.[25]

Under the Camp David accords, Palestinian rights were to be defined via negotiations; the U.S. non-paper, however, anticipated a Security Council forum. Such a venue implied the possibility of sanctions and would take the issue out of the negotiating approach underlying the Camp David process, where the parties had implicit vetoes over undesirable outcomes. Had the mention of legitimate rights been connected to the Camp David process, it would have been more valid than imbedding the reference in a Security Council framework. And because the council had never adopted a resolution affirming "the legitimate rights of Palestinians," it may have been a major concession to the Palestinians for the United States to include this phrase in its non-paper without consulting with Israel.

The U.S. position also could have been taken as acquiescence to the idea of giving the Security Council authority to deal with the modern Palestinian issue as opposed to the "Palestine question," that has long been on the council's agenda. This question has included such concerns as the partition of the former British Mandate of Palestine into an Arab and a Jewish state, as well as the disposition of refugees as a result of the creation of Israel.

The American argument was weak in denying that it had not violated the 1975 understanding by which it had agreed to consult with Israel on any revisions of Resolution 242. The administration's reasoning was that because there was no actual intent to revise 242, there was no violation. The American rationale was stronger, however, in denying that it conferred the attributes of states onto a people, deftly and explicitly distinguishing between characteristics of states (sovereignty, territorial integrity, and political independence) and rights of peoples (justice). In other words, favoring justice for peoples need not require statehood according to the traditional U.S. position. The bottom line was that the administration was willing to make a basic trade-off. It would accept the risks of appearing to violate the 1975 understanding and perhaps allowing the Security Council to enter the negotiations, for the expected benefit of delaying or even derailing the Franco-Egyptian locomotive that had been picking up steam as the Israeli siege tightened.

The War for the American Public

In the war for Washington, the PLO had some diplomatic leverage to inspire behind-the-lines moves on its behalf but virtually no domestic political support within the American people. A Gallup poll of June 11-14, 1982, taken after the first week of the war in Lebanon, indicates that American sympathies broke down as follows: 52 percent pro-Israel, 29 percent neutral, and 10 percent pro-Arab. With respect to the specific countries and organizations, Israel and Egypt received positive ratings of about 80 percent, Saudi Arabia almost 60 percent, Syria 26 percent, and the PLO only 15 percent. Support for Israel actually increased from the period following the 1973 War until the Lebanon War--from 1974 to 1982. Although almost as many Americans disapproved (35 percent) as approved (40 percent) of Israel's 1982 invasion of Lebanon, this action did not alter basic patterns of support for nations and organizations in the area. There was no avalanche of pro-Palestinian, anti-Israel sentiment occasioned by the war. Indeed, 57 percent of those interviewed agreed that Israel was right to take "defensive" action in Lebanon because the PLO regularly had shelled northern Israel. Finally, 68 percent agreed with the proposition that "you have to admire the military skill Israel showed in defeating its opposition in Lebanon."[26]

And even before the invasion of Lebanon, Israel had bombed the PLO's Beirut positions and headquarters in July 1981. But the relatively mild bombing at that time caused an even greater negative reaction among the American public than the massive attack a year later. Fifty percent of Americans surveyed believed the Beirut bombing was unjustified, and only 31 percent felt that it was warranted. That survey also found no change in the basic orientation of Americans toward nations and organizations in the region, with Israel still receiving over five times more support than the Palestine Liberation Organization. The president was well acquainted with these Gallup poll findings, and the administration quickly terminated its feelers toward the PLO once these probes leaked during the third week of July 1982.

Following the extended siege of Beirut in August 1982, support for Israel did sag, but it subsequently rebounded to former levels. During September, after the massacre of Palestinians by Lebanese rightist militia units aligned with Israel, only 32 percent of the respondents expressed pro-Israel sympathies, and 28 percent were pro-Arab. But the effect of the massacre was not long term. In a survey taken four months later (January 21-30, 1983), 49 percent were pro-Israel, and only 12 percent expressed a pro-Arab attitude. These results roughly matched those of polls taken during October 1980, July 1981, and June 1982.[27]

The pattern of resurgent American support for Israel throughout the Lebanon War discussed here is reaffirmed by a scholar of public opinion and foreign policy, Eytan Gilboa: "For a brief period of time, the [American] public criticized Israel and expressed considerable sympathy for the Arabs and Palestinians, but after several weeks, public opinion returned to its traditional patterns."[28] Gilboa's findings and analysis reinforce a conclusion of this study--as a result of the lack of support in the American public, the PLO's war for Washington suffered. Its diplomatic leverage at 1600 Pennsylvania Avenue and in the Foggy Bottom section of Washington was not matched by political clout on Main Street America.

The Battle for Israeli Public Opinion

Because the PLO lacked domestic political support in the American public, the administration had difficulty playing the Palestinian card and pressuring Israel to back down from its threat to invade West Beirut. Jerusalem not only held an approximately 5-to-1 advantage over the PLO among the American populace, it also had the overwhelming support of its own people in its effort to destroy the armed Palestinian presence in Lebanon. Such backing further deflated Washington's attempt to put the squeeze on Jerusalem. Had the Israeli public been divided by the war in Lebanon, Jerusalem could have been vulnerable to Washington's influence. To gauge public opinion within Israel, the Modi'in Ezrahi Applied Research Centre conducted a survey on June 21-30, 1982, among 1,233 adults, and the DAHAF Research Institute conducted a poll during the first week in July among 1,164 adults. Both surveys underrepresented the 18-39 age group because of the war, but, nevertheless, they were probably valid indications of the Israeli attitudes about the war effort.

These polls found that three weeks after Israel's invasion, its public overwhelmingly supported the action. In spite of widespread criticism of the magnitude of the war, the Israeli public denied that it was disproportionate or had tarnished the image of Israel on the world stage. Moreover, two out of three Israelis were optimistic about the likely results of the Lebanese action, believing that: (1) the Palestinian threat would be removed from Lebanon, (2) an independent Lebanese government would be formed that would oust the Syrians, and (3) that new government would sign a peace treaty with Israel. In the midst of war, a clear majority opposed withdrawing from Lebanon until a suitable political solution had been found.

In sum, not only did Jerusalem have large-scale backing among the American people, its policies also were overwhelmingly popular among Israelis. Therefore, Jerusalem was relatively immune from Washington's political pressures. In contrast, the PLO enjoyed little support among the American people; rather, its backing came from international political constituencies that were unable to deliver Washington on behalf of that organization. The PLO even lacked support from the local Arab population of Beirut, and Syria's "backing" was questionable, to say the least. Thus, this organization was relatively vulnerable to Israel's military coercion and unable to apply effective diplomatic counterpressure on Washington. Israel's military force in Lebanon, combined with domestic political support in the States, produced a mixture that was more potent than PLO diplomatic leverage in the war for Washington.

Conclusions

The Israeli siege of Beirut, the American squeeze on Jerusalem, and the PLO war for Washington were interwoven elements in a crescendo of military and diplomatic activities during late July and early August of 1982. Underlying the siege, the squeeze, and the war was the issue of relative leverage. Could Jerusalem's military pressure pry the PLO from its foothold in West Beirut before the PLO's diplomatic clout pried Washington away from Jerusalem? In fact, the answer was yes. Similarly, would Jerusalem's diplomatic isolation allow Washington to pressure Israel to lift its siege before the PLO yielded to Israel's terms? The answer here was no.

8

The Endgame

Every War Must End

Fights, Games, and Debates

Although it is true that every war must end, it is often unclear to the combatants if they have entered what chess players call the "endgame"--a concluding phase when both players retain a comparable number of pieces. As applied here, the endgame refers to the time in the Lebanon conflict when the end of war was in sight and the antagonists perceived that they were relatively balanced in overall influence. The approach of the endgame signals the transition from a fight to a bargaining game of competition and cooperation to a debate about the future.[1]

Uncertainty arises because the side that begins a war cannot end it alone. As strategist Fred Ikle writes, "Those with power to start a war frequently come to discover that they lack the power to stop it."[2] Israel had begun the war in Lebanon, but it had to share with the PLO the power to end it. A tacit bargain between these two was necessary before the endgame could commence. Once American diplomats detected such an implicit accord in August 1982, they began to describe the period that followed as the endgame.

Although the Israel Defense Forces had an overwhelming military advantage, PLO fighters integrated themselves within the Lebanese civilian population in such a fashion that it would require house-to-house battles to dislodge them. The outcome of such an action not only would have been a high Lebanese civilian death toll but additional Israeli casualties as well. In effect, the PLO had neutralized Jerusalem's conventional military advantage by using West Beirut civilians as a shield to blunt the Israeli sword. The PLO also attempted to check Israel's military superiority with diplomatic pressure in the capitals of the great powers, particularly in Washington. So, as the endgame approached, the two

177

contestants had an equivalent set of pieces to move on the global chess board.

As August 1982 began, the Palestinian mainstream had made considerable progress in transforming a losing fight in Beirut into a chess game where a draw was conceivable. The PLO began to curb Israel's military power and to initiate a new debate over the future of the Palestinians. The fact that they had no place to go was used as an argument for the need to establish a Palestinian homeland. Without making any major concessions, the centrists had manipulated the siege of West Beirut to constrain a final Israeli assault. They also were able to paint Israel as an immoral giant in diplomatic isolation.

Ironically, as long as the siege lasted, the PLO would reap substantial dividends. If Jerusalem were to launch an all-out assault, however, the PLO could have lost those benefits and more. Centrists, led by Chairman Arafat, reasoned that the more protracted the blockade of West Beirut, the greater the political bonus they would receive for departing. The PLO Chairman hoped that a UN resolution, Saudi-Egyptian-French lobbying, a crisis in American-Israeli relations, or a combination of these elements would compel Washington to extend some measure of recognition to his organization.

At a minimum, Arafat hoped that such factors would prompt Washington to commit itself formally to support the concept of Palestinian self-determination, beyond the general euphemisms used to describe Palestinians in United Nations Resolution 242 and in the Camp David peace process. With good cause, the chairman believed that were he to leave Beirut without concrete political gains (that is, on his knees), his status and influence within the Palestinian movement would be jeopardized and his centrist diplomatic approach to Israel undermined. Thus, Arafat tried to initiate a grand, though indirect, debate on mutual recognition between the PLO and Israel. In this way, he hoped, diplomatic momentum would lead to an American-Palestinian dialogue and to an irreversible movement toward the creation of a Palestinian state.

Jerusalem wished to avoid a debate, especially one involving Washington, over both the siege of Beirut and the peace process. Israel attempted to maintain the credibility of its military force at the forefront of bargaining and wanted the PLO to be so preoccupied with Jerusalem's military threat that it would have neither the time nor the inclination to take part in any grand debate. Israeli goals included the destruction of the Palestinian armed presence in Lebanon, the dispersal of PLO fighters throughout the Arab world and a consequent weakening of the Palestinian claim to nationhood, and the transformation of Lebanon from a potential confrontation state into one that was in tacit alignment with Israel. As Israeli foreign policy specialist Avner Yaniv suggests, the elimination of the PLO from Lebanon would reduce the pressure on Israel either to engage in historic peace negotiations with that organization or face the prospect of impaired relations with the United States.[3] Moreover, a new Lebanon, free of the PLO, could emerge under the control of the rightist militia leadership of Bashir Gemayel, who already was in league with his counterparts in Israel.

Although Jerusalem's objectives and strategies were relatively coherent during the endgame, those of Washington were confused by bureaucratic politics. Some American officials, such as the shuttle diplomat Habib, sought to use the threat of further Israeli force to compel a rapid PLO exit without any political compensation in the Arab-Israeli peace process. Other officials in Washington tried to deflate the credibility of Israel's threat currency. Their goal was to provide the equivalent of a flight ticket for the PLO exodus-- a political plus in the peace process to make up for a military minus in Lebanon. Not only were there differences between officials in Washington and Habib, there was an apparent split within the Habib mission itself. Reflect upon the mission's approach to the role of the United Nations.

UN Security Council

The Security Council adopted Resolution 516 (the vote was 15 to 0) on August 1, 1982, calling for military observers to monitor a cease-fire in Beirut. On August 4, the Security Council approved Resolution 517. The vote was 14 to 0 with the United States abstaining because it failed to criticize the Palestine Liberation Organization for breaking the cease-fire and stalling its withdrawal from Beirut and Lebanon. Once again, the UN condemned Israel, demanded a cease-fire and withdrawal of Israeli forces from Lebanon, authorized the secretary general to increase the number of UN observers in and around Beirut, and, in the event of noncompliance by any of the parties, promised to consider adopting effective measures in accordance with the provisions of the UN Charter. This phrase alludes to sanctions that would be imposed on Israel under Chapter 7 of the UN Charter. After meeting for five hours on August 5, the Israeli Cabinet decided not to heed the Security Council calls.[4] Jerusalem reasoned that the presence of observers would signal to the PLO that it was under no obligation to depart from Beirut.

When the August resolutions on observers were approved, it was the first time the council had agreed to install even a symbolic UN presence in the Lebanese capital. One journalist wrote that Israel had opposed any role for United Nations observers for two reasons. First, Jerusalem did not want to collide with even a symbolic UN presence; second, Israel wanted an American-led multinational force, not a United Nations group, to supervise the pullout of the PLO from Beirut.[5] Although the UN observers under Resolution 516 would not have had such a supervisory task, their presence in Beirut might have encouraged demands in New York for the UN troops in Lebanon to broaden their existing mandate and oversee the departure of PLO fighters.

Regarding the decisionmaking process that produced the U.S. vote in favor of observers, UN delegates were awakened at 3:30 A.M. on August 1 after reports of Israel's intensive armored, air, and sea attacks on West Beirut. Five hours later, the delegates negotiated the text of the cease-fire/observers resolution. The secretary general would have drawn cease-fire observers from the United Nations Truce Supervision Organization (UNTSO). This body consisted of 298 officers from 17 countries, including the United States and the Soviet Union, and it was headquartered in Jerusalem. It was set up in 1948 to oversee the end of the first Arab-Israeli war.

The U.S. permanent representative to the United Nations, Ambassador Jeane J. Kirkpatrick, prevailed over the other delegates to delete language critical of Israel; she also obtained assurances that the observers would be limited to the Beirut area, although the resolution referred to all military activities across the Lebanese-Israeli border. Between 4:00 and 8:00 A.M. on August 2, there was a flurry of messages among American diplomats in Washington, New York, and Beirut to determine the U.S. position on the draft that was to become Resolution 516. The United States voted with a unanimous council, despite the fact that Habib was not part of the consensus within the American government that produced the vote in favor of observers. While the delegates were being awakened, Habib called State at 3:15 A.M. The special envoy said that he was not comfortable with the insertion of U.N. observers; at that point, he doubted that they would enhance his efforts. Habib feared that the presence of the observers would, in fact, augment the intransigence of the PLO.

As Habib was in Beirut calling State to lobby against the introduction of UN observers, his deputy, Ambassador Morris Draper, was in Jerusalem arguing in favor of such observers. According to Israeli sources, Draper justified the UN presence by saying that it helped to facilitate the entry of Italian troops into the Multi-National Force (MNF) that was being formed to monitor the withdrawal of the PLO outside the UN context. Moreover, Draper said that UN observers would not intervene between the Israeli and PLO forces; rather, they could be placed at key observation points. Contradicting his assertion that the observers would not be a shield, however, Draper admonished the Israeli leadership to avoid falling on its own sword in opposing the UN observer force. That is, if Jerusalem's opposition left open the option of a military attack, such an assault could result in casualties and have other harmful effects on Israel. So, while Habib opposed UN observers, Draper simultaneously favored them. The differences between Habib and Draper were overtaken by events--Israel's military movements that resulted in a resumption of hostilities. As a result, by August 5, Habib also was recommending the deployment of UN observers to monitor the cease-fire. Israel had lost yet another friend in court.

U.S. National Security Council

Bureaucratic politics were not confined to relations between State and the Habib mission nor within the mission itself. Such politics also dominated a White House where the Special Situations Group met on August 4 at 7:15 A.M. Initially chaired by the vice president, this session became a de facto National Security Council meeting when the president arrived at 8:30 A.M., after having been informed of the escalating fighting at 6:15 A.M. by National Security Adviser Clark. Due to the importance of this meeting, several press accounts later appeared, based upon officially inspired leaks on its outcome. By combining several of these accounts with interviews of participants, it was possible to reconstruct portions of the discussions.

At first, principals at the August 4 meeting believed that an all-out assault on Beirut had begun. Later information indicated that the military activity was not as intense as had been thought. The meeting's agenda included a review of the chronology of events, Ambassador Habib's request for a strong letter that would threaten sanctions if Israel failed to provide him with enough time and quiet to conclude the negotiations, and a discussion of alternatives.

Such options consisted of: (1) a public statement that condemned Israeli actions and called for strict observance of the cease-fire, (2) a letter from the president that included strong language but no threat to Prime Minister Begin concerning the consequences on American-Israeli relations of a continued lack of cooperation by Jerusalem, and (3) a suspension of arms shipments to Israel and the imposition of other unilateral American sanctions, independent of UN actions. A fourth option that briefly entered the discussion was the possibility of pulling Habib out. This idea was shot down because it might have been misconstrued as giving a green light for an Israeli invasion. The withdrawal of Habib, however, became a live option one week later, during the final escalation of fighting.

According to some of the participants, the star of the August 4 meeting was Ambassador Kirkpatrick. In a brilliant presentation of globalist views, she ably filled the void left by Haig's departure. Speaking out as if she were the new secretary of state, the UN Ambassador presented a tough brief against the PLO, concluding that it was hardly an agrarian land reform organization. She also stood up to the call for unilateral sanctions against Israel if it attacked West Beirut. The advocates of sanctions at the meeting had failed to take into account the lack of domestic political support for such tough measures against an ally.

Indeed, the National Security Council session heard a report that Israel's approval rating on Capitol Hill continued to be high despite press accounts of alleged atrocities during the siege of West Beirut. Even some key Republicans, such as Majority Leader of the Senate Howard Baker, believed that Jerusalem should have ordered an attack on West Beirut even before the August 4 meeting at the White House. The fact that domestic politics were addressed at the council session suggests that they may have played a role in the decisionmaking process; however, it is difficult to determine the weight of politics relative to national security considerations in decisions made at that meeting.

Not only were American politics discussed at the White House, but Israeli politics were treated as well. Some officials sided with Kirkpatrick against sanctions, correctly reasoning that they would strengthen Prime Minister Begin domestically without forcing compliance. The group then decided to recommend to Reagan that he issue a public declaration and send yet another private message to Begin.

The president's public statement of August 4, 1982, described the movement of Israeli forces beyond their cease-fire lines around Beirut the night before. It was only two days earlier that he had told Foreign Minister Shamir of the necessity of reestablishing and maintaining a strict cease-fire in place. Although the president tried to balance his statement with a call on the PLO to stop delaying its withdrawal from Beirut, his declaration was not well received in Israel and did not result in Jerusalem's compliance. For Israel to ignore the United States is puzzling to those who believe that the dependence of a small state automatically translates into influence for the large benefactor, but such is rarely the case.

Alliance Politics and Leverage

Sanctions Against Allies

Relations between Israel and the United States can be compared to those among the countries of an alliance, such as the North Atlantic Treaty Organization. In both cases, the United States often attempts to gain the compliance of a reluctant ally. In this respect, reconsider the National Security Council meeting of August 4 that decided against recommending sanctions to the president. American officials in Tel Aviv had met with their Israeli counterparts just prior to that decision and hinted via a diplomatic demarche that sanctions might be imposed.

Reiterating earlier U.S. statements that had appeared in the press, Israeli sources reported that the American diplomats had stressed that a military assault on West Beirut would have grievous consequences for the bilateral relationship. These diplomats blamed the resumption of fighting on Israeli movements that had broken the existing cease-fire. Jerusalem's response was less than candid: It suggested that the Israel Defense Forces moved into two empty positions in reaction to PLO shelling, which in turn prompted a sharp exchange of infantry fire. Because it had not called in air, naval, or heavy artillery, Jerusalem claimed that it had exercised the restraint that Washington requested. American diplomats supposedly replied that there was a perception in Washington that the Israel Defense Forces had deliberately and hypocritically launched an attack; in no way could Jerusalem argue that in so doing it was using U.S.-controlled arms for defensive purposes.

To strengthen the effect of the demarche, the American envoys in Tel Aviv noted that a White House meeting would take place shortly, thereby implying that sanctions might be considered. The U.S. diplomats reportedly said that the government of Israel had a major credibility problem. The bottom line of this approach from a unified administration was that Washington wanted Jerusalem to cease all forms of military attack immediately: Everything--even movements without firing--should stop now. Somewhat shaken by the strong demarche, the Israelis indicated that they would go immediately to the prime minister.

Israel's Noncompliance

Begin's public response to the president's public statement of August 4 and the American diplomats' demarche in Tel Aviv was, "'Nobody should preach to us.'"[6] Begin's private response to Reagan's message of August 4 was no less subtle: "'Jews do not kneel but to God.'"[7] Nevertheless, the prime minister did issue orders to halt any further advance into West Beirut. But American diplomats in East Beirut reported that Israeli forces still continued to move into the port area. The credibility gap was widening, and the same American diplomats that met in Tel Aviv had yet another meeting with Israeli officials--this time including Defense Minister Sharon himself. Though he loudly denied the reports and subjected the Americans to a verbal tirade, Sharon quietly began to mass three divisions around Beirut.[8] By assembling these additional forces, he laid his cards on the table with the expectation that Arafat would drop out of the game. Sharon's more immediate aims were to increase the pressure on the PLO and prepare for an advance into West Beirut.

As the Lebanese leadership observed the massing of Israeli forces, some of them complained to Ambassador Habib, questioning why the United States would tolerate such misbehavior. According to Lebanese sources, the leadership held that Sharon was winning the race against a political settlement; American sources add that all of the Lebanese leaders believed the United States could stop Israel's flagrant, deliberate, and hypocritical breaking of the cease-fires.

Accordingly, Lebanon's Prime Minister Wazzan called Habib to plead that something be done to stop the bombardment. Meanwhile, Habib wondered how the Lebanese could retain their faith in the U.S. ability to stop the Israeli onslaught in view of

America's apparent impotence. By then, he reportedly thought that there was no way that Israel's use of American-origin equipment could be characterized as defensive. Rather, it was offensive in every sense of the word--militarily, politically, and morally. In his considered judgment, Habib felt that the time had come for the United States to put a stop to Israel's use of force, even employing whatever pressure was necessary to do so--code words for advocating sanctions.

Given the president's private conversations with Israeli Foreign Minister Shamir, U.S. public statements, and letters from the president and secretary of state to Prime Minister Begin, Special Envoy Habib believed that the United States could no longer accept Israel's disregard of American views. Because Habib, in effect, had come down on the side of a virtual cutoff of all economic and military assistance, Washington decided to threaten sanctions from the highest levels and in the strongest terms. Israeli noncompliance with American demands finally caused Habib to support sanctions himself.

The White House backed up the president's tough statement of August 4 with public hints that military assistance would be cut off. Washington took the position that the concept of a cease-fire was becoming discredited by disproportionate Israeli bombing and artillery attacks. And not only were these assaults extracting unacceptable human costs, they were making negotiations nearly impossible. Should these practices continue, Washington said, it would become increasingly difficult to defend the proposition that Israel's use of American-supplied arms was for defensive purposes. Therefore, the sides must come to the diplomatic table for a solution and not rely on military means. But almost as if some villain were trying to sabotage the progress Habib had made in obtaining the PLO agreement to withdraw, Israeli forces again moved forward into West Beirut and maintained a deadly and vastly disproportionate artillery barrage when the PLO reacted to the Israeli moves.

A Critique of the American Approach

That Washington was running out of patience was understandable, but its diplomacy of pressuring Israel in the midst of the siege was flawed. Two false assumptions underpined the U.S. approach: (1) an incorrect belief that American diplomatic moves to negotiate a settlement were incompatible with continued

Israeli military pressure, and (2) an invalid view of the efficacy of leverage, that is, a false expectation that a U.S. threat to cut off Israel during a war would be perceived as credible and compelling by both Jerusalem and the American public. National Security Council staffers who criticized the issuance of such threats in the crisis contended, to no avail, that Jerusalem would call Washington's bluff and raise the ante by increasing its military pressure to force a final diplomatic showdown with the PLO. This was, indeed, the outcome.

In an editorial and in an essay on the same day by William Safire, conservative columnist and former speechwriter for President Nixon, the *New York Times* reinforced the internal NSC staff reservations about American policy.[9] The editorial stated that:

> While Israel moves in tanks to squeeze West Beirut, President Reagan moves from impatient scowls to vague threats to squeeze Israel. He says the Israeli advances are unhelpful to efforts to get the P.L.O. out of Lebanon. Yet it is only the Israeli threat that makes the P.L.O. willing to consider withdrawal.

In line with the *Times* editorial, Safire came out in favor of an American diplomatic policy that used, instead of criticized, Israel's military force. He contended that it was a mistake for the administration to state publicly that negotiation was the only way to induce the PLO to depart from West Beirut: "The only incentive for the P.L.O. to release its hostage city is the certainty that the soft American hostage policy will be followed by the hard Israeli hostage policy. Anything that undermines that certainty--such as tough talk by Mr. Reagan warning Israel not to attack--destroys the chances of a peaceful withdrawal." The *Times* had come down solidly on the side of a blend of diplomacy and force, contrary to the administration's policy of using its diplomacy to undercut the potential efficacy of Israel's force employment and threat to escalate.

On the same day as the *Times* editorial and Safire critique, the *Wall Street Journal* published an editorial that advocated a mix of diplomacy and force as it blasted the administration for inadvertently giving the PLO the hope it needed to continue its holdout in West Beirut.[10] The *Journal* facetiously held that coupling public complaints against Israel with a call for the PLO to leave Beirut made sense only if one believed that American words would be more effective than Israeli shells in persuading the PLO to withdraw. Finally, the *Journal* concluded that the U.S. desire to stop the fighting may have won commendation at home and abroad, but the contradictory approach of balancing criticism of Israel and the PLO only caused confusion and prolonged the bloodshed.

An editorial in the *Washington Post* three days later took the administration to task for agreeing with Israel's goals yet publicly complaining about its use of military force.[11] The Post contended that the administration found itself in the hopeless contradiction of endorsing Jerusalem's aims while attempting to control its tactics in Lebanon. The editorial said that American protests encouraged the PLO to hang on and thus stirred Israel to press harder, which actually may have increased the number of casualties. Thus, three national newspapers had come out against the Reagan administration's approach to Lebanon that unwisely decoupled diplomatic negotiations from the use of force.

To add to the confusion over what Washington's policy was regarding diplomacy and force, there were reports of a White House meeting on August 5, 1982, with American Jewish leaders. After the session, the group's spokesman, Julius Berman, promptly announced that the United States agreed with Israel on the need for continued military pressure on the PLO as a condition for the diplomatic solution that both countries sought. On the next day, the *Washington Post* reported the delegation as saying that the president was not considering sanctions at this time.[12] The Reagan administration took a hard line on Israel in Tel Aviv and Jerusalem but a softer line to the pro-Israel lobby in Washington. In so doing, it aligned itself with diplomatic cherubs abroad by criticizing Israel publicly and with political angels at home by winking at Israel's "sins" before a powerful domestic political constituency.

One approach to resolving the issue of where the U.S. stood on continued Israeli military pressure was considered but not implemented. This preferred strategy called for U.S. leaders to refrain from public comments critical of Israel's behavior while making clear in diplomatic channels with Jerusalem that its conduct was unacceptable. Also, the administration should communicate to the PLO, via governments in direct contact with that group, that there was a high risk of an assault on West Beirut unless there was a prompt diplomatic resolution of the problem of Palestinian fighters--a risk that could have been factored into the American approach to handling the confrontation. The continued Israeli military presence and occasional outbreaks of violence were, in themselves, a clear form of pressure, but they were diminished by public American criticism.

This alternative approach actually coincided with press guidance that State prepared to minimize the public flap brewing about the meeting at the White House with the Jewish leaders.   State, however, undermined the thrust of its own guidance that combined diplomacy with force when the department simultaneously opposed military action that resulted in loss of innocent civilian lives and set back the prospects for successful negotiations.   To follow a balanced policy and avoid choosing between Israel and the PLO, the administration temporized, satisfied neither, and helped prolong the fighting.   Meanwhile, the threat of sanctions hung in the air.

The General Futility of Sanctions

Press accounts confirmed that Washington was considering sanctions against Jerusalem.   A journalist for the *New York Times*, Bernard Weinraub, quoted from portions of the president's strongly worded message to Jerusalem, but unnamed administration officials denied that the president had mentioned punitive measures directly in his call for a strict observance of the cease-fire.[13]   Although the president did not explicitly mention sanctions, there was no doubt that euphemisms for punishing Israel would be interpreted as such by Prime Minister Begin.

Although punitive measures were discussed, they were not implemented for several reasons.   First, prior experience had shown the uselessness of such punishment as a deterrent to future transgressions by Jerusalem.   For example, the suspension of deliveries of jet aircraft to Israel after its air raids on an Iraqi nuclear installation and on Palestinian positions in Beirut during the summer of 1981 had failed to deter Jerusalem's annexation of the Golan Heights from Damascus that December.   Moreover, American decisions taken earlier in the war to suspend shipments of cluster munitions and delay formal notification to Congress of a scheduled sale of seventy-five F-16 fighter bombers for delivery in 1985 had not deterred Jerusalem from intensifying its military pressure during the first week of August 1982.

A second reason for not imposing additional sanctions was that they may have had the unintended effect of encouraging escalation. Hedrick Smith of the *New York Times* quoted unnamed senior officials as fearing that a new halt of arms shipments might backfire, touching off precisely the kind of an all-out assault on

West Beirut that the administration hoped to prevent.[14] In effect, Washington's moves to embargo arms shipments or otherwise pressure Jerusalem could boomerang and reinforce the hawks there who were convinced that the future credibility of Israel's threats required an all-out assault on West Beirut. Thus, threatening Israel with a loss of aid in the midst of a crisis could have had the ironic effect of stimulating the very intensification of fighting Washington wanted to deter.

A third reason for hesitating to oppose strong and explicit sanctions is that they are not an effective lever in general nor for crisis management in particular. Furthermore, given the closeness of the U.S.-Israel alignment, sanctions generally are applied in a half-hearted fashion. Yet as a former NSC aide to Presidents Nixon and Carter, William Quandt, states: "'American pressure [on Israel] has worked on occasion....But to be credible it has to be consistent.'"[15] In that respect, President Eisenhower effectively pressured Israel to withdraw from the Sinai in 1957, and President Carter did the same to get Israel out of Lebanon in 1978.

Despite these precedents, the dominant school of thought among Washington officials during the 1981-1982 period opposed tough and specific sanctions in favor of America's most powerful point of leverage with an ally--a call into question of the "general bilateral relationship." This phrase is actually a euphemism for sanctions, but it is not as likely to provoke a negative Israeli reaction as specific threats. Smith, in this regard, quotes from Reagan's personal message to Begin that unnecessary bloodshed might put the "relationship" between the two countries in jeopardy. (See the next section for an elaboration of the "bilateral relationship" between America and Israel.)

In the Israeli press, editorials generally suggested that the president's harsh messages encouraged the PLO to stall in Beirut. That organization would claim a political victory by having provoked a crisis in American-Israeli relations; therefore, the PLO would not evacuate the city. The Israeli press read in the president's tone the implication that Jerusalem could no longer depend on what it had seen as tacit American approval of Israel Defense Forces actions in Lebanon. Despite the increasingly intense red light coming from 1600 Pennsylvania Avenue, however, there was a growing public consensus in Israel that an assault on West Beirut was necessary to oust the armed Palestinians. This popular sentiment reinforced Defense Minister Sharon's efforts to win the prime minister's full support for such an operation.

And when the ultranationalist Tehiya Party joined the government coalition, the influence of hawks in both the cabinet and in the Knesset--Israel's parliament--increased. Sharon supposedly had concluded that, because U.S.-Israeli relations were already strained, it was time to finish the destruction of the Palestine Liberation Organization. Thus, Israel's movements on August 3-4 were interpreted by American intelligence agencies as steps designed to bifurcate West Beirut. Beyond that, these moves brought the Israel Defense Forces and the PLO into such close proximity that an escalation of hostilities was virtually unavoidable.

Jerusalem's Dilemma: Attack or Wait?

Israel's choices boiled down to whether to invade West Beirut or delay. In spite of the seeming inevitability that the fighting would intensify, Prime Minister Begin had considerable domestic leeway in deciding to accept a de facto freeze in the Beirut situation and letting the confrontation simmer. American officials believed that Israel's only alternative to launching an assault on Beirut was to allow negotiations to drag on and permit sporadic outbreaks of violence that would signal Jerusalem's intent to wait it out. Letting the siege simmer would be consistent with the prime minister's penchant for temporizing, would delay significant Israeli losses, and would defer for a while a crunch in Jerusalem's relations with Washington.

And not surprisingly, the fighting had strengthened Begin's domestic political hand, at least in the short term. It consolidated his hold on the politically significant Jews who were born in Arab countries--the Sephardim. These Oriental Jews were steadfastly loyal to the Likud Party in general and to the prime minister in particular. This loyalty stemmed from the hard-line stance shared by the Sephardim and Likud against radical Arab countries and the Palestine Liberation Organization.

Thus, Begin's political hand received an unexpected set of cards which he could play at will, and his economic hand was in relatively good order as well. Washington knew that the government of Israel could insulate its economy from the war even as late as August, mainly because of its highly selective and limited mobilization. Once the threat of general war with Syria receded in late June, a limited mobilization was sufficient to handle the invasion of Lebanon against the Palestine Liberation Organization. The cabinet quickly scaled down the number of reserve units assigned to operations in

Lebanon, and the brunt of the fighting was handled by regular units on active duty before the war had begun in June. At the end of July, the cabinet enacted a law raising the rate of value-added tax to 15 percent and collecting a 2 percent tax on the sale of securities on the stock exchange, in order to help finance the growing cost of the war.[16]

As of the first week of August, Israel's Finance Minister Aridor estimated the total cost of the war at about $1 billion. Government subsidies on basic commodities had to be reduced because of Israel's growing budget deficit. Such reductions raised the consumer price index 50 percent, and plans were made between January and August 1982 to help finance the war via additional cutbacks in subsidies. Apart from direct costs, however, the war had only a marginal impact on the economy as of August. Because the economy was not much of an immediate constraint on Jerusalem's war effort, Washington considered relations with the United States as one of the few factors that might restrain Israel.

The main reason why Begin might have chosen to let the confrontation continue without a major assault was to protect Israel's bilateral relationship with the United States. A noted scholar on Israel's foreign policy, Michael Brecher, characterizes the U.S.-Israeli relationship as a "dominant bilateral system." That is, the total pattern of interactions makes the United States the main external factor in Israel's foreign policy decisionmaking.[17] However, although the bilateral relationship is preeminent, it cannot always be converted into political influence as readily as Washington would like.

Especially in a crisis over security issues, the United States cannot count on successfully invoking "the relationship" in its bargaining with Israel. Despite such limits, Begin could be expected to go a long way to prevent a sharp deterioration of the relationship, provided that in doing so he would not permit the PLO to slip out of the siege. In other words, putting the assault option on the back burner and letting the situation simmer might give the prime minister a means to escape from the dilemma of either having to jeopardize relations with Washington or letting the PLO escape.

Last Moves of the Endgame

In the final stages of the endgame, the prime minister of Israel and the chairman of the PLO shared a common interest in delaying an assault by the Israel Defense Forces on West Beirut. For Begin, delay was an interim solution, posed by the problem of having to choose between assault and U.S. support. For Arafat, delay was a temporary measure to avert a Hobson's choice between destruction and flight. While the centers converged on both sides, so did the extremes. Israeli hard-liners, led by Defense Minister Sharon, readied their engines in anticipation of getting a green light to race into West Beirut. Palestinian hawks and their Iraqi patrons saw an Israeli assault as a means to destroy the PLO center, embarrass Syria, and allow a radical Palestinian leadership aligned with Iraq to take over the movement. The extremists wanted all-or-nothing outcomes, but centrists were willing to accept compromise solutions rather than destroy their opponents. So, interlocking dilemmas made it difficult to reach the final stages of the endgame.

The PLO Versus the Government of Lebanon

Progress toward the endgame was slow, in part, because PLO commitments lacked credibility: Its leadership had signed worthless agreements with the government of Lebanon during 1969, 1973, and 1977. These accords ostensibly were designed to restrict PLO activities, for example, by controlling the use of heavy weapons and preventing military personnel from using refugee camps as training facilities. In each case, the PLO broke the promises it had made in the signed agreements. The Cairo Agreement of 1969, signed by Arafat and the head of the Lebanese Armed Forces, called on the PLO to refrain from shelling Israeli targets from inside Lebanon, building or operating military bases in southern Lebanon, and conducting military training in Palestinian refugee camps. But, rather than adhere to this binding accord, the PLO conducted military training in refugee camps in the south and turned southern Lebanon into a launching pad for raids into northern Israel.

During May 1973, the government of Lebanon ordered its army to move against PLO military bases in the refugee camps. Palestine Liberation Army (PLA) forces entered Lebanon from Syria and fought briefly with the Lebanese army, prompting negotiations sponsored by the Arab League, as well as a cease-fire. The Malkert Agreement of 1973 emerged from these negotiations. It stipulated that the PLO would remove heavy weapons from refugee camps, stop all military activities in Lebanon, and cease using the camps for military training. Once again, the PLO declined to implement an agreement. This time, however, the

Lebanese rightist Phalange militia took on the responsibility of disciplining the armed Palestinians.

As noted in Chapter 1, the Palestinian armed presence in Lebanon helped to bring about the civil war of 1975-1976. After Syria's intervention against the PLO in 1976, Arab League summit conferences in Cairo and Riyadh formally terminated the war and established a committee to monitor the implementation of the 1969 Cairo Agreement. Although Arafat promised to cooperate with this committee, he failed to do so, and it ultimately faded into oblivion. Meanwhile, the PLO built up a military infrastructure in the south and periodically clashed with Israel's rightist Lebanese militia and other Lebanese as well.

And the failure of the PLO to implement the Cairo Agreement led to another accord after fighting escalated during July 1977. Syria again convened a conference at Shtaura for the purpose of controlling the Palestinian armed presence in Lebanon, and the leadership once more pledged to limit its activities there. Not surprisingly, the organization broke yet another commitment to the Arab states in general and to the government of Lebanon in particular with a series of military actions against Israel that set the stage for Jerusalem's invasions of 1978 and 1982.

A Multinational Shield for a Palestinian Sword?

With good reason, Jerusalem was quite reluctant to accept a PLO agreement with the government of Lebanon. The organization could promise to depart and then break the accord under the protection of multinational units operating between Israeli and PLO forces. Secretary Shultz sent a letter to Prime Minister Begin on August 7, urging his government to accept an American evacuation plan designed to guard against the "agree-then-stall" scenario. A reporter for the *New York Times*, Bernard Weinraub, summarized Shultz's letter to Begin. Written in response to a message from the prime minister delivered to the secretary on August 6, the Shultz communication recognized the government of Israel's concern that an international force entering Beirut prior to a PLO evacuation could serve as a screen behind which it could delay departure.[18]

The Habib withdrawal package, however, addressed the issue of the PLO's agree-then-stall pattern, supposedly with minimal risks for Israel. Moreover, the Shultz letter to Begin admitted that the PLO had used delaying tactics in prior situations but argued that it was now committed to evacuation. The United States, the government of Lebanon, and the PLO all wanted the international force to enter as the PLO withdrew. No contingent of such forces-- American, French, or Italian--would allow itself to be used as a shield by a PLO sword (the Palestinian combatants) to delay the inevitable. Contrary to the Shultz assurance, however, the pledge by Paris not to allow the PLO to use a French presence for stalling was disingenuous at best. Unbeknownst to the United States during that time, French diplomats were encouraging the Palestinian leadership to draw out the negotiations in order to obtain political compensation from the United States.

Timing for the Introduction of a Multinational Force

The last moves of the endgame depended on the resolution of two interrelated queries: (1) When should the multinational force arrive? and (2) Where would the PLO fighters and leadership go? Regarding the timing issue, the PLO attached the utmost significance to having these external units in place at precisely the same time as its withdrawal occurred, but Jerusalem wanted the outside force to enter after the departure was completed. The United States proposed that the multinational force be in place midway through the pullout, that is, five to seven days after the departure began. France, however, was prepared to come in on the day the PLO was ready to depart--D-Day. Indeed, the French conditioned their participation on a D-Day arrival. The PLO timetable as of August 4 called for a French contingent to arrive in Beirut on D-Day as a precursor of the main multinational force that the PLO had agreed could arrive on D+5, that is, five days after the pullout began.

The PLO and Israel were not the only ones concerned about the timing of the arrival of an international force. Thomas Friedman of the *New York Times* noted that the Sunni Moslems of West Beirut also wanted the outside force in place when the evacuation began.[19] The Moslem leadership feared that, if the departure occurred before the international force arrived, the Israeli army and its Lebanese rightist allies might try to occupy West Beirut and impose hegemony there, as in other traditionally Moslem areas of Lebanon. Marvine Howe, also of the *Times*, concurred with Friedman's analysis and added that Moslems, particularly Druse who had been fighting alongside Palestinians, were afraid that, if the PLO fighters withdrew before the multinational force arrived, Israelis and Lebanese rightists would carry out reprisals.[20]

Destination for Palestinian Departees

In addition to the problem of timing, the destination issue contributed to a deadlock in the negotiations. As of the first week of August, administration officials considered the Egyptian connection crucial to the disposition of the Palestinian combatants. The PLO leadership proposed on August 3 that the fighters evacuate to Jordan, Iraq, Egypt, and Syria; this proposal, however, was merely a diplomatic gambit designed to stall the negotiations because these countries had not firmly acknowledged that they would accept the combatants. As of August 10, Israeli intelligence believed that the PLO had become convinced of Jerusalem's determination to destroy it. But only after the intense fighting of the week before did the leadership decide to leave. Despite its intent to order the take-off from Beirut, the combatants had nowhere to land. Thus, it was doubtful if the Habib withdrawal plan would succeed without a firm commitment by Arab countries to receive PLO combatants. Though the commitments had not been nailed down by August 8, reports surfaced that Syria had agreed to take the PLO leadership and some 2,000 fighters and that Jordan would take those with the Kingdom's passports. Although Egypt indicated that it would accept a portion of the combatants, Cairo continued to insist on extracting a political price from the United States before actually accepting them. Cairo also sought a formal request from the PLO, which had broken its ties with the government of Egypt after its peace accord with Israel.

It was ironic that Egypt attempted to link the fate of Lebanese civilians and the PLO to some broad peace settlement during 1982. The Camp David accords of 1978 included a framework for addressing the Palestinian question but eschewed any meaningful linkage of a peace agreement between Egypt and Israel, on the one hand, and resolution of the Palestinian issue, on the other. One reason why Egypt linked PLO withdrawal from Beirut to a political payment to the Palestinians in the Arab-Israeli peace process was that Cairo was reluctant to see the dispersal of PLO fighters. This unwillingness, however, was not based upon any altruistic, pro-Palestinian feelings. Rather, Egypt considered the spread of discontented Palestinians as a potential source of instability. Therefore, evacuation and dispersal of the PLO fighters were worse options than an Israeli military solution from the perspective of some moderate Arab states.

Egypt's attempt to tie its acceptance of PLO combatants to a general settlement of the Palestinian issue was a clear sign that the destination problem remained unsolved. Thus, despite Washington's indication to Israel that the PLO had accepted the necessity of departure, the deadlock continued. Jerusalem rightly believed that there were no firm destination countries, except perhaps Jordan, for those Palestinian fighters holding the Kingdom's passports.

But it was neither Jordan nor Egypt but rather Syria that was the key player in the Lebanese card game. Syria's large military presence in Lebanon during 1982 was a wild card that could remain unplayed yet exert influence once Israel had withdrawn as it had after the 1978 incursion into Lebanon. In this sense, military power casts a political shadow well beyond the actual reach of the forces themselves. Since President Assad was well aware of the link between power and purpose, it was inconceivable that he would withdraw his own forces without receiving in exchange a political payment, in the form of a return of the Golan Heights or at least the negotiations for their return. The Syrian presence in the Bekaa Valley and in northern Lebanon during 1982 could have been used as a bargaining chip, at a minimum, to induce an Israeli pullout from Beirut and the Lebanese approaches to Damascus. In fact, it was unnecessary for Assad to withdraw any of his forces when the Israelis left in the mid-1980s due to the intense pressure of the Lebanese Shi'a and other local groups under the influence of Syria and Iran.

Damascus had expressed an interest in accepting the PLO's headquarters but not its combatants. President Assad wanted to control the organization and convert it into a radical tool of Syrian foreign policy without the security problems associated with large numbers of disgruntled armed Palestinians. Syria was clear in its reluctance to receive the fighters. Nevertheless, the administration hoped that it would accept up to 1,000 combatants in a collective Arab relocation plan. Habib was informed on July 23 that Palestinian members of the Syrian-backed Palestine Liberation Army and Saiqa units would be able to depart for Syria; it would take two or three more weeks, however, to ensure that Syria, in fact, would accept those Palestinians. Also during the third week of July, Saudi and Syrian foreign ministers in Washington proposed an "interim stop" solution--the so-called Tripoli Option, by which Palestinian fighters would leave Beirut for the isolated northern Lebanese port city of Tripoli. However, even Arab support for that option faded quickly into the sunset, as fear persisted that the PLO would come under the sway of Syrian-backed Lebanese in the Tripoli area.

In the State Department's planning, the idea dawned of using Syria as a temporary staging area for PLO fighters in transit to Jordan and Egypt. Combatants en route to Jordan would travel overland through Syria, those on the way to Egypt would go via air from Damascus, and fighters destined for Syria would travel by boat to Latakia on the Mediterranean coast or by way of the Beirut-Damascus Highway. President Reagan mentioned this possibility in a July 28 press conference, and a State Department spokesman publicly discussed this plan the next day. In addition, there were public comments on background by an unnamed official from the Department that Syria might be utilized as a temporary staging area for PLO fighters who eventually might go on for resettlement in such countries as Jordan, Egypt, Saudi Arabia, or Iraq. Damascus, however, from the highest levels down, had rejected such an arrangement. Even a rapid transit of combatants through the Damascus airport had not been settled in the negotiations. Thus, State had engaged in a bout of wishful thinking regarding Syria's conciliatory behavior. The prospect that Damascus would cooperate without negative incentives, such as the threat of force, vanished as quickly as a mirage in the desert. Indeed, the military preparations Syria began in late July suggested an even harder line toward Israeli actions in Lebanon.

The Syrian Surface-to-Surface Missile Threat to Israel

A serious confrontation developed between Damascus and Jerusalem concerning Israel's air operations over Lebanon. Syria stated that it had never agreed that Israel had an unimpeded right to operate military aircraft within Lebanon.[21] August 1982 found a major change in the status quo. Syria's surface-to-air missile (SAM) line of defense in the Bekaa Valley of Lebanon had been eliminated, and Israel and Syria were in a state of indirect confrontation in that area. Therefore, Israeli air operations took on a different character--they became more threatening to Syrian forces in the Bekaa than they had been before the invasion when these forces operated under a protective Syrian missile umbrella.

In late July, Syria engaged in activities that were interpreted by Israel as preparations for launching SCUDs, Soviet-supplied surface-to-surface (SS) missiles. With a range of some 300 kilometers and an accuracy of only about 700 meters, they could strike at virtually any large target within Israel. Because the accuracy of the SCUD decreases with range, it would be more suitable for random use against cities than military targets. In effect, then, the only mission for the SCUDs that made sense would be to deter an Israeli invasion that threatened the Syrian armed forces with total destruction. Damascus surely had to be aware that the offensive use of SCUDs would prompt a major response from Jerusalem. In this connection, the Israel Defense Forces Radio reported that a senior security figure had warned the Syrians that if they tried to use SCUDs, they would have to pay a very high price.[22] During the early phase of Israel's invasion, all of Syria's 18 SCUDs were moved from their permanent garrison and training area north of Damascus to hardened sites 20 kilometers south of the city--the same sites Damascus had used during the May 1981 SAM-site crisis.

Two hypotheses formed in Washington and Jerusalem to explain the 1982 movement of the surface-to-surface missiles. One offered a nonhostile, defensive explanation for the movement: SCUDs were transferred to secure sites during times of crisis as a standard operating procedure. The other hypothesis was that, because the missiles were moved to a less vulnerable location and closer to Israel, the SCUDs were being prepared for offensive use. The nonhostile explanation dominated Washington discussions, and the hostile one prevailed in Jerusalem. The actual combat deployment followed public warnings by Syria on the weekend of July 24 that it had weapons that had not yet been employed.

In prior situations where there was a risk that Syria might use SCUD missiles, Jerusalem had sometimes issued private warnings through third parties, as well as public announcements to reinforce deterrence by indicating possible military retaliation. In addition to the surface-to-surface threat to its cities, Jerusalem now faced a surface-to-air capability from within Syria and Lebanon that placed Israeli aircraft over Lebanon at risk. Henry Kamm of the *New York Times* reported that Israeli jets had once again destroyed Syrian surface-to-air missiles in Lebanon.[23] On July 30 at 2:00 P.M. local time, Israel Radio broadcast a warning that Damascus should refrain from launching its surface-to-air missiles against Israeli aircraft operating over Lebanon. In fact, Jerusalem did not need to use public channels to deliver such a warning. But by doing so, it may have been trying to enhance deterrence by demonstrating a public resolve that locked it into a position of having to fight a general war in the event that Syria used the SCUDs. Begin may have been building up domestic support not only to deter Damascus but also to strengthen his hand in Lebanon vis-a-vis the PLO and Washington. On the same day that it went public, Jerusalem asked a third country to transmit the same threat.

Before a clear warning could be transmitted on Israel's behalf, Syria seized the occasion to issue one of its own: The absence of a missile umbrella in Lebanon compelled Damascus to take all available "defensive" measures because of the increased threat posed by Israel. Thus, air attacks on Syrian territory, whether preemptive or retaliatory, would be a dangerous aggravation that could result in war. Contributing to the tensions, several hundred demonstrators in Damascus stoned the American, Jordanian, and Saudi embassies to protest Israel's invasion of Lebanon.

Syrian Compliance with Israeli Coercive Diplomacy

The *New York Times* reported that, despite rising enmity bordering on overt hostilities between Damascus and Jerusalem (or perhaps because of such tensions), Syria was now willing to accept all the Palestinian combatants from West Beirut that the leaders of the Palestine Liberation Organization wanted to send.[24] But doubts remained in Israel concerning PLO destination sites. After Ambassador Habib presented to Israel a joint American, French, and Italian plan for the withdrawal of the PLO from Beirut and the deployment of a multinational force, Israeli sources reported that Defense Minister Sharon refuted optimistic reports of the Habib negotiations. Sharon claimed that there could be no accord because the Arab states still had not agreed to accept PLO combatants.

In light of the diplomatic impasse on the destination of the fighters and the renewed sparring between Israel and Syria over missiles, Minister Sharon unleashed Israeli armed forces during August 9-12 in the war's final, spasmodic outburst of military activity. On August 9, Israeli planes struck at the PLO behind Syrian lines. Rather than responding with force, Damascus chose diplomacy and publicly stated that it would accept some of the PLO fighters and leaders. As if in response to Syria's conciliatory gesture, Israeli jets resorted to additional force the next day: Its jets bombed West Beirut for eleven consecutive hours, causing the government of Lebanon to suspend negotiations once again.

Israel's Noncompliance with American Diplomacy

According to an August 12 report from Jerusalem, President Reagan sent messages to Prime Minister Begin stating that Jerusalem must adhere to an immediate, strict cease-fire "in place" (that is, no firing or movement allowed). Moreover, the sting in the tail was that the entire relationship between the United States and Israel was at stake if military eruptions continued.[25] As reported in the *Middle East Policy Survey* of August 13, 1982 (no. 62), the president complained that his words to Prime Minister Begin had fallen on "deaf ears," and the president warned that the entire relationship between the two countries was at stake. At this crucial moment in the Habib mission, with the parties only a few days from settling the final points of his package plan, Israel's military activities again had stopped the negotiations. Finally, as Jerusalem Radio reported, if Israeli air force bombings of Beirut continued, the United States would stop negotiations on removing the Palestinian combatants from West Beirut and might order Habib back to Washington.[26]

An editorial in the *Washington Post* also reported that the president had threatened to end the Habib mission unless the bombing ceased.[27] The government of Israel took this threat far more seriously than earlier hints of a cutoff in military assistance because Habib had accomplished so much by mid-August that Jerusalem wished to preserve. Here, the lesson on alliance politics is that a superpower's leverage over an ally depends upon: (1) the credibility that the threat will be implemented, (2) the importance of the objective, (3) the context in which a threat or actual punishment is made, and (4) the perceived link between the threat or punishment and the misbehavior.

Jerusalem believed Washington's threat to withdraw Habib. Bringing home the special envoy would entail fewer political costs for the administration than implementing such sanctions as suspending military deliveries to Israel. The pro-Israel lobby's influence would have more impact in an arms sales issue where Congress has a direct role to play than in a diplomatic question, such as where Habib should be stationed at any point in time. And the success of the mission may have been even more important for Israel than for the United States by mid-August. At that time, Jerusalem had refrained from taking West Beirut partly because of its apprehension about conducting house-to-house battles.

The reluctance to take casualties coincides with a predilection to avoid further strains in Israel's alignment with the United States.[28]

Once Habib had accomplished so much with the help of Israeli military pressure, Jerusalem had no desire to forfeit these achievements. So, circumstances were more conducive to Israeli compliance with American preferences in the middle of August than they had been in June or July. Some Israelis even acknowledged a clear connection between withdrawing Habib to Washington and Jerusalem's transgressions in Beirut: With bombs falling on the parties, it was not only difficult to hold meetings but also unlikely that concessions would be made.

The Skyjacking of the Israeli Air Force

Despite the fact that American influence over Israel had increased, the two allies' policies did not converge immediately. Unbeknownst to the United States, the Israel Air Force had been "skyjacked" by Defense Minister Sharon. Technically empowered to do so at the time, he ordered what later became "unauthorized" attacks against West Beirut and air strikes on Palestinians behind Syrian deployment areas. Washington was cognizant of a general split within the cabinet but unaware of the magnitude of the gap between Sharon and his colleagues, and the United States became concerned about Jerusalem's overall intentions in light of its extraordinary military activities. It was not that Washington was short of information about bureaucratic politics in Jerusalem. Rather, the failure lay in the communications link, or lack thereof, between the defense minister and his own peers. The cabinet itself was caught unawares.

Washington believed that Jerusalem's goal in attacking the armed Palestinians behind Syrian lines on August 9 may have been to keep sufficient pressure on the PLO to cause it to leave Lebanon altogether. Conversely, there was unsubstantiated speculation that the attacks may have been designed to bolster Palestinian hard-liners, thereby rendering a negotiated settlement so unlikely that Israel could impose a final military solution. Israel's air strikes of August 9 also brought the Syrian factor to centerstage again after a week of relative quiet. Hitting PLO positions in Syrian areas of Lebanon sent a clear signal to Damascus that Palestinian violations of the eastern front cease-fire had to stop.

According to Israeli sources, one of Sharon's goals was to show Damascus that his forces were not a paper tiger bound by endless, U.S.-sponsored cease-fire agreements--that the option to pursue a military solution to the problem of West Beirut was alive and well.

A tactical purpose was to preempt Syrian forces from making a flanking maneuver against the Israel Defense Forces. In this regard, Sharon used the ruse of needing a convenient place to deploy tanks and equipment in order to make his own flanking moves against Syrian forces in the Bekaa. The United States, however, was not taken in by this parking-place ploy. Such movements confronted Damascus with a major military threat to its forces without an Israeli deployment per se north of the Beirut-Damascus Highway. In fact, the actions indicated that Jerusalem might hope to capture the Bekaa Valley's capital city of Zahle.

Israel's military movements in the north also bolstered Jerusalem's candidate--the rightist Phalange leader, Bashir Gemayel--in the Lebanese presidential elections that were scheduled to begin August 19. The military actions made it easier for parliamentary deputies who were likely to support Gemayel, including those from Zahle, to travel to Beirut and participate in the elections to be held in the National Assembly building. Reflect upon what was taking place on the ground: Israel's navy had landed armored personnel carriers across the beach north of Beirut near Junieh and made subsequent southward movements, and Sharon had ordered a fresh mechanized brigade to the north. The seaborne transport of armored personnel carriers was interpreted by the U.S. Defense Department as a response to the navy's institutional need to get involved in the only war they had. The overall consensus in Washington, however, was that Jerusalem was using military forces to make it difficult for the isolated parliamentary deputies from northern Lebanon, who opposed Bashir, to take part in the presidential elections.

Beirut-Damascus-Amman Roads as "Political Socializers"

Goaded by Sharon's actions, Damascus seemed to be moving in the direction of a political solution that included Syria as a destination point for Palestinian departees. But if the Beirut-Damascus Highway became the route that PLO centrists were to traverse, Palestinian extremists might take Damascus-Amman roads. In other words, the highways would reflect the political socialization of the Palestinian combatants from centrist (upon departing Beirut) to radical (after a stay in Syria.) Amman did not want an influx of radicalized Palestinians who could destabilize Jordan, and it became concerned that Syria was playing too prominent a role in Palestinian relocation planning.

Although there was no love lost between King Hussein and Chairman Arafat, the king believed the chairman's survival was necessary if Jordan were to be involved in the peace process, for example, by obtaining a green light from the PLO mainstream movement for the Kingdom to negotiate with Israel. If Arafat were politically mutilated in Beirut and then entombed in Damascus, Assad would be able to coerce Arab moderates through his control of the Palestinian movement. Hussein suspected, moreover, that Israel was attempting to block a prospective American-Palestinian political dialogue, and that Israel would be satisfied with the elimination of the centrist wing of the PLO or its radicalization under Syrian suzerainty. Press accounts suggested that King Hussein formally offered asylum for perhaps as many as 1,500 Palestinian fighters in West Beirut who held Jordanian passports. The prospect of their return to Amman produced mixed emotions in the Kingdom. Although sympathy for the PLO was widespread and had grown since the Israeli bombardment of Beirut, native Jordanians of Bedouin heritage worried about the destabilizing risks posed by an influx of Palestinian combatants.

Who's at the Helm in Jerusalem?

Israeli forces made military gains on the ground in Lebanon. Bashir made inroads in his quest for the presidency there. And Hussein's fears that Syria would dominate the PLO grew. Concurrently, Sharon began to lose political ground within Israel. In a special session convened at noon on August 12, the cabinet voted 15-to-2 to reject his proposal for additional military moves against West Beirut. This vote suggested that a consensus had developed within the government in favor of the political solution represented by Habib's proposals. The cabinet delegated to Prime Minister Begin formal responsibility for decisions on any further use of air strikes in Lebanon.

The issue of ministerial responsibility highlights the central theme of leadership. Although the question of "who's at the helm?" points to President Reagan's limited involvement in American decisionmaking, this query applies to Prime Minister Begin, as well. Consider Sharon's manipulation of Begin to allow Israeli forces to go all the way to Beirut and Sharon's use of air power for an intense bombing campaign of which Begin was unaware. These events imply a lack of leadership on Begin's part that mirrors Reagan's laid-back management style.[29]

To Sharon's surprise, he found himself attacked from all sides in a stormy session of the cabinet. Pursuing a strategy of winner-take-all, he had requested the very vote that he then lost by the 15-to-2 margin. Oddly enough, had he not demanded a vote and thereby precipitated an immediate debate, Sharon may not have lost his implicit mandate to prosecute the war at will. The architect of the war stood isolated, only supported by the newest member of the cabinet, Minister of Science Yuval Neuman, who represented the small right-wing Tehiya Party. The prime minister was furious with his defense minister because Begin was blindsided by Sharon's decision to apply massive artillery and air fire power in West Beirut on August 12. In a stunning critique, Begin told Sharon that he was representing the cabinet vis-a-vis the army, not the other way around.[30] To demonstrate his displeasure further, Begin noted that other defense ministers had resigned under fire and that the current incumbent could leave at any time.

Jerusalem Radio reported a harsh, though ironically amusing, exchange between the embattled defense minister and Interior Minister Yosef Burg.[31] Burg contended that Sharon had acted contrary to the line adopted by the government; Sharon countered that Burg relied too heavily on reports from his mother-in-law. The implication was that Burg's relatives may have been listening to news reports and rumors from the front, rather than relying on Sharon-approved military intelligence. The coup de grace occurred when hard-line Foreign Minister Shamir asked his political ally Sharon to explain why he had not consulted with the prime minister before carrying out a particularly destructive mission in Beirut. By this point, virtually the entire government believed that its forces thereafter should react only if they were fired upon, that the cabinet should not have to learn about military actions from the news media, and that it was almost time to allow diplomacy to wrap up an agreement.

Although the August 12 special session of the cabinet leaned toward a political solution, it was not until its meeting three days later that the government finally made enough concessions for Ambassador Habib's evacuation and resettlement plan to be implemented. Following the special session, negotiations resumed. The PLO sent Habib a timetable for withdrawal, and the government of Lebanon announced that Damascus, indeed, was prepared to remove its troops and the Palestinian forces under Syrian command from West Beirut. Habib met twice with Begin in early August 1982. In the second session, Begin finally agreed to the introduction of the multinational force on D-Day, day one of the PLO departure. This concession was significant because, previously, Israel had demanded that the outside force could enter only after the evacuation was completed.

Yet another sting in the tail, however, was that as part of any settlement, Jerusalem wanted the Syrian military to leave Lebanon entirely. Ultimately, Jerusalem insisted only that Syrian forces leaving Beirut should go directly to Damascus, rather than deploying with Syrian units elsewhere in Lebanon. As a matter of principle, Israel's first demand regarding the withdrawal of all Syrian forces was a nonstarter; it was a nonnegotiable demand as far as Damascus was concerned because it considered its military presence to be legal under an Arab League mandate that ended the 1975-1976 Lebanon civil war. As a practical matter, moreover, Israel's second demand need not have been negotiated: Syrian units in Beirut were so battered that it was highly likely that they would return straight to Damascus to be reconstituted.

By now, the players had begun the last moves of the endgame, as evidenced by a dispute between Washington and Jerusalem over the relatively trivial issue of who would receive the credit for the move toward "peace." Prime Minister Begin's aides put the word out among the diplomatic corps that the cabinet had acted to end the bombing of Beirut well before a presidential call to the prime minister. The Israeli press carried a report that the White House had stage-managed a confrontation between Reagan and Begin to convey the impression that Jerusalem had ended its siege due to Washington's squeeze.[32]

More was at stake here than the reputations of two sensitive leaders. Israel was concerned that its enemies might infer that it was bowing to U.S. pressure. Indeed, such a perception had bolstered Palestinian morale in West Beirut and may have contributed to a further delay in the PLO withdrawal. To counter this, the Israeli press report, based on an official leak in Jerusalem, claimed that the decision to end the bombing was passed to the U.S. embassy in Tel Aviv "well before" President Reagan's call to Prime Minister Begin. The prime minister himself said that:

Even in the most critical days, more than once, when President Reagan appealed to me we did whatever was necessary without giving in; let no one tell me that we bowed before the United States; this government did not give in to any pressure whatsoever.[33]

Begin also claimed that a call received at 2:15 P.M. from American Ambassador Samuel Lewis about the bombing had hindered the cabinet from stopping the air raids because the ministers thought it might appear that Israel was knuckling under to U.S. pressure. An Israeli journalist, Moshe Zaq, added that Washington leaked to the press its tough message to Jerusalem only after it was certain that Israel had halted the bombing, in an attempt to obtain credit in the Arab world for restraining Israel.[34] It was true that Jerusalem tried to manage the news to avoid the impression that it could be delivered by Washington. Conversely, it was also true that the United States wanted to take credit in American domestic political circles and in the Arab world for finally ending the war.

Conclusions

The American element was only one factor contributing to Israel's decision to end the siege. The most important reason why the cabinet stopped the air raids and ended the blockade of Beirut was that the government had achieved most of the goals it had sought. Jerusalem's reluctance to spill additional blood and expend treasure for marginal returns coincided with its aversion to placing further strain on U.S.-Israel relations.

As in every war, the fighting in Lebanon had to end eventually, and Israel decided to take its perceived gains rather than risk additional losses as the war wound down. Also, the PLO began to cooperate with Israel in a mutual recognition of the endgame, signaling that the transition from a fight to a competitive and cooperative bargaining game to a debate over the future had begun.

The defeat and flight of the PLO, the proven impotence of Syrian forces in Lebanon, and the apparent Israeli dominance seemed to create a different political/military environment for Lebanon. Rightist-Christian militias aligned with Israel were up and in; leftist-Moslem factions associated with Syria were down and out. However, Lebanese political instability, abetted by Syrian and Iranian terrorism, rose again as an obstacle to the preservation of the status quo. The strategic problem posed by the PLO's use of Lebanon as a platform to launch attacks on Israel had been greatly lessened by war, although a new wave of instability made it difficult to preserve the gains of warfare. The balance of power as the fighting ended, though, was but a single frame in a video. That is, there was a fragile structure of relations at war's end.

With respect to a shifting balance of power in Lebanon, Thomas Friedman of the *New York Times* reported that several Israeli specialists had advised their Defense Ministry to consider blockading the Phalangist port of Junieh or even severing Jerusalem's long-standing ties with the rightists in the hope of creating better relations with the rising Shi'a Moslem forces of Lebanon.[35] In fact, Israel's military defeat of the PLO in Lebanon during 1982 allowed the Shi'a to expand their power base; this faction then used that platform to force the ouster of Israeli troops from most of Lebanon. To complete the circle, Jerusalem temporarily assisted the Shi'a in a challenge to a new alliance--Lebanese rightists, Iraq, and the Palestine Liberation Organization. Thus, Israel's erstwhile allies, the Lebanese rightists, now were aligned with its enemy--the Palestine Liberation Organization.

By the spring of 1987, the Israeli-Shi'a alignment would break down, and the Shi'a would again turn on Israel in the south. Lebanon would become a battleground in a proxy war between Iraq, on one side, and Syria and Iran, on the other side. This time, however, the United States and Israel would watch from the sidelines as a coalition of factions supported by Iran and Syria fought Lebanese rightist militias aligned with Iraq. So, as the 1980s came to a close, Lebanon would return, once again, to a familiar state of turmoil.[36] Meanwhile, in the immediate aftermath of the 1982 war, officials in Washington began to take stock of the lessons of Lebanon.

9

Lessons of Lebanon

Bureaucratic Politics and Foreign Policy

From the opening gambits of the parties engaged in tacit bargaining to the final moves of the endgame there, Lebanon offers valuable lessons on policymakers, processes, and policies. A main principle concerns the way in which bureaucratic political processes explain foreign policy. As a key decisionmaker, the president must persuade other national security officials to operate according to White House priorities. And if he succeeds, foreign policy may be the product of presidentially inspired process, rather than the result of bureaucratic politics among cabinet-level aides.

From the 1981 Missiles of May crisis through 1982's guns of June and August endgame, Ronald Reagan was involved less in matters regarding Lebanon than in his other presidential duties. Hence, bureaucratic processes generally determined American policy toward Lebanon. The interplay of leadership and politics was manifest in the debate over the SAM-site game. Recall that the central issue there was whether a Syrian surface-to-air missile could take out an Israeli attack aircraft before that plane could down the missile. Specifically, Washington officials had hoped to determine if the SAM-site game would lead to a general war that would be harmful to American interests in the Middle East or if Israel could attack the missiles without damaging the U.S. agenda.

Regionalists Versus Globalists

The bureaucratic lineup within the administration featured a regionalist-versus-globalist split on the missile confrontation. Regionalists viewed the conflict from the standpoint of the local actors and considered the Syrian missiles to be a way for Damascus to defend its troops against the threat of Lebanese rightist militias. Because the missiles were thought to serve defensive purposes, regionalists did not believe they were a threat to Israel. Thus, these officials were reluctant to give Jerusalem a green light to

209

attack the weapons or to associate U.S. diplomacy with Israel's threats to use force.

Globalists saw the conflict as one between Soviet-backed Syria and American-supported Israel and viewed the presence of the missiles as an effort by Damascus to gain a strategic advantage over Jerusalem. Globalists, therefore, were willing to give Israel a go-ahead to take out the missiles. At a minimum, they advocated a policy of reinforcing Jerusalem's threats to use military action with U.S. diplomacy.

When a premature consensus, led by the regionalists, developed on the need for Israel to refrain from using force, the president failed to have his staff challenge it. This was consistent with his propensity to avert war but compromised the principles of supporting an ally and enforcing the tacit accord between Israel and Syria that had been negotiated via the good offices of the United States. Overlaying the split between regionalists and globalists, there was also a dispute between State and Defense about Syria's missiles in Lebanon and a prospective Israeli response.

State Versus Defense

Compared to Defense, Secretary Haig's State Department was less worried that Israeli military action in Lebanon would harm American relations with other Arab states in the area, such as the Gulf states. Therefore, in early May of 1981, the Department of State was willing to contemplate an Israeli air strike against Syrian missiles in Lebanon, even one employing American-origin equipment.

With a traditional focus on the Gulf, the Department of Defense feared that an Israeli strike would complicate U.S. negotiations with Gulf states regarding the use of their facilities in the event of a Soviet invasion of Iran. Additionally, Defense believed that an Israeli attack would prevent Gulf nations from taking part in joint military planning to prepare for such a Soviet-Iranian contingency. As a result, the Department of Defense strongly opposed an Israeli air strike against Syrian missiles that used American-origin equipment.

Without active lobbying from the White House, those at State who favored Israel's use of force and who wanted to bolster Jerusalem's threats with American diplomacy lost out to the coalition that sought to restrain Israel. Subsequently, a State/Defense consensus evolved for Jerusalem to avoid the use of force--an unchallenged bureaucratic consensus that was guided neither by a coherent set of presidential priorities nor coordinated by the National Security Council staff. As the crisis escalated, however, the White House role would grow.

The White House as Power Broker

The complexity of American policymaking in regard to Lebanon can be seen in the diverse stands of the White House, State, and Defense on Israel's war against the PLO in Lebanon. The White House saw the crisis as an occasion to seize power, and, with the split between State and Defense, it eventually evolved as power broker. Led by McFarlane, the National Security Council created structures designed to moderate State's views and to secure wider interagency backing for them.

One consequence of the augmented White House role was the isolation of Defense, as a White House/State coalition developed. With the help of the White House, State's view of the crisis as an opportunity to enhance the security of America's friends in the area and facilitate the Arab-Israeli peace process became the interim approach of the Government.

State was willing to take advantage of Israel's use of force to achieve U.S. goals in the region, but the Department of Defense was not. Always reluctant to see its forces used, even for American diplomatic purposes, Defense was particularly opposed to taking advantage of a crisis initiated by Israel. Both the Office of the Secretary of Defense and the Organization of the Joint Chiefs of Staff accused State of rationalizing Israel's invasion to derive political benefits.

The Department of Defense viewed the missile crisis as an opportunity to advocate arms sales to Jordan and exert pressure for such sanctions as canceling or delaying arms transfers to Israel. Moreover, Defense strongly opposed the introduction of American military forces as part of a State-designed peacekeeping operation that was intended to facilitate the PLO withdrawal from Lebanon. Again, bureaucratic politics and the absence of leadership at the top worked hand in hand to thwart the rational formulation of foreign policy. But despite the lack of presidential initiative, the White House staff, in the role of power broker, was in a position to develop a working coalition with State against Defense.

The White House and State Versus Defense

Bureaucratic politics in foreign policy also may be seen in the disagreement within the administration over the sale of cluster bomb munitions to Israel. Given Jerusalem's use of cluster-type weapons in the Lebanon War, there was a "flap" in Washington over how to punish Israel. At issue in the administration was whether to discontinue cluster bomb sales altogether or maintain a suspension then in effect for another six months.

Once again, State and the White House were aligned against Defense. The Department of State and the NSC staff argued that to cancel the sale and prohibit future ones would give Israeli hawks a pretext to invade West Beirut at a time when the administration was trying to convince Jerusalem not to do so. But both the Office of the Secretary of Defense and the Organization of the Joint Chiefs of Staff held that only a cutoff of sales to Israel would allow the Arab states of the Gulf to join the United States in military contingency planning.

While Defense was arguing that Gulf states would refuse to take part in joint contingency planning with Washington unless cluster weapon sales to Israel were discontinued, those nations began to step up such planning in response to Iran's gains in its war against Iraq. To the extent that the Gulf states were aware of the rationale Defense used in its efforts to block arm sales to Israel, they actually may have constrained their participation in joint planning with the United States. In any event, the argument Defense used in the Washington debate was inconsistent with its activities in the Gulf. This logical inconsistency ultimately contributed to the rise of the White House as power broker. Furthermore, as the coalition between the White House and State solidified, the issue of who had access to the president loomed even larger than before.

Proximity to the President

In Washington, as in any capital, "access to the throne" is a sign of power. But when policy changes as a consequence of who has the ear of the president last and for the longest period of time, this indicates a flaw in the policy process. American responses to Israel's invasion of Lebanon from June 6 to 18, 1982, came from an interagency process, initially led by State under Haig but subsequently led by the White House as Haig's influence waned. Although he was on the way out, Haig was with the president at an economic summit in Europe, far from a Washington bureaucracy that was hostile to Israel. Captive to Haig's policy views while in Europe, Reagan followed an approach that was relatively permissive towards Israel's invasion. Accordingly, American diplomacy supported Israel's use of force in the first week of hostilities.

Upon returning from the economic summit, Haig tried to regain the lead, but he could not do so in full measure. His fall from grace coincided with the rise of Weinberger as a key player when the president returned from abroad. Policy tilted against Israel when the bureaucracy hostile toward Israel (that is, a Defense-led coalition) was able to regain its access to the president. American policy changed abruptly, now moving at cross-purposes with Israel's use of force. As State and Defense jockeyed for the lead, this gave the National Security Council staff an opportunity to take advantage of the escalating crisis in order to pursue political/military contingency planning.

The Politics of Contingency Planning

In the national security decisionmaking process, contingency planning includes the specification of ranked objectives, a consideration of events or contingencies that might affect these goals, and an assessment of options in terms of such criteria as anticipated benefit and risk (expected loss). In the contingency planning for the Missiles of May crisis, there was some agreement among the principals on purposes but little on the rank order or weight to give each aim; therefore, it was difficult to make trade-offs.

The president favored the short-term goals of avoiding and limiting war but was silent on the need to deny the Soviet Union political benefits if fighting commenced between Israel and Syria. The secretary of state wanted to use the threat of war to stimulate the peace process, but he did not take into account the impact of war on the administration's strategy for a Soviet invasion of Iran. The secretary of defense stressed the implications of war between Israel and Syria for Gulf contingencies, but he failed to see the value of using the Lebanon crisis as an opportunity to further the Arab-Israeli peace process.

Given the assortment of aims advanced by the national security group, President Reagan should have communicated his priorities and authorized his staff to reconcile the objectives of other senior players with this agenda. But he neither specified his priorities nor charged his staff with coordinating the interagency process. Moreover, in an environment of relative presidential disinterest, the NSC staff lacked the political clout to harmonize the interagency process on its own. Without such orchestration, policy inconsistency abounded.

Inconsistent Consensus

Policy inconsistency is the logical incongruity that may result from political infighting. President Reagan's laid-back management style assumed that coherent policies would flow from the bargaining within his national security team. In fact, though, what developed was an inconsistent consensus. On the one hand, most agreed on the need to prevent war between Israel and Syria; on the other hand, there was a shared assumption that, if diplomacy failed to induce Damascus to withdraw its missiles from Lebanon, Jerusalem had a right to remove the missiles with force. Implicit in this contradiction in American policy were two messages for Israel--a public call for restraint and a private acknowledgement of a legitimate right to use force. Such contradictory messages gave factions within the government of Israel a justification for advocating the use of force.

Another illustration of inconsistent consensus that should have been made coherent by the National Security Council staff was the administration's winter 1982 assessment of Israel's goals in Lebanon. Washington believed that Jerusalem intended to drive the PLO beyond artillery range of Israel's northern border with Lebanon. But the United States also knew that Israel wished to destroy the Palestinian leadership. Because most of the Palestinian leaders resided in Beirut or could be expected to flee there in a crisis, the Israel Defense Forces would be inclined to take the fighting to Beirut. The Washington consensus was inconsistent in concluding that Israel's goals would be geographically limited and yet still targeted on the Beirut-based Palestinian leadership.

Twin explanations for such inconsistency are politics and leadership. Those who wished to give Israel a green light to take out Syria's missiles assumed that Jerusalem's objectives were limited; therefore, its prospective military action would be proportionate to some Palestinian provocation. But those who wanted to restrain Jerusalem believed that its aims were relatively unlimited; thus, Israel would tend to act out of proportion to provocation. Each group used its assumptions in its fight for control over policy. But rather than adopting either group's position, the president tended to avoid choice and thereby permit policy inconsistency. So, bureaucratic politics operated in the context of lax leadership at the top and produced inconsistent consensus.

Incoherent Policy

The flip side of inconsistency is incoherence. Inconsistency concerns contradictory policy; incoherence is policy confusion. And just as inconsistency may stem from politics, so may incoherence. An example of incoherent American policy may be found in events surrounding the May 1982 visit of Israeli Defense Minister Sharon. During the visit, Secretary of Defense Caspar Weinberger refused to follow talking points developed through an interagency process. The intent of this guidance was to have Weinberger inform Sharon that the administration was now ready to implement the strategic cooperation accord between Israel and the United States, which had been frozen after Israel annexed the Golan Heights of Syria in December 1981. Because Weinberger's own staff had "signed off" on these talking points, it was reasonable to expect that the secretary would follow this guidance.

Sharon had already heard that Washington was about to implement the accord; therefore, Weinberger's refusal to inform his Israeli counterpart to that effect demonstrated the confusion among American policymakers and showed that the administration was not a unitary actor. Following through on the agreement was meant to be a signal of a rapprochement in American-Israeli relations. What Weinberger actually did, however, only increased tensions within the alignment: He alluded to the possibility of further American sanctions against Israel in the event that it harmed the "vital interests" of the United States.

The agreed-upon talking points had been forwarded to the Pentagon by Deputy National Security Adviser Robert McFarlane. Although he was the principal at the White House on Middle East policymaking, McFarlane was not considered a bureaucratic equal to Weinberger. Hence, McFarlane was unable to get the secretary's compliance concerning the interagency-approved guidance. And while McFarlane was being bested in a contest for power with Weinberger, Haig was sending Sharon a contradictory message.

Unlike Defense and regionalists in his own Department of State, Haig was willing to harmonize American diplomacy with Israel's threats to use force against Syria's missiles. During his meeting with Sharon, the secretary tried to get the minister to accept a formula that would calibrate Israeli force in proportion to Palestinian provocation. So, while Haig was giving a conditional green light to Sharon for a limited military operation in response to an attack against Israel, Weinberger was threatening sanctions if Jerusalem did anything that would harm American interests (that is, any actions that Weinberger disapproved). Bureaucratic politics explain the incoherent American policy towards Lebanon, and White House preoccupation with other priorities allowed politics to reign.

Multiple Voices

When there are several speakers trying to present policy, it is not surprising if doubts arise on exactly what that policy is. Such confusion highlights the role of politics in foreign policy. The funeral of King Khalid of Saudi Arabia provided an opportunity for multiple voices to speak on behalf of the United States. The American delegation to the funeral in Riyadh included Vice President George Bush, Secretary of Defense Weinberger, Chairman of the Senate Foreign Relations Committee Senator Charles Percy, and Deputy Assistant to the President McFarlane. While Secretary of State Haig and Ambassador Habib were attempting to reinforce Israel's military pressure on the PLO and win acceptance for Jerusalem's terms for a cease-fire and withdrawal, other officials in the delegation may have implied to the Saudis that the United States would compel Israel to accept different terms. And by sending contradictory messages, the delegation undercut Israel's coercive diplomacy. Meanwhile, the United States was unable to induce Israel to accept a cease-fire, and the confusion in American policy only encouraged the PLO to continue fighting.

The different policies expressed by Haig in Washington and Weinberger in Riyadh indicate the range of opinion within the administration and the absence of a central authority to harmonize these views. Haig was more likely than Weinberger to support the orchestration of American diplomacy with Israel's force. But the funeral in Saudi Arabia allowed Defense to enter the policy process as a major player because it occurred in the Middle East during the fighting in Lebanon. And with Weinberger and Percy on the Delegation, it was weighted in favor of pressuring Israel to accept a cease-fire and permitting the PLO to remain intact as a political/military organization. Neither Haig nor Habib was in Saudi Arabia for the funeral, so the Department of State's views were underrepresented relative to those of Defense.

Although it is useful to focus attention on the role of multiple speakers in the politics of policymaking, consider the critical part played in the American approach to Lebanon by one official--Robert McFarlane. As a member of the U.S. delegation in Riyadh, a reputed ally of Haig, and the White House principal most knowledgeable about Lebanon, McFarlane was in a position to prevent the confusion in U.S. policy. Clearly, he failed to do so.

The Flaws of McFarlane

Although groups are an obvious part of all institutions and bureaucratic dynamics, it is helpful to focus on those individuals who play major roles in the current case or may have a counterpart in a future administration.

The discussion in prior chapters has treated such key decisionmakers as Reagan, Haig, Shultz, Weinberger, Kirkpatrick, and Habib. Whatever their faults, none of these officials were as central to the failure of American policy in Lebanon as was Robert McFarlane. The focus here falls upon him because of the pivotal part he played in the Lebanon drama, as well as in the transition from Lebanon to another policy failure--Iran. In other words, evidence from McFarlane's exploits should be studied to understand how patterns of decisionmaking begun in Lebanon can help explain subsequent events in Iran and may actually help avoid mismanagement in the future.

Intelligence and Policy: Lebanon

One of McFarlane's principal flaws was that he tended to use intelligence information only when it was consistent with his policy objectives. He used intelligence as a weapon in bureaucratic warfare, rather than as a tool for rational decisionmaking. In light of the president's understandable need to perform other duties, it is not surprising that his aides would be tempted to misuse intelligence, and, certainly, others have employed it in a self-serving fashion. But McFarlane's actions are particularly troublesome given his role as Deputy and, later, National Security Adviser to the president. For a supposedly honest broker of information and analysis to abuse that assignment is unacceptable.

McFarlane is not alone in using intelligence to reinforce policy; indeed, this is a general pattern found in individuals under various circumstances. As research in cognitive psychology confirms, people tend to act on the basis of value preferences, rather than on the grounds of information.[1] They consequently tend to downgrade intelligence in and of itself or use it only if it is consistent with their own value preferences. McFarlane's sins, however, go well beyond a mere deemphasis of intelligence. He actually manipulated the intelligence process to produce information that would justify his bureaucratic ambitions or achieve policy aims for which there was little consensus in the administration, in the absence of such "massaged" intelligence.

Because value preferences dominated information in U.S. policymaking on Lebanon, intelligence agencies entered the decisionmaking process as balancers when there were policy disputes among the departments. Therefore, intelligence estimates on Lebanon played a minor role except when they were used by a winning coalition to reinforce its policy preferences. The dominant alignment in the American policy process on Lebanon generally included McFarlane.

In bureaucratic politics, one technique for influencing decisions is for proponents of a specific policy to request a study from intelligence officials that is likely to support their conclusions at an advantageous time.[2] One way that McFarlane gained an advantage was by altering scheduled intelligence reporting requirements. He often ordered planned reports of intelligence estimates to appear earlier than scheduled. For example, it was common knowledge that war prospects were going up, and a formal report citing such increased probabilities would favor McFarlane's bureaucratic goal--seizing the action from State. As a result, McFarlane tasked the intelligence community to make a Special National Intelligence Estimate on the likelihood of an Israeli attack against the PLO in Lebanon. He then used this Special Estimate to control the policy process.

In addition to abusing the intelligence scheduling process, McFarlane frequently ignored intelligence data when it did not accord with his policy preferences. He and Secretary of State George Shultz pushed for U.S. participation in a peacekeeping force for Lebanon despite intelligence reports that indicated it would encounter insurmountable difficulties. A senior editor of the

Washington Post, Bob Woodward, wrote that a CIA estimate on July 23, 1982, had warned that the peacekeeping forces in Lebanon would encounter "intractable" political and military problems.[3] If Woodward was correct, Shultz and McFarlane pursued their policy of placing Americans in peacekeeping forces in Lebanon and ignored intelligence to the contrary.

Evidence of the minor role intelligence played in the policy process led by Shultz and McFarlane also may be found in the case of the Israel-Lebanon Treaty of May 17, 1983. Woodward points out that Shultz was confident Damascus could not exercise veto power over a settlement, and the United States had more influence over Syria than anyone realized. Contrary to the secretary's optimism, however, Woodward notes that the CIA viewed a settlement as a "nonstarter." Report after report said that Syria would not go along; furthermore, the State Department's intelligence branch agreed.[4] In other words, the 1983 Israel-Lebanon Treaty was pursued as a policy option despite an intelligence consensus that Syria would not permit it to be effective and that Damascus had the military capabilities in Lebanon to enforce its veto.

A plausible reason why a policy could be adopted in the face of intelligence that warned against it lies in the alignment of Shultz at State and McFarlane at the White House. This coalition could allow intelligence to be ignored because it was McFarlane's job to make certain that pessimistic intelligence, like that reported by Woodward, was used to evaluate policy options on a government-wide basis. But he failed to incorporate such intelligence in the policy process for Lebanon as an honest broker should have done. Thus, the Shultz/McFarlane alignment could achieve its policy goal irrespective of intelligence to the contrary. A similar pattern occurred in McFarlane's use of intelligence in the policy process for Iran.

Intelligence and Policy: Iran

In the 1985-1987 arms-for-hostages exchange between Washington and Teheran, the way in which intelligence was utilized in the interagency process was similar to that of the Lebanon situation five years earlier. In both cases, intelligence was either ignored or employed largely to reinforce policies already selected on the basis of value preferences. There was no rational incorporation of preference with expectation.

The decision to sell American arms to Iran was not based upon U.S. intelligence assessments. Although the Central Intelligence Agency played a major part in the covert delivery of arms, it did little in terms of conducting independent analyses to inform the policy process. The Agency did not give policymakers intelligence assessments to indicate that arms transfers to Iran would likely bring the release of American hostages in Lebanon, a strengthening of "moderates" in Iran, or a tilt of that country back toward the American sphere. These three desirable outcomes, in fact, constituted McFarlane's policy preferences on Iran. But rather than vindicating these assumptions, American intelligence actually invalidated them.

Under McFarlane's supervision, the NSC staff willingly used the CIA's capacity to conduct covert actions for the clandestine arms transfers, but it failed to use the Agency's analytic capability to evaluate the likely success of the sales. According to the Tower Commission Report, in October 1984 the intelligence community produced a Special National Intelligence Estimate on Iran that challenged White House assumptions about the arms transfer.[5] The intelligence community, in fact, provided a valid critique of the premises underlying an arms-for-hostages exchange with Teheran. But McFarlane ignored that assessment and plunged ahead with the arms sale on the basis of policy values, uninformed by intelligence.

A further illustration of the dominance of McFarlane's values over intelligence on Iran appeared in the Report of the Senate Intelligence Committee. The committee addressed the question of whether or not the Iran initiative was based on adequate and effectively used intelligence.[6] The hearings established that a National Intelligence Estimate published in April 1985 showed that Israel had its own rationale to promote the sale of arms to Iran. Jerusalem's reasons only partially overlapped with American interests. According to the report, the White House official with the action on the initial sales, National Security Adviser McFarlane, testified that he had not seen any analysis on that National Intelligence Estimate.

On the one hand, McFarlane may have turned aside information that called attention to the value conflict implicit in the Iran arms deal. In this regard, the Senate Intelligence Committee hearings concluded that McFarlane and his colleagues either had failed to use the available intelligence on Israeli policy toward Iran, or greatly discounted the intelligence when they made decisions on the Iran arms sale.[7]

On the other hand, critical uncertainties identified by lower-level experts could have been deemphasized when transmitted to and summarized for top level officials.[8] Given McFarlane's position as a primary customer for such important documents as National Intelligence Estimates and in view of the sensitive nature of Iranian matters, however, it is doubtful that the NSC staff or the CIA itself would allow him to remain unaware of such crucial information. It is possible that McFarlane examined the information, decided it was not in keeping with his goal of giving an opening to Iranian "moderates," and proceeded to ignore the intelligence and deny that he had seen it.

Another example of McFarlane's misuse of his position at the White House by tampering with the process of intelligence estimation for bureaucratic advantage also concerns Iran. According to the Tower Commission Report, on August 31, 1984, McFarlane requested an interagency analysis of American relations with Iran after the death of the Ayatollah Khomeni.[9] Among other things, the McFarlane-initiated study, presented in October, concluded that the possibility of resuming American arms shipments to Iran depended upon its willingness to restore formal relations with the United States. The study conveys a sense of the administration's inability to affect events in Iran.

Displeased with this pessimistic intelligence assessment, McFarlane's NSC staffer, Howard Teicher, began to work closely with the CIA's national intelligence officer for the Near East and South Asia, Graham Fuller, to prepare another Special National Intelligence Estimate. Their goal may have been to come up with an intelligence estimate that would be more in accord with McFarlane's preferred policy of selling arms to Iran.

In May 1985, the intelligence community circulated a revised Special National Intelligence Estimate on post-Khomeni Iran. It concluded that (1) the United States lacked a capability to counter expected Soviet moves in the unstable climate that was predicted to follow Khomeni's death, and (2) friendly states, such as Israel, might be able to fill a military gap for Iran, for example, by selling American-origin arms to Iran even if the United States could not make the sale directly. McFarlane clearly needed this revised estimate in his struggle to dominate the Iranian policy process because both Shultz at State and Weinberger at Defense were opposed to selling American arms to Iran.

In sum, then, McFarlane had denied seeing intelligence reports for which he was a primary consumer, had manipulated their scheduled appearance, and had massaged intelligence data to fit his policy preferences. He was the official responsible for the alteration of the schedule for the Lebanon Estimate and the Iranian Estimate, as well as the person who, incredibly, denied having access to this Iranian Estimate. Just as McFarlane ignored the proper linkage of intelligence and policy, so, too, did he mismanage American diplomatic and military tools of statecraft in dealing with Lebanon.

Force Without Intelligence or Diplomacy

When McFarlane came to the White House from State in early 1982, there was considerable excitement in the building because this marine with diplomatic experience seemed to be just the right person to help the president and Judge Clark create a coherent national security policy. Unfortunately, McFarlane was not up to the task. Although he began his White House career as an aide to Henry Kissinger and gained prominence as counselor to Alexander Haig at State, McFarlane was neither a Kissinger nor a Haig. Nonetheless, he tried in vain to reprise the roles of these two giants upon gaining access to the Oval Office under Reagan. When he replaced Habib as presidential envoy to the Middle East, McFarlane also retained his White House title as Deputy National Security Adviser; thus, he was in a position to coordinate military planning and diplomatic negotiations in preparation for presidential decisionmaking. One of his principal failures, however, was his inability to balance diplomacy and force.

From the time McFarlane took over as the special envoy, he made repeated calls for the use of force in Lebanon. The *Middle East Policy Survey* of September 16, 1983 (no. 87), reports that McFarlane also urged the United States to take an active military role there. Beginning with the National Security Council meeting that he attended as special envoy on September 3 and another council meeting on September 10, he consistently advocated American military action. At first, he argued for the use of the U.S. Marines in order to reverse the deteriorating political and military situation in Lebanon.

These Council meetings featured discussions of the Israeli decision to pull its forces from the Chouf Mountains, just southeast of Beirut. The Israel Defense Forces had withdrawn from their forward positions along the Beirut-Damascus Highway to positions below the Awali River, near the town of Sidon on the coast in southern Lebanon. The Israeli pullback from central Lebanon created a power vacuum that was filled by warring Lebanese factions. Druse combatants, supported by Syria, the PLO, and Shi'ite militias, fought against Lebanese rightists. The Druse coalition began to prevail, giving McFarlane a pretext to make an even stronger case for a U.S. military role.

McFarlane suggested that American marines and the Lebanese army take up positions abandoned by the departing Israelis in order to avert bloodshed. But when fighting did occur, McFarlane changed his rationale for using the marines. Now, he wanted them there to maintain a cease-fire he claimed to be arranging on the ground. In sum, McFarlane initially advocated the deployment of U.S. forces to deter hostilities and later suggested that these forces be used to maintain a cease-fire that had not even been brokered.

In a naive attempt to fashion a coercive diplomacy strategy, McFarlane claimed that only an American show of force would compel Syria to consider a political option, for example, a cease-fire between the Druse and the government of Lebanon forces. That approach was innocent because it failed to take into account the high motivation of the Druse to replace the Israelis and the relatively large Syrian military presence (compared to the small American ground combat force deployed in Lebanon at the time.)

Fortunately, there was a well-conceived consensus in the administration against the McFarlane recommendations. It rested on the inability to calculate the chances for success of such an American show of force. Furthermore, State Department officials strongly opposed McFarlane's suggestions because it was unclear to them what it would take to coerce Syria. Both Secretary of State Shultz and Secretary of Defense Weinberger also opposed McFarlane because the use of American naval and air power against what they called "co-mingled" civilian/military positions would likely result in Lebanese casualties.

After losing in the National Security Council, McFarlane departed for Lebanon and continued his efforts to find justification for the redeployment of American marines. Recall that he initially wanted them to be deployed to arrest a deteriorating situation and deter fighting; then he suggested they should be used to enforce a cease-fire that had not been nailed down. Now he was advocating that they be used as a show of force to coerce Syria.

At last, McFarlane found a persuasive reason to employ the marines as a result of a battle for a Chouf mountain village called

Souk el-Garb. The *New York Times* bureau chief in Lebanon, Thomas Friedman, faults McFarlane for involving the United States military in the fight over Souk el-Garb. According to Friedman, this involvement changed the local perception of American marines deployed in Lebanon from neutral peacekeepers to just another warring faction.[10] And, once the marines were perceived as part of the factional strife, they became vulnerable to attack.

Soon after the fighting began on September 19, 1983, the Lebanese commander-in-chief, who belonged to the rightist group, implied that he would like to see the U.S. Marines directly involved in the fighting on the side of the Lebanese army because Syria was actively supporting his Druse adversary. Despite prior opportunities to do so, the United States generally had declined to be drawn into the factional strife of Lebanon. This would change, however, when McFarlane misused his authority as special envoy and became the equivalent of an "artillery spotter" for the Lebanese rightists.

Syrian- and Palestinian-backed Druse units had begun an artillery and ground assault on a Lebanese army unit that controlled a ridge overlooking Beirut. The Lebanese commander told McFarlane's military aide that a "massive" offensive had been launched against his men; further, he said that they could only hold out for about a half an hour more and that he needed U.S. help immediately. McFarlane received the information from his military aide at the nearby residence of the American ambassador. According to Friedman:

> Without seeking any independent confirmation of [the Lebanese commander-in-chief's] assessment, McFarlane ordered the Marine commander in Beirut to have the navy ships under his authority fire in support of the Lebanese army.[11]

To his credit, the American marine commander in Beirut strenuously but unsuccessfully opposed McFarlane's order on the grounds that it would make American troops party to what was intra-Lebanese factional fighting and that the Lebanese Muslims would not retaliate against U.S. ships at sea but against American marines on shore. Overruling this prophetic advice, McFarlane had the guided missile cruisers *Virginia*, *John Rodgers*, and *Bowen*, as well as the destroyer *Radford*, fire 360 5-inch shells at the Druse-Syrian-Palestinian forces.

In the wake of the Druse assault, McFarlane had sent from Beirut what came to be known in the Reagan administration as the "sky is falling cable," a message that precipitated the widespread use of American force, including the battleship *New Jersey,* to shell the Lebanese countryside. Subsequently, however, the administration learned that only eight Lebanese army troops had been killed and twelve wounded in the fighting of September 19, 1983, that gave rise to the extensive use of American force.

In addition to Friedman, Charles Babock and Don Oberdorfer of the *Washington Post* hold McFarlane accountable for recommending American air strikes and naval gunfire without waiting for an intelligence assessment of the consequences of such force employment. The perception of the United States troops as combatants, in fact, provided an excuse for the bombing of 241 American marines in their Beirut barracks by a terrorist acting on behalf of Syria and/or Iran about a month after McFarlane recommended the use of force. With respect to the connection between Lebanon and Iran, moreover, Babock and Oberdorfer consider that McFarlane's cable to use force was but a small step on the long road toward the NSC's "cult of secrecy" and the eventual Iran-contra debacle.[12] Ultimately, McFarlane's flaws played a critical role in American policy's failure in both Lebanon and Iran.

A basic assumption of the present inquiry is that people and process interact to help shape outcomes. When individuals manipulate the process for their own ends, the outcomes often suffer. More egregious than the president's innocent omissions are McFarlane's sins of commission. His misuse of intelligence directly harmed the policy process. And McFarlane's lack of success in balancing force and diplomacy for Lebanon was also manifest in his arms-for-hostages scheme for Iran. He used too much force in relation to diplomacy for Lebanon and too little force in comparison to diplomacy for Iran.

After the bombing of the American Embassy Annex and Marine barracks in Beirut during April and October 1983, respectively, the Habib diplomatic approach acceded to the McFarlane military approach. Five weeks after his first visit to the area as Habib's replacement in August 1983, a period of escalating American force with little diplomacy began. Unwilling to pay the price in additional American blood, the president then ordered the marines to withdraw offshore until circumstances permitted the ships to sail away unobtrusively from what seemed, at year's end, to be a Lebanese quagmire.

By summer 1985, Israel had followed the American withdrawal. Lebanese factional instability, coupled with state-sponsored terrorism, had made it unattractive for either Washington or Jerusalem to maintain a visible military presence in Lebanon. In Washington, the State-dominated phase of U.S. diplomacy uncoordinated with Israeli force was followed by a period of White House-led military action with scant regard for diplomatic activity.

With McFarlane abusing the process of American policymaking on eastern Mediterranean issues, the U.S. ship of state listed precariously from side to side. As a result, policy careened from Habib, as diplomatic troubleshooter for the U.S. government, to McFarlane, as artillery spotter for the government of Lebanon. Regarding American policymaking in the Gulf, McFarlane initiated a process whereby the ship of state eventually lurched from clandestine arms and intelligence support for Iran in its land war with Iraq, to alignment with Iraq in its naval war with Iran by escorting Kuwaiti ships disguised as American vessels.[13] In both the eastern Mediterranean and the Gulf, McFarlane failed to incorporate the best intelligence into the policy process or coordinate diplomatic policy with military force. As a result, McFarlane failed his president and his country.

Conclusions: Lessons of Lebanon

Given the possibility for failure by any one individual among the top presidential advisers, the interagency process is a key to the effective management of national security affairs. Accordingly, reflect upon the three questions that structure this volume: (1) Which leaders should regulate the traffic at the intersection of political/military affairs? (2) Why do such officials make the decisions that they do regarding diplomacy and force? and (3) How does crisis affect both process and choice?

First, the president and national security council principals, such as the secretary of state and secretary of defense, should lead an interagency process designed to harmonize political and military affairs. The national security adviser should operate as an honest broker in the interagency process not as an independent policy formulator.

Second, presidents need to be aware of how difficult it is to combine diplomacy and force because of bureaucratic politics. Recognizing this, they may be prepared to structure the interagency process in order to synthesize these two tools of statecraft.

Third, crisis has a direct impact on process and policy. Crises are policyforcing events that allow the White House to assume the lead. In the absence of White House leadership, other cabinet-level officials tend to do the bidding of their respective units. And when a lack of leadership and bureaucratic politics converge, as in the Lebanon case, policymakers may not take advantage of the opportunity presented by crisis. Because such policyforcing events may become a permanent part of the international political landscape, however, future presidents should have ample opportunity to seize the occasion crisis affords to blend diplomacy and force into effective foreign policy.

The Lebanon case reveals a national security decisionmaking style that is a map for mismanagement--a precursor to the Iran affair a half-decade later and to the Lebanons and Irans of the future, unless presidents learn the lessons of Lebanon in the 1980s. The issue of "who's at the helm?" does, indeed, matter. Without an effective White House staff at the tiller, the American ship of state is likely to capsize in the dangerous waters of national security affairs.

Notes

Preface

1. Henry Kissinger, *White House Years* (Boston: Little, Brown and Company, 1979) and *Years of Upheaval* (Boston: Little, Brown and Company, 1982); Zbigniew Brzezinski, *Power and Principle: Memoirs of the National Security Advisor 1977-1981* (New York: Farrar Straus Giroux, 1983); Robert Pastor, *Condemned to Repetition* (Princeton, N.J.: Princeton University Press, 1987); Constantine Menges, *Inside the National Security Council* (New York: Simon and Schuster, 1988); Gary Sick, *All Fall Down: America's Tragic Encounter with Iran* (New York: Random House, 1985); William Quandt, *Camp David: Peacemaking and Politics* (Washington D.C.: The Brookings Institution, 1986).

2. Ze'ev Schiff and Ehud Ya'ari, *Israel's Lebanon War* (New York: Simon and Schuster, 1984), and Rashid Khalidi, *Under Siege: P.L.O. Decisionmaking During the 1982 War* (New York: Columbia University Press, 1986).

Introduction

1. Alexander Haig, *Caveat* (New York: McMillan Publishing Company, 1984), p. 85.

2. Stanley Miller, *The Mary Celeste: A Survivor's Tale* (New York: St. Martin's Press, 1980), p. 51.

Chapter 1

1. See Walid Khalidi, *Conflict and Violence in Lebanon* (Cambridge, Mass.: Harvard University Press, 1979), pp. 67-82, for a description of Lebanese militias.

2. Helena Cobban, *The Palestinian Liberation Organisation: People, Power, and Politics* (Cambridge, England: Cambridge University Press, 1984), pp. 68-69.

3. Itamar Rabinovich, *The War for Lebanon, 1970-1985* (Ithaca, N.Y.: Cornell University Press, 1985), p. 89.

4. Cobban, *op. cit.*, p. 66.

5. Rashid Khalidi, *Under Siege: P.L.O. Decisionmaking During the 1982 War* (New York: Columbia University Press, 1986, p. 33.

6. Khalidi, p. 194, footnote 20, and Cobban, *op. cit.*, p. 108.

7. Cyrus Vance, *Hard Choices: Critical Years in American Foreign Policy* (New York: Simon and Schuster, 1983), p. 209.

8. Also see Jimmy Carter, *Keeping Faith: Memoirs of a President* (Toronto: Bantam Books, 1982), pp. 310-311.

9. Vance, *op. cit.*, p. 209.

10. See Rabinovich, *op. cit.*, pp. 98, 110, as well as Schiff and Ya'ari, *op. cit.*, p. 20.

11. Schiff and Ya'ari, *op. cit.*, p. 33.

12. Rabinovich, *op. cit.*, pp. 167-181.

13. Schiff and Ya'ari, *op. cit.*, p. 33.

14. Rabinovich, *op. cit.*, p. 115.

15. See Ole Holsti, *Crisis, Escalation, War* (Montreal: McGill University Press, 1972), as well as Michael Brecher and Patrick James, *Crisis and Change in World Politics* (Boulder, Colo: Westview Press, 1986).

16. Acknowledgements are due to Professor Janice Stein of the University of Toronto for her comments comparing the 1967 and 1982 cases. Also see Janice Stein and Raymond Tanter, *Rational Decision-Making: Israel's Security Choices, 1967* (Columbus OH: Ohio State University Press, 1980) for an analysis of the 1967 war.

17. Also see Bernard Gwertzman, "A Special U.S. Envoy Will Go to the Mideast," *New York Times*, 6 May 1981, p. 23.

18. Despite the fact that Palestinians made conciliatory statements toward Jordan at the fifteenth session of the Palestinian National Council in Damascus and the fact that Syria is an adversary of Jordan, there is no evidence linking inter-Arab politics with Syria's missile deployment in Lebanon--e.g., to defend PLO combatants there. Indeed, circumstantial evidence suggests no connection between the two sets of events. The fourteenth session of the Council took place in Damascus during January 1979. Its concluding statements contained a reference to political cooperation with Jordan as long as Amman did not take part in the American-inspired Camp David peace process. Despite this pronouncement, Syria did not take any actions comparable to the deployment of its missiles in Lebanon to curry the favor of the Palestinians vis-a-vis Jordan. For information on the evolution of the Palestinian National Council's statements on Jordan, see Cobban, *op. cit.*, pp. 86, 103, 108.

19. Kissinger, *op. cit.*, 1982, pp. 478-479.

20. Journalists Marvin Kalb and Bernard Kalb in their biography authorized by Kissinger, *Kissinger* (Boston: Little, Brown and Company, 1974), p. 467, back his claim that he attempted to facilitate the resupply of Israel. An international relations scholar, Walter Laqueur, *Confrontation: The Middle East War and World Politics* (London: Wildwood House and Sphere Books, 1974), p. 147, contends that Kissinger sought to delay arms transfers for Israel in order to find a diplomatic solution with Soviet assistance. Because the assertions of Kissinger and the Kalb brothers are consistent with Kissinger's general reluctance to use arms shipments to Israel for diplomatic leverage, their version may be the valid historical account.

Chapter 2

1. James McCartney, "Did the U.S. Consider War on Syria?" *Miami Hearld*, 28 January 1982, pp. 1 and 7A.

2. Haig, *op cit.*, p. 332.

3. Schiff and Ya'ari, *op. cit.*, p. 76.

4. Daniel Ellsberg, *Papers on the War* (New York: Simon and Schuster, 1972), p. 102; cf. Leslie Gelb with Richard Betts, *The Irony of Vietnam: The System Worked* (Washington, D.C.: The Brookings Institution, 1979), pp. 17-18.

5. In addition to the issue of sending dual messages in the May 1981 missile crisis, the topic recurs in the discussion of the June 1982 war in Chapter 5.

6. Bernard Gwertzman, "Begin Is Said to Tell Reagan That Israel Faces Peril as in 1967," *New York Times*, 9 May 1981, p. 6.

7. John Kifner, "Syria Tells Israel It Won't Withdraw Missiles in Lebanon," *New York Times*, 9 May 1981, pp. 1, A6.

8. As quoted in Michael Brecher, *Decisions in Israel's Foreign Policy* (New Haven, Conn.: Yale University Press, 1975), p. 393. Brecher's footnote is omitted here.

9. Henry Kissinger, *White House Years* (Boston: Little, Brown and Company, 1979), pp. 607-608.

10. Alan Dowty, *Middle East Crisis: U.S. Decision-making in 1958, 1970 and 1973* (Berkeley: University of California Press, 1984), p. 378.

11. Kissinger, *op. cit.*, p. 629; Bernard Kalb and Marvin Kalb, *Kissinger* (Boston: Little, Brown and Company, 1974), pp. 206-207.

12. William Quandt, *Decade of Decisions* (Berkeley: University of California Press, 1977), p. 124.

13. Seymour Hersh, *The Price of Power: Kissinger in the Nixon White House* (New York: Summit Books, 1983), p. 246.

14. Kifner, *op. cit.*

15. SANA [official Syrian news agency], *Foreign Broadcast Information Service*, 8 May 1981 (hereinafter abbreviated as *FBIS*).

16. William Quandt, "Lebanon, 1958, and, Jordan 1970," in Bary Blechman and Stephen Kaplan, eds., *Force Without War: U.S. Armed Forces as a Political Instrument* (Washington, D.C.: The Brookings Institution, 1978), p. 236.

17. Blechman and Kaplan, *op. cit.*, pp. 118-119.

18. Schiff and Ya'ari, *op. cit.*, p. 35.

19. *Ibid.*

20. As shown on the map of Lebanon in Figure 1, Tyre is in southern Lebanon on the Mediterranean coast just south of the Litani River; Tripoli is in northern Lebanon on the coast just south of the Syrian border.

21. Richard Straus and Kenneth Wollack, *Middle East Policy Survey* (hereinafter abbreviated as *MEPS*), 2 July 1981, no. 35.

22. Schiff and Ya'ari, *op. cit.*, p. 37.

23. *Ibid.*, p. 65.

24. *MEPS*, 18 December 1981, no. 46.

25. Israeli Radio in Hebrew on 6 December 1981, *FBIS*, 7 December 1981, p. I 4.

26. Ariel Sharon, *Warrior* (New York: Simon and Schuster, 1989), p. 426.

27. *Ibid.* Sharon's footnote is omitted here.

28. Jerusalem, Government Press Office in English, 15 December 1981, *FBIS*, 18 December 1981.

29. *Ibid.*

30. Schiff and Ya'ari, *op. cit.*, pp. 42, 47-48.

Chapter 3

1. Marvine Howe, "Israeli Action Cited in Golan Heights," *New York Times*, 21 December 1981, p. A21.

2. Bernard Nossiter, "Syria Pushes Hard U.N. Line Over Golan," *New York Times*, 6 January 1982, p. A 3.

3. David Landau, "Prime Minister Begin to Meet with Habib 8 March," *Jerusalem Post*, in English, 8 March 1982, p. 2; *FBIS*, 8 March 1982, p. I 7.

4. David Shipler, "Israel Is Said to Weigh an Invasion of Lebanon If P.L.O. Raids Go On," *New York Times*, 10 February 1982, pp. 1, A 10.

5. *Ibid.*

6. Haig, *op. cit.*, p. 332.

7. Beirut Domestic Radio Service in Arabic on 9 March 1982, *FBIS*, 10 March 1982, p. G 1.

8. Amman Domestic Radio Service in Arabic on 5 March 1982, *FBIS*, 8 March 1982, p. F 1.

9. Jerusalem Domestic Radio Service in Hebrew on 7 March 1982, *FBIS*, 8 March 1982, p. 1 7.

10. John Kifner, "Syrian President Reported to Face Harsh Challenges," *New York Times*, 18 May 1986, pp. 1, A 6.

11. Damascus Radio Service in Arabic on 3 March 1982, *FBIS*, 4 March 1982, p. H 1.

12. Damascus Radio Service in Arabic on 4 March 1982, *FBIS*, 5 March 1982, p. H 1.

13. Dennis Ross, "Acting with Caution: Middle East Policy Planning for the Second Reagan Administration," *Policy Papers--Number One* (Washington, D.C.: The Washington Institute for Near East Policy, 1985), pp. 10-12. The Ross approach of using internal danger to facilitate international diplomacy is similar to that of strategist, Thomas Schelling. Consult his book, *Arms and Influence* (New Haven, Conn.: Yale University Press, 1966), pp. 69-78 regarding the concept of "compellence" as a strategy that combines disincentives and incentives to compel adversaries to act. Deterrence is a strategy to induce opponents to refrain from acting, but "compellence" is designed to get them to take some action. For constraints on deterrence and "compellence," see Alexander George, David Hall, and William Simons, *The Limits of Coercive Diplomacy* (Boston: Little, Brown and Company, 1971).

14. Malcom Kerr, *The Arab Cold War: Gamal 'Abd al-Nasir and His Rivals, 1958-1970* (London: Oxford University Press, 1971), pp. 125-128.

15. Cf. Syrian private sources cited in the text with Damascus Radio Service, *op. cit.*, 4 and 5 March 1982.

16. Jerusalem Domestic Radio Service in Hebrew on 8 March 1982, *FBIS*, 9 March 1982, p. I 2 .

17. Also consult *MEPS*, 18 December 1981, no. 46.

18. Bernard Gwertzman, "U.S. Officials Fear Israel-Syria Clash," *New York Times*, 5 May 1982, p. A 11.

19.   Jerusalem Domestic Television Service in Hebrew on 8 March 1982, *FBIS*, 9 March 1982, p. I 1.

20.   Jerusalem Domestic Radio Service in Hebrew on 7 March 1982, *FBIS*, 8 March 1982, p. I 7.

21.   *Ibid.*

22.   Jerusalem Domestic Radio Service in Hebrew on 4 March 1982, *FBIS*, 8 March 1982, p. I 7.

23.   Landau, *op. cit.*, p. 2.

24.   John Devlin, *Syria: Modern State in an Ancient Land* (London: Westview Press, 1983), p. 129.

25.   Henry Kissinger, *Years of Upheaval* (Boston: Little, Brown and Company, 1982), p. 659.

26.   William Quandt, *Saudia Arabia in the 1980's* (Washington, D.C.: The Brookings Institution, 1981), p. 34.

27.   Jimmy Carter, *The Blood of Abraham* (Boston: Houghton Mifflin Company, 1985), p. 191.

28.   *MEPS*, 23 April 1982, no. 54.

29.   Ross, *op. cit.*, p. 19.

Chapter 4

1.   John Brecher, et. al., "The Birth Pangs of a New Policy," *Newsweek*, 13 September 1982, p. 13.

2.   Henry Kissinger, "From Lebanon to the West Bank to the Gulf," *Washington Post*, 16 June 1982, p. A15.

3.   Don Oberdorfer, "Israeli-Palestinian Cease-fire Termed 'Fragile' by Habib," *Washington Post*, 19 March 1982, p. A26.

4.   Helena Cobban, *Palestinian Liberation Organisation* (Cambridge, England: Cambridge University Press, 1984), p. 140; William Quandt, et. al., *The Politics of Palestinian Nationalism* (Berkeley: University of California Press, 1973), pp. 71.

5.   Schiff and Ya'ari, *op. cit.*, p. 99.

6.   *Ibid.*, p. 100.

7.   Jerusalem Domestic Radio Service in Hebrew on 15 April 1982, *FBIS*, 16 April 1982, p. I1.

8.   *MEPS*, 23 April 1982, no. 54.

9.   Tunisia Domestic Radio Service in Arabic on 7 June 1982, *FBIS*, 8 June 1982, has an account of Prime Minister Mzali's visit to Washington.

10.   John Steinbruner, *The Cybernetic Theory of Decision* (Princeton, N.J.: Princeton University Press, 1974), p. 16.

11.   See Roy Godson, ed., *Intelligence Requirements for the 1980's: Elements of Intelligence* (Washington, D.C.:   National Strategy Information Center, 1979); *Intelligence Requirements for the 1980's: Analysis and Estimates* (Washington, D.C.:   National Strategy Information Center, 1980); *Intelligence Requirements for the 1980's: Intelligence and Policy* (Lexington, Mass.:   Lexington Books, 1986).

12.   International Institute of Strategic Studies (IISS), *The Military Balance, 1972-1973* (London: IISS, 1973), p. 36, and IISS, *The Military Blance, 1981-1982* (London: IISS, 1981), p. 57.

13.   Janice Stein and Raymond Tanter, *Rational Decision-Making: Israel's Choices, 1967* (Columbus, Ohio: Ohio State University Press, 1980), pp. 137-156.

14.   Moshe Dayan, *Story of My Life* (Jerusalem: Steimatsky's Agency Ltd., 1976), p. 251.

Chapter 5

1.   Jerusalem Domestic Radio Service in Hebrew on 31 May 1982, *FBIS*, 1 June 1982, pp. I 5-6.

2.   Consult Ariel Sharon, *op. cit.*, p. 436, for his rationale to make war on the PLO in Lebanon.

3.   Haig, *op. cit.*, p. 335.

4.   Sharon, *op. cit.*, p. 451.

5.   Jerusalem Domestic Radio Service in Hebrew on 31 May 1982, *FBIS*, 1 June 1982, pp. I 5-6.

6.   Sharon, *op. cit.*, p. 487.

7.   Schiff and Ya'ari, *op. cit.*, p. 76.

8.   *Ibid.*, pp. 74-75.

9.   Sharon, *op. cit.*, p. 451.

10.   Schiff and Ya'ari, *op. cit.*, p. 76.

11.   Steven Weisman, "Summit Chiefs Shocked by Invasion of Lebanon," *New York Times*, 7 June 1982, p. A14.

12.   Hedrick Smith, "U.S. Asks Pullout," *New York Times*, 8 June 1982, pp. 1, A14.

13.   Damascus Domestic Radio Service in Arabic on 9 June 1982, in *FBIS*, 10 June 1982, p. H4.

14.   Israel Defense Forces Radio (hereinafter abbreviated as IDF Radio) in Hebrew on 9 June 1982, *FBIS*, 10 June 1982, p. I 1.

15.   Edward Cody, "Israelis Seem to Rule Out Hunt for PLO," *Washington Post*, 18 June 1982, p. 1, and David Ottaway, "Peace Effort in Lebanon Is Stalled," *Washington Post*, 19 June 1982, p. 2.

16. Schiff and Ya'ari, *op. cit.*, p. 98.

17. Haig, *op. cit.*, p. 318; *MEPS*, 18 June 1982, no. 58.

Chapter 6

1. Haig, *op. cit.*, p. 344.

2. *Ibid.*, p. 343.

3. Jerusalem Domestic Radio Service in Hebrew on 17 June 1982, 1500 Greenwich Mean Time (GMT), *FBIS*, 18 June 1982, pp. I1-3.

4. *Ibid.*, 1725 GMT.

5. Jerusalem Domestic Television Service in Hebrew on 23 June 1982, *FBIS*, 24 June 1982.

6. IDF Radio in Hebrew on 23 June 1982, *FBIS*, 24 June 1982.

7. Don Oberdorfer, "Begin Vows Israel Won't Enter Beirut," *Washington Post*, 25 June 1982, pp. A 1, 26.

8. Haig, *op. cit.*, pp. 344-345.

9. Bernard Gwertzman, "Haig Is Said to Have Felt Jealous of Mideast Role," *New York Times*, 29 June 1982, p. A8.

10. John Goshko, "Haig Resigns at State; Shultz Is Named," *Washington Post*, 26 June 1982, pp. 1, A13.

11. United States Senate, Committee on Foreign Relations, *Testimony of the Secretary of State Alexander M. Haig*, 97th Cong., 1st sess., 12 November 1981. U.S., Congress, Senate, Committee on Foreign Relations, *Statement of the Secretary of State-Designate on the Nomination of George P. Shultz of California to be Secretary of State*, 97th Cong., 2nd sess., 13-14 July 1982.

12. *Ibid.*

13. *MEPS*, 13 August 1982, no. 62.

14. Rashid Khalidi, *Under Siege: P.L.O. Decisionmaking During the 1982 War* (New York: Columbia University Press, 1986), p. 164.

15. *Ibid.*, p. 13, 41.

16. *Ibid.*, p. 23.

17. *Ibid.*, pp. 110-113.

18. *Ibid.*, p. 85. Khalidi's footnote is omitted here.

19. Haig, *op. cit.*, p. 345.

20. Kuwait Domestic Radio Service in Arabic on 21 July 1982, *FBIS*, 22 July 1982.

21. Riyadh Domestic Television Service in Arabic on 21 July 1982, *FBIS*, 22 July 1982, pp. C 1-2.

22. Rashid Khalidi, *op. cit.*, p. 136; p. 142; pp. 148-149.

Chapter 7

1. Schiff and Ya'ari, *op. cit.*, p. 227.

2. Bob Woodward, *Veil: The Secret Wars of the CIA 1981-1987* (New York: Simon and Schuster, 1987), p. 217.

3. *New York Times*, 16 July 1982, p. A4.

4. "Israel Mutual Defense Agreement," *U.S. Treaties and Other International Agreements* (Washington D.C.: Government Printing Office, 1952), vol. 3, pp. 4985-4987.

5. United States Department of State, "Report of the Acting Secretary of State to the Speaker of the House of Representatives and to the Chairman of the Senate Foreign Relations Committee," 15 July 1982.

6. Judith Miller, "U.S. Bars Cluster Shells for Israel Indefinitely," *New York Times*, 28 July 1982, p. A16.

7. Bernard Gwertzman, "U.S. Insists Arabs Must Have Given Havens to P.L.O. Fighters," *New York Times*, 20 July 1982, pp. 1, 11.

8. Thomas Friedman, "Clash at Airport: Habib Arranges Truce," *New York Times*, 2 August 1982, pp. 1, 7.

9. Bernard Weinraub, "A Grim Reagan Calls for a Halt to the Fighting," *New York Times*, 2 August 1982, pp. 1, 6.

10. Tel Aviv, ITIM Radio Service in Hebrew on 5 August 1982, *FBIS*, 6 August 1982, p. I 5.

11. John Goshko, "Reagan Warns Israel on Beirut," *Washington Post*, 3 August 1982, pp. A 1, 12.

12. Bernard Gwertzman, "U.S. Shift on P.L.O.," *New York Times*, 8 July 1982, pp. A 1, 7.

13. *Washington Post*, 1 August 1982, p. A18.

14. *New York Times*, 24 July 1982, pp. 1, 25.

15. William Branigan, "Palestinians Say U.S. Responsive on Terms," *Washington Post*, 22 July 1982, pp. 1, 25.

16. Leslie Gelb, "Habib Expands Role in Shaping Lebanon Policy," *New York Times*, 23 July 1982, p. A 1, 4.

17. Jonathan Randall, "Arafat Reportedly Signs Agreement to Withdraw," *Washington Post*, 4 July 1982, pp. A 1, 8.

18. Cairo MENA Radio Service in Arabic on 24 July 1982, *FBIS*, 26 July 1982, p. D 1.

19. Also consult Beirut Domestic Radio Service in Arabic on 14 July 1982, *FBIS*, 15 July 1982, p. G 2.

20. Cairo MENA Radio Service in Arabic on 24 July 1982, *FBIS*, 26 July 1982, p. D 1.

21. Cf. Cairo MENA Radio Service in Arabic on 16 June 1982 and 18 August 1982, *FBIS*, 17 June 1982 and 19 August 1982, respectively.

22. Hassan Bin Talal, "Mideast Flashpoints," *New York Times*, 6 August 1982, p. 23.

23. United Nations Security Council, "Draft Resolution No. S/15317" (New York: United Nations, 1982).

24. Raymond Cohen, *Theatre of Power: The Art of Diplomatic Signalling* (London: Longman, 1987), p. 153.

25. William Quandt, *Camp David: Peacemaking and Politics* (Washington, D.C.: The Brookings Institution, 1986), p. 379.

26. The interviews were of 1,504 adults, 18 years and older, of whom 1,399 (92 percent) were aware of events in the Middle East. Interviewers conducted surveys in more than 300 scientifically selected locations across the United States. For results based on the "aware group sample," one can say with 95 percent confidence that the error attributable to sampling and other random effects could be three percentage points in either direction, i.e., there is a 3 percent margin of error in the poll.

27. As with the poll reported in Note 26, the 1983 survey has a margin of error of three percentage points and is based on personal interviews with 1,515 adults.

28. Eytan Gilboa, *American Public Opinion Toward Israel and the Arab-Israeli Conflict* (Lexington, Mass.: Lexington Books, 1987), p. 321.

Chapter 8

1. Regarding the endgame in arms control negotiations, see Strobe Talbott, *Endgame* (New York: Harper and Row, 1979), p. 17. For general applications of the theory of games, consult Anatol Rapoport, *Fights, Games, and Debates* (Ann Arbor: The University of Michigan Press, 1960), and Robert Axelrod, *The Evolution of Cooperation* (New York: Basic Books, 1984).

2. Fred Ikle, *Every War Must End* (New York: Columbia University Press, 1971), p. 106.

3. Avner Yaniv, *Dilemmas of Security: Politics, Strategy, and the Israeli Experience in Lebanon* (New York: Oxford University Press, 1987), p. 22, and *Deterrence Without the Bomb: The Politics of Israeli Strategy* (Lexington, Mass.: Lexington Books, 1987). Also, consult Ilan Peleg, *Begin's Foreign Policy, 1977-1983* (New York: Greenwood Press, 1987), p. 149.

4. James Clarity, "Israelis Turn Down Calls for Observers in Beirut," *New York Times*, 5 August 1982, pp. 1, 4.

5. Bernard Nossiter, "Nobody Should Preach to Us on Attacks or Seizures," *New York Times*, 5 August 1982, pp. 1, 2.

6. Schiff and Ya'ari, *op. cit.*, pp. 221-222.

7. *Ibid.*, p. 222.

8. *Ibid.*

9. *New York Times* editorial page, 5 August 1982, and William Safire, "Remember Desert One," *New York Times*, 5 August 1982, p. 19.

10. *Wall Street Journal*, editorial page, 5 August 1982.

11. *Washington Post*, editorial page, 8 August 1982.

12. John Goshko and Don Oberdorfer, "U.S. Urges Pullback, Two Week Pause," *Washington Post*, 6 August 1982, pp. A 1, 12.

13. Bernard Weinraub, "Reagan Urges Prompt P.L.O. Pullout," *New York Times*, 5 August 1982, p. 1.

14. Hedrick Smith, "Problems with Israel," *New York Times*, 5 August 1982, p. 14.

15. Terence Smith, "When Pressuring Israel Fails, Choices Are Few," *New York Times*, 8 August 1982, p. 1, section 4.

16. Israel Defense Forces Radio Service in Hebrew on 25 July 1982, at 1245 GMT, *FBIS*, 26 July 1982, p. I 1.

17. Michael Brecher, *The Foreign Policy System of Israel* (New Haven, Conn.: Yale University Press, 1972), pp. 7, 43-46, as well as his *Decisions in Israel's Foreign Policy* (New Haven, Conn.: Yale University Press, 1975), p. 112.

18. Bernard Weinraub, "Shultz Urges Begin to Accept U.S. Pledges," *New York Times*, 9 August 1982, p. 6.

19. Thomas Friedman, "Egypt and Syria Reported Opening Doors to the P.L.O.," *New York Times*, 9 August 1982, pp. 1, 12.

20. Marvine Howe, "Lebanese Sees U.S. at Fault If the Plan Fails," *New York Times*, 9 August 1982, p. 6.

21. For the Israeli view of the implicit agreement between Jerusalem and Damascus, see Avner Yaniv, *Deterence Without the Bomb: The politics of Israeli Strategy* (Lexington, Mass.: Lexington Books, 1987), p. 212. He writes that Israel allowed Syria to deploy forces into Lebanon during 1976 within four restrictions. One constraint on the Syrian military in Lebanon was that Israeli aircraft would have complete freedom to carry out flights over Lebanese territory. Because the placement of Syrian missiles in Lebanon impaired Israel's freedom of access over Lebanon, these missiles were in violation of the tacit accord between Damascus and

Jerusalem. Also see Yair Evron, *War and Intervention in Lebanon* (London: Croom Helm, 1987), pp. 190-191.

22. Israel Defense Forces Radio Service in Hebrew on 25 July 1982 at 1510 GMT, *FBIS*, 26 July 1982, p. I 2.

23. Henry Kamm, "Israelis Say Jets Again Destroyed Syrians' Missiles," *New York Times*, 25 July 1982, pp. A1, 13.

24. *New York Times*, 11 August 1982.

25. Jerusalem Domestic Radio Service in Hebrew on 12 August 1982 at 1720 GMT, *FBIS*, 13 August 1982, p. I 1.

26. *Ibid.*

27. *Washington Post*, editorial page, 16 August 1982.

28. With regard to American-Israeli alliance politics, see Wolf Blitzer, *Between Jerusalem and Washington* (New York: Oxford University Press, 1985).

29. For an analysis of the respective management styles of Ronald Reagan and Menachem Begin, consult John Tower, Edmund Muskie, and Brent Scowcroft, *The Tower Commission Report* (New York: Bantam Books, 1987), as well as Amos Perlmutter, *The Life and Times of Menachem Begin* (New York: Doubleday, 1987).

30. Jerusalem Domestic Radio Service in Hebrew on 12 August 1982 at 1705 GMT, *FBIS*, 13 August 1982, p. I 4.

31. *Ibid.*

32. *Jerusalem Post* in English, *FBIS*, 16 August 1982, pp. 1, 2.

33. *Ibid.*

34. Ma'ariv in Hebrew, *FBIS*, 17 August 1982, p. I14.

35. Thomas Friedman, "New Lebanon Allies: Christians and the P.L.O.," *New York Times*, 8 January 1987, pp. 1, 9.

36. Ihsan Hijazi, "In Lebanon, a New Chance for the Old War," *New York Times*, 8 January 1988, p. E 3.

Chapter 9

1. Paul Slovic and Sarah Lichtenstein, "Relative Importance of Probabilities and Payoffs in Risk-Taking," *Journal of Experimental Psychology*, vol. 3, no. 78 (1968), as well as Daniel Kahneman and Amos Tversky, "On the Psychology of Prediction," *Psychological Review*, vol. 80, no. 4 (1973).

2. Morton Halperin, *Bureaucratic Politics and Foreign Policy* (Washington, D.C.: The Brookings Institution, 1974), p. 161, as well as Graham Allison, *Essence of Decision: Explaining the Cuban Missile Crisis* (Boston, Mass.: Little, Brown and Company, 1971), pp. 117-123, and Jeffrey Richelson, *The U.S. Intelligence*

Community (Cambridge, Mass.:   Ballinger Publishing Company, 1985), p. 245.

3. Bob Woodward, *Veil: The Secret Wars of the CIA 1981-1987* (New York: Simon and Schuster, 1987), p. 286.

4. *Ibid.*, p. 248.

5. John Tower, Edmund Muskie, and Brent Scowcroft, *op. cit.*, pp. 105, 112, 114.

6. *New York Times*, 19 January 1987, p. A1.

7. *Ibid.*

8.   Alexander George, *Presidential Decisionmaking in Foreign Policy: The Effective Use of Information and Advice* (Boulder, Colo.: Westview Press, 1980), p. 21, as well as Avi Shlaim, "Failures in National Intelligence Estimates: The Case of the Yom Kippur War," *World Politics* (April 1976), pp. 348-380.

9. John Tower, Edmund Muskie, and Brent Scowcroft, *op. cit.*, p. 104.

10. Thomas Friedman, *From Beirut to Jerusalem* (New York: Farrar Straus Giroux, 1989), pp. 200-201.

11. *Ibid.*

12.   Charles Babock and Don Oberdorfer, "The NSC Cabal: How Arrogance and Secrecy Brought on a Scandal," *Washington Post*, 21 June 1987, p. B 1.

13.   Henry Kissinger, "Wandering in the Gulf," *Washington Post*, 21 June 1987, p. B 7.

Bibliography

Allison, Graham. *Essence of Decision: Explaining the Cuban Missile Crisis*. Boston: Little, Brown and Company, 1971.

Axelrod, Robert. *The Evolution of Cooperation*. New York: Basic Books, 1984.

Babock, Charles, and Don Oberdorfer. "The NSC Cabal: How Arrogance and Secrecy Brought on a Scandal," *Washington Post*, 21 June 1987, p. B1.

Beirut Domestic Radio Service in Arabic on 9 March 1982, translated in *Foreign Broadcast Information Service* (hereinafter abbreviated as *FBIS*), 10 March 1982, p. G1.

_____ on 14 July 1982, translated in *FBIS*, 15 July 1982, p. G2.

Blechman, Barry, and Stephen Kaplan, eds. *Force Without War: U.S. Armed Forces as a Political Instrument*. Washington, D.C.: The Brookings Institution, 1978.

Blitzer, Wolf. *Between Washington and Jerusalem: A Reporter's Notebook*. New York: Oxford University Press, 1985.

Branigin, William. "Palestinians Say U.S. Responsive on Terms," *Washington Post*, 22 July 1982, pp. 1, 25.

Brecher, John, et al. "The Birth Pangs of a New Policy," *Newsweek*, 13 September 1982, p. 26.

Brecher, Michael. *Decisions in Israel's Foreign Policy*. New Haven, Conn.: Yale University Press, 1975.

_____. *The Foreign Policy System of Israel: Setting, Images, Process*. New Haven, Conn.: Yale University Press, 1972.

Brecher, Michael, and Patrick James. *Crisis and Change in World Politics*. Boulder, Colo.: Westview Press, 1986.

Brzezinski, Zbigniew. *Power and Principle: Memoirs of the National Security Advisor 1977-1981*. New York: Farrar Straus Giroux, 1983.

Cairo MENA Radio Service in Arabic on 16 June 1982, translated in *FBIS*, 17 June 1982, p. D 3.

_____ on 24 July 1982, translated in *FBIS*, 26 July 1982, p. D1.

243

_____ on 18 August 1982, translated in *FBIS*, 19 August 1982, p. D.

Campbell, Colin. "Jordanians Torn on Greeting P.L.O.," *New York Times*, 18 August 1982, p. 15.

Carter, Jimmy. *Keeping Faith: Memoirs of a President.* Toronto: Bantam Books, 1982.

_____. *The Blood of Abraham.* Boston: Houghton Mifflin Company, 1985.

Claiborne, William. "Israel Hits PLO Sites in Beirut Killing 45," *Washington Post*, 5 June 1982, pp. A 21, 23-24.

Clarity, James. "Israelis Turn Down Calls for a Pullback and U.N. Observers," *New York Times*, 6 August 1982, pp. 1, 4.

_____. "Nobody Should Preach to Us on Attacks or Seizures," *New York Times*, 5 August 1982, pp. 1, 2.

Cobban, Helena. *The Palestinian Liberation Organisation: People, Power, and Politics.* Cambridge, England: Cambridge University Press, 1984.

Cody, Edward. "Israelis Seem to Rule Out Hunt for PLO," *Washington Post*, 18 June 1982, p. 1.

Cohen, Raymond. *Theatre of Power: The Art of Diplomatic Signaling.* London: Longman, 1987.

Damascus Domestic Radio Service in Arabic on 3 March 1982, translated in *FBIS*, 4 March 1982, p. H1.

_____ on 4 March 1982, translated in *FBIS*, 5 March 1982, p. H 1.

_____ on 9 June 1982, translated in *FBIS*, 10 June 1982, p. H 4.

Dayan, Moshe. *Story of My Life.* Jerusalem: Steimatsky's Agency Ltd., 1976.

Devlin, John. *Syria: Modern State in an Ancient Land.* London: Westview Press, 1983.

Dowty, Alan. *Middle East Crisis: U.S. Decision-making in 1958, 1970 and 1973.* Berkeley: University of California Press, 1984.

Ellsberg, Daniel. *Papers on the War.* New York: Simon and Schuster, 1972.

Engelberg, Stephen. "Iran and Iraq Got 'Doctored' Data, U.S. Officials Say," *New York Times*, 12 January 1987, pp. 1, 9.

Evron, Yair. *War and Intervention in Lebanon.* London: Croom Helm, 1987.

Friedman, Thomas. "Clash at Airport: Habib Arranges Truce," *New York Times*, 2 August 1982, pp. 1, 7.

_____. "U.S., France and Lebanon Discuss Details for Withdrawal by P.L.O.," *New York Times*, 8 August 1982, pp. 1, A6.

_____. "Egypt and Syria Reported Opening Doors to the P.L.O.," *New York Times*, 9 August 1982, pp. 1, 12.

_____. "New Lebanon Allies: Christians and the P.L.O.," *New York Times*, 8 January 1987, pp. 1, 9.

_____. "Confusion and Israeli Role," *New York Times*, 13 January 1987, pp. 1, 8.

_____. *From Beirut to Jerusalem*. New York: Farrar Straus Giroux, 1989.

Gelb, Leslie. "Habib Expands Role in Shaping Lebanon Policy," *New York Times*, 23 July 1982, pp. 1, A4.

_____, and Richard Betts. *The Irony of Vietnam: The System Worked*. Washington, D.C.: The Brookings Institution, 1979.

George, Alexander. *Presidential Decisionmaking in Foreign Policy: The Effective Use of Information and Advice*. Boulder, Colo.: Westview Press, 1980.

Gilboa, Eytan. *American Public Opinion Toward Israel and the Arab-Israeli Conflict*. Lexington, Mass.: Lexington Books, 1987.

Godson, Roy, ed. *Intelligence Requirements for the 1980's: Elements of Intelligence*. Washington, D.C.: National Strategy Information Center, 1979.

_____. *Intelligence Requirements for the 1980's: Analysis and Estimates*. Washington, D.C.: National Strategy Information Center, 1980.

_____. *Intelligence Requirements for the 1980's: Intelligence and Policy*. Lexington, Mass.: Lexington Books, 1986.

Gordon, Michael. "1980 Soviet Test: How to Invade Iran," *New York Times*, 15 December 1986, p. A12.

_____. "At Foreign Policy Helm: Shultz vs. White House," *New York Times*, 26 August 1987, p. 6.

Goshko, John. "Reagan Warns Israel on Beirut," *Washington Post*, 3 August 1982, pp. 1, A12.

_____, and Don Oberdorfer. "U.S. Urges Pullback, Two-Week Pause," *Washington Post*, 6 August 1982, pp. 1, A25.

_____. "Haig Resigns at State; Shultz Is Named," *Washington Post*, 26 June 1982, pp. 1, A13.

Gwertzman, Bernard. "U.S. Officials Fear Israel-Syria Clash," *New York Times*, 5 May 1981, p. A11.

_____. "A Special U.S. Envoy Will Go to Mideast," *New York Times*, 6 May 1981, p. 23.

_____. "Begin Is Said to Tell Reagan That Israel Faces Peril As in 1967," *New York Times*, 9 May 1981, p. 6.

_____. "Mood Is 'Angry' As Begin Meets Panel of Senate," *New York Times*, 23 June 1982, pp. 1, A8.

_____. "Haig Is Said to Have Felt Jealous of Mideast Role," *New York Times*, 29 June 1982, p. A8.

_____. "Getaway Day for Haig, with Yet More Ambiguity," *New York Times*, 2 July 1982, p. 2.

_____. "U.S. Shift on P.L.O.," *New York Times*, 8 July 1982, pp. 1, A7.

_____. "U.S. Insists Arabs Must Have Given Haven to P.L.O. Fighters," *New York Times*, 20 July 1982, pp. 1, 11.

Haig, Alexander. *Caveat.* New York: McMillan Publishing Company, 1984.

Halperin, Morton. *Bureaucratic Politics and Foreign Policy.* Washington, D.C.: The Brookings Institution, 1974.

Harif, Yosef, and Razi Guterman. "Begin Determined to Remove All Foreign Forces," *Ma'ariv*, 18 June 1982, pp. 1, 11, translated in *FBIS*, 18 June 1982.

Hersh, Seymour. *The Price of Power: Kissinger in the Nixon White House.* New York: Summit Books, 1983.

Hijazi, Ihsan. "In Lebanon, a New Chance for the Old War," *New York Times*, 5 June 1988, p. E3.

Holsti, Ole. *Crisis, Escalation, War.* Montreal: McGill University Press, 1972.

Howe, Marvine. "Israeli Action Cited in Golan Heights," *New York Times*, 21 December 1981, p. A21.

_____. "Lebanese Sees U.S. at Fault If Plan Fails," *New York Times*, 9 August 1982, p. 6.

Hudson, Michael. *The Precarious Republic.* New York: Random House, 1978.

Ikle, Fred. *Every War Must End.* New York: Columbia University Press, 1971.

Inderfurth, Karl, and Loch Johnson. *Decisions of the Highest Order: Perspectives on the National Security Council.* Pacific Grove, Calif.: Brooks/Cole Publishing Company, 1988.

International Institute for Strategic Studies. *Military Balance 1972-1973.* London: International Institute for Strategic Studies, 1973.

_____. *Military Balance 1980-1981*. London: International Institute for Strategic Studies, 1981.

Israel Defense Forces Radio Service in Hebrew on 10 June 1982, translated in *FBIS*, 10 June 1982, p. I1.

_____ on 23 June 1982, translated in *FBIS*, 24 June 1982, p. I2.

_____ on 25 July 1982 at 1245 GMT, translated in *FBIS*, 26 July 1982, p. I1.

_____ on 25 July 1982 at 1510 GMT, translated in *FBIS*, 26 July 1982, p. I2.

Israeli Radio in Hebrew, 6 December 1981, translated in *FBIS*, 7 December 1981, p. 14.

Jerusalem Domestic Radio Service in Hebrew, 7 March 1982, translated in *FBIS*, 8 March 1982, p. 17.

_____ on 8 March 1982, translated in *FBIS*, 9 March 1982, p. I7.

_____ on 15 April 1982, translated in *FBIS*, 16 April 1982, p. I1.

_____ on 31 May 1982, translated in *FBIS*, 1 June 1982, pp. I5-6.

_____ on 17 June 1982, translated in *FBIS*, 18 June 1982, pp. I1-3.

_____ on 12 August 1982 at 1500 and 1705 Greenwich Mean Time (GMT), translated in *FBIS*, 13 August 1982, p. I4.

_____ on 12 August 1982 at 1720 GMT, translated in *FBIS*, 13 August 1982, p. I1.

_____ on 13 August 1982, translated in *FBIS*, 14 August 1982, p. I5.

Jerusalem Domestic Television Service in Hebrew on 8 March 1982, translated in *FBIS*, 9 March 1982, p. I1.

_____ on 22 June 1982, translated in *FBIS*, 23 June 1982.

Jerusalem Government Press Office in English, 15 December 1981, in *FBIS*, 18 December 1981.

Jordanian Domestic Radio Service in Arabic on 5 March 1982, translated in *FBIS*, 8 March 1982, p. F1.

Kahneman, Daniel, and Amos Tversky. "On the Psychology of Prediction." *Psychological Review* 80, no. 4 (1973): 237-251.

Kalb, Marvin, and Bernard Kalb. *Kissinger*. Boston: Little, Brown and Company, 1974.

Kamm, Henry. "Israelis Say Jets Again Destroyed Syrians' Missiles," *New York Times*, 25 July 1982, pp. 1, A13.

Kerr, Malcolm. *The Arab Cold War: Gamal'Abd al-Nasir and His Rivals, 1958-1970.* London: Oxford University Press, 1971.

Khalidi, Rashid. *Under Siege: P.L.O. Decisionmaking During the 1982 War.* New York: Columbia University Press, 1986.

Khalidi, Walid. *Conflict and Violence in Lebanon.* Cambridge, Mass.: Harvard University Press, 1979.

Kifner, John. "Syria Is Resisting Pressure to Remove Missiles in Lebanon," *New York Times*, 5 May 1981, pp. 1, A9.

_____. "Syria Tells Israel It Won't Withdraw Missiles in Lebanon," *New York Times*, 9 May 1981, pp. 1, A6.

_____. "Syrian President Reported to Face Harsh Challenges," *New York Times*, 18 May 1986, pp. 1, 16.

Kissinger, Henry. *White House Years.* Boston: Little, Brown and Company, 1979.

_____. *Years of Upheaval.* Boston: Little, Brown and Company, 1982.

_____. "From Lebanon to the West Bank to the Gulf," *Washington Post*, 16 June 1982, p. A15.

_____. "Wandering in the Gulf," *Washington Post*, 21 June 1987, p. B7.

Kuwait Domestic Radio Service in Arabic on 21 July 1982, translated in *FBIS*, 22 July 1982.

Landau, David. "Prime Minister Begin to Meet with Habib 8 March," *Jerusalem Post*, 8 March 1982, p. 2, translated in *FBIS*, 8 March 1982.

Laqueur, Walter. *Confrontation: The Middle East War and World Politics.* London: Wildwood House and Sphere Books, 1974.

Lescaze, Lee. "Habib Reports Lebanon Crisis Has Cooled," *Washington Post*, 12 December 1981, p. A2.

McCartney, James. "Did U.S. Consider War on Syria?" *Miami Herald*, 28 January 1982, pp. 1, 7A.

Menges, Constantine. *Inside the National Security Council.* New York: Simon and Schuster, 1988.

Miller, Judith. "U.S. Bars Cluster Shells for Israel Indefinitely," *New York Times*, 28 July 1982, p. A16.

Miller, Stanley. *The Mary Celeste: A Survivor's Tale.* New York: St. Martin's Press, 1980.

Neustadt, Richard. *Presidential Power: The Politics of Leadership.* New York: John Wiley & Sons, Inc., 1960.

New York Times, 10 January 1982; 16 July 1982; 24 July 1982; 5 August 1982; 11 August 1982; 19 January 1987; 10 March 1987.

Nossiter, Bernard. "Syria Pushes Hard U.N. Line over Golan," *New York Times*, 6 January 1982, p. A3.

_____. "U.N. Votes for Observers in Beirut," *New York Times*, 2 August 1982, pp. 1, 6.

Oberdorfer, Don. "Israeli-Palestinian Cease-Fire Termed 'Fragile' by Habib," *Washington Post*, 19 March 1982, p. A26.

_____. "Begin Vows Israel Won't Enter Beirut," *Washington Post*, 25 June 1982, pp. 1, A26.

Ottaway, David. "Peace Effort in Lebanon Is Stalled," *Washington Post*, 19 June 1982, p. 1.

Pastor, Robert. *Condemned to Repetition*. Princeton, N.J.: Princeton University Press, 1987.

Peleg, Ilan. *Begin's Foreign Policy, 1977-1983*. New York: Greenwood Press, 1987.

Perlmutter, Amos. *The Life and Times of Menachem Begin*. New York: Doubleday, 1987.

Quandt, William. *Decade of Decisions*. Berkeley, Calif.: University of California Press, 1977.

_____. "Lebanon 1958 and Jordan 1970," cited by Barry Blechman and Stephen Kaplan, eds. *Force Without War: U.S. Armed Forces as a Political Instrument*. Washington, D.C.: The Brookings Institution, 1978, pp. 222-288.

_____. *Saudi Arabia in the 1980s: Foreign Policy, Security and Oil*. Washington, D.C.: The Brookings Institution, 1981.

_____. *Camp David: Peacemaking and Politics*. Washington, D.C.: The Brookings Institution, 1986.

Quandt, William, Fouad Jabber, and Ann Mosely Lesch. *The Politics of Palestinian Nationalism*. Berkeley: University of California Press, 1973.

Rabinovich, Itamar. *The War for Lebanon, 1970-1985*. Ithaca, N.Y.: Cornell University Press, 1985.

Randall, Jonathan. "Arafat Reportedly Signs Agreement to Withdraw," *Washington Post*, 4 July 1982, pp. 1, A18.

Rapoport, Anatol. *Fights, Games, and Debates*. Ann Arbor: The University of Michigan Press, 1960.

Richardson, David. "'Source': White House 'Stage-Managed' Confrontation," *Jerusalem Post*, 16 August 1982, pp. 1, 2, translated in *FBIS*, 16 August 1982.

Richelson, Jeffrey. *The U.S. Intelligence Community*. Cambridge, Mass.: Ballinger Publishing Company, 1985.

Riyadh Domestic Television Service in Arabic on 21 July 1982, translated in *FBIS*, 22 July 1982, pp. C1-2.

Ross, Dennis. "Acting with Caution: Middle East Policy Planning for the Second Reagan Administration," *Policy Papers-Number One*. The Washington Institute for Near East Policy, 1985, pp. 1-45.

Safire, William. "Remember Desert One," *New York Times*, 5 August1982, p. 19.

SANA [official Syrian news agency], translated in *FBIS*, 8 May 1981.

Schiff, Ze'ev, and Ehud Ya'ari. *Israel's Lebanon War*. New York: Simon and Schuster, 1984.

Schiffer, Shim'on. "Report on Israeli Radio," 1 June 1982, translated in *FBIS*, 1 June 1982, pp. I5-6.

Sciolino, Elaine. "Latin Peace Plan Divides U.S. Aides," *New York Times*, 19 March 1987, p. 8.

Sharon, Ariel. *Warrior*. New York: Simon and Schuster, 1989.

Shipler, David. "Israel Is Said to Weigh an Invasion of Lebanon If P.L.O. Raids Go On," *New York Times*, 10 February 1982, pp. 1, A10.

Shlaim, Avi. "Failures in National Intelligence Estimates: The Case of the Yom Kippur War." *World Politics* (April 1976): 348-380.

Shlaim, Avi, and Raymond Tanter. "Decision Process, Choice, and Consequences: Israel's Deep-Penetration Bombing in Egypt, 1970." *World Politics* 30 (July 1978): 483-516.

Sick, Gary. *All Fall Down: America's Tragic Encounter with Iran*. New York: Random House, 1985.

Slovic, Paul, and Sarah Lichtenstein. "Relative Importance of Probabilities and Payoffs in Risk-Taking." *Journal of Experimental Psychology* 3, no. 78 (1968): 1-18.

Smith, Hedrick. "Problems with Israel," *New York Times*, 5 August 1982, p. 14.

_____. "U.S. Asks Pullout," *New York Times*, 8 June 1982, pp. 1, A14.

Smith, Terence. "When Pressuring Israel Fails, Choices Are Few," *New York Times*, 8 August 1982, sec. 4, p. 1.

"Sources Claim 'Slow Death' of Normalization," *Ar-Rayah*, 7 July 1982, p. 6, translated in *FBIS*, 8 July 1982.

Spiegel, Steven. *The Other Arab-Israeli Conflict: Making America's Middle East Policy, from Truman to Reagan*. Chicago: The University of Chicago Press, 1985.

Stein, Janice, and Raymond Tanter. *Rational Decision-Making: Israel's Security Choices, 1967.* Columbus, Ohio: The Ohio State University Press, 1980.

Steinbruner, John. *The Cybernetic Theory of Decision: New Dimensions of Political Analysis.* Princeton, N.J.: Princeton University Press, 1974.

Straus, Richard, and Kenneth Wollack, eds. *Middle East Policy Survey* (hereinafter abbreviated as *MEPS*) no. 29, 10 April 1981.

_____. *MEPS*, no. 31, 8 May 1981.

_____. *MEPS*, no. 32, 22 May 1981.

_____. *MEPS*, no. 33, 5 June 1981.

_____. *MEPS*, no. 35, 2 July 1981.

_____. *MEPS*, no. 37, 31 July 1981.

_____. *MEPS*, no. 39, 11 September 1981.

_____. *MEPS*, no. 40, 25 September 1981.

_____. *MEPS*, no. 43, 6 November 1981.

_____. *MEPS*, no. 44, 20 November 1981.

_____. *MEPS*, no. 46, 18 December 1981.

_____. *MEPS*, no. 47, 15 January 1982.

_____. *MEPS*, no. 49, 12 February 1982.

_____. *MEPS*, no. 51, 12 March 1982.

_____. *MEPS*, no. 54, 23 April 1982.

_____. *MEPS*, no. 57, 4 June 1982.

_____. *MEPS*, no. 58, 18 June 1982.

_____. *MEPS*, no. 61, 30 July 1982.

_____. *MEPS*, no. 62, 13 August 1982.

_____. *MEPS*, no. 70, 17 December 1982.

_____. *MEPS*, no. 87, 16 September 1983.

Talal, Hassan Bin. "Mideast Flash Points," *New York Times*, 6 August 1982, p. 23.

Talbott, Strobe. *Endgame.* New York: Harper and Row, 1979.

Tel Aviv ITIM Radio Service in Hebrew on 5 August 1982, translated in *FBIS*, 6 August 1982, p. I5.

Tower, John, Edmund Muskie, and Brent Scowcroft. *The Tower Commission Report.* New York: Bantam Books, 1987.

Tunisian Domestic Radio Service in Arabic on 7 June 1982, translated in *FBIS*, 8 June 1982, p. Q2.

United Nations Security Council, Draft Resolution No. S/15317.

United States Department of State. "Israel Mutual Defense Assistance Agreement," *U.S. Treaties and Other International Agreements*, volume 3, no. 4, 1952, pp. 4985-4987.

_____. *Report of the Acting Secretary of State to the Speaker of the House of Representatives and to the Chairman of the Senate Foreign Relations Committee*, 15 July 1982.

United States Senate, Committee on Foreign Relations. *Testimony of the Secretary of State Alexander M. Haig*, 97th Cong. 1st sess., 12 November 1981.

_____. *Statement of the Secretary of State-Designate on the Nomination of George P. Shultz of California to be Secretary of State*, 97th Cong. 2nd sess., 13-14 July 1982.

Vance, Cyrus. *Hard Choices: Critical Years in American Foreign Policy*. New York: Simon and Schuster, 1983.

Wall Street Journal, (editorial), "Prolonging the Agony," 5 August 1982.

Washington Post, (editorial), "The Tragedy of Lebanon," 8 August 1982, p. C6; as well as 1 August 1981; 28 September 1981; 29 September 1981; 5 December 1981; 16 August 1982.

Weinraub, Bernard. "A Grim Reagan Calls for a Halt to the Fighting," *New York Times*, 2 August 1982, pp. 1, 6.

_____. "Reagan Urges Prompt P.L.O. Pullout," *New York Times*, 5 August 1982, p. 1.

_____. "Shultz Urges Begin to Accept U.S. Pledges," *New York Times*, 9 August 1982, p. 6.

Weisman, Steven. "Summit Chiefs Shocked by Invasion of Lebanon," *New York Times*, 7 June 1982, p. A14.

Woodward, Bob. *Veil: The Secret Wars of the CIA 1981-1987*. New York: Simon and Schuster, 1987.

Wright, Robin. *Sacred Rage: The Crusade of Modern Islam*. New York: Linden Press/Simon and Schuster, 1985.

Yaniv, Avner. *Deterrence Without the Bomb: The Politics of Israeli Strategy*. Lexington, Mass.: Lexington Books, 1987.

_____. *Dilemmas Of Security: Politics, Strategy, and the Israeli Experience in Lebanon*. New York: Oxford University Press, 1987.

Zaq, Moshe. "The Agreement--and the End," *Ma'ariv*, 17 August 1982, p. 5, translated in *FBIS*, 16 August 1982, p. I14.

Zumwalt, Elmo. "Israel and the U.S. Gained in Lebanon," *New York Times*, 19 November 1982, p. 35.

Index

and Soviet-Syrian relations, 40–41, 44
subversion policy of, 75
Syrian relations, 34–35, 73–78, 87, 100, 106, 219
and UN Resolution 242, 171, 172
UNTSO. *See* United Nations, Truce Supervision Organization

Vance, Cyrus, 12–13
Veliotes, Nicholas, 6, 125
Vietnam, 34

Wall Street Journal, 186–187
Washington Post, 53, 55, 187, 200
Watkins, James, 70

Weinberger, Caspar, 6, 70, 72, 109–110, 125, 134–135, 136, 213, 215, 216, 221, 223
Weinraub, Bernard, 188, 193
Weizman, Ezer, 56, 57
West, Francis (Bing), 6
West Bank, 13, 36, 89, 91, 119, 125, 159
Wolfowitz, Paul, 6, 70
Woodward, Bob, 219

Ya'ari, Ehud, 15, 16, 53, 58, 95, 113, 153
Yaniv, Avner, 179

Zahle, 15, 16, 17, 49, 202
Zaq, Moshe, 206

DUE